POVERTY AND SOCIAL EXCLUSION IN THE NEW RUSSIA

Poverty and Social Exclusion in the New Russia

Edited by
NICK MANNING
NATALIYA TIKHONOVA

Translations by Karen George

ASHGATE

Published by
Ashgate Publishing Limited
Gower House
Croft Road
Aldershot
Hants GU11 3HR
England

Ashgate Publishing Company
Suite 420
101 Cherry Street
Burlington, VT 05401-4405
USA

Ashgate website: http://www.ashgate.com

British Library Cataloguing in Publication Data
Poverty and social exclusion in the new Russia
  1. Poverty - Russia (Federation) 2. Marginality, Social -
  Russia (Federation) 3. Russia (Federation) - Social
  conditions - 1991-
  I. Manning, Nick, 1951- II. Tikhonova, N.E.
  362.5'0947

Library of Congress Cataloging-in-Publication Data
Poverty and social exclusion in the new Russia / edited by Nick Manning, Nataliya Tikhonova ; translations by Karen George.
      p.   cm.
  Includes bibliographical references and index.
  ISBN 0-7546-3739-5
  1. Poverty--Russia (Federation) 2. Social isolation--Russia (Federation) I. Manning, Nick P. II. Tikhonova, N.E. III. Title.

HC340.12.Z9P658 2004
305.5'69'0947--dc22   2004007713

ISBN 0 7546 3739 5

Printed and bound by Athenaeum Press, Ltd.,
Gateshead, Tyne & Wear.

Contents

List of Figures

List of Tables

List of Contributors

Peter Abrahamson, PhD, is Associate Professor in Sociology, University of Copenhagen. His research concentrates on comparative studies of contemporary welfare societies: theoretical and empirical studies on poverty, social exclusion, and well-being of families.

Nadia Davidova is Senior Research Fellow, Institute for Multidisciplinary Social Studies, Russian Academy of Sciences. She has published more than 30 works in Russia and the UK including contributions to Manning, N., Shkaratan, O., and N. Tikhonova (eds.) *Work and Welfare in the New Russia*, 2000; Alcock, P., and G. Craig (eds.) *International Social Policy*, 2001; Gorshkov, M., and N. Tikhonova (eds.) *Woman of New Russia: Who is She? By What Does She Live? To What Does She Aspire?*, 2002, *State Social Policy and Household Strategies of Survival*, 2003, with O. Shkaratan, T. Sidorina and N. Tikhonova. She is interested in social problems and policies during the 1990s, particularly the issues of unemployment, poverty, health and gender inequalities, and regional differentiation. She has a PhD in sociology from the Institute of Sociology, Russian Academy of Sciences (2001).

Karen George has a BA in Russian from the University of London, and has been a member of the Institute of Linguists since 1993. During the 1980s, she worked in welfare rights in the public sector; from 1993 to 2001, she was a part-time lecturer in social policy at the University of Kent. She has many published translations in the social sciences, including *Work and Welfare in the New Russia* by Nick Manning, Ovsey Shkaratan and Nataliya Tikhonova (Ashgate, 2000) and *European Cities: social conflicts and governance* by Patrick Le Galès (Oxford University Press, 2002), which was awarded the Stein Rokkan Prize for comparative research by the International Social Science Council.

Nick Manning has been engaged in research on social issues in Russia since 1979 (*Socialism, Social Welfare and the Soviet Union*, 1980, with Vic George; *The New Eastern Europe: past, present and future for social policy*, 1992, with B. Deacon, *et al.*; *Environmental and Housing Movements, grassroots experience in Hungary, Russia and Estonia*, 1997, edited with K. Lang-Pickvance and C. Pickvance; *Work and Welfare in the*

New Russia, 2000, with Ovsey Shkaratan and Nataliya Tikhonova). He also works in the fields of medical sociology and health policy, and social theory and social policy, and has written or edited more than 20 books. Since 1995 he has been Professor of Social Policy and Sociology at the University of Nottingham, UK, and is seconded as head of Research and University Liaison to the Nottinghamshire Healthcare NHS Trust, 2003-2006.

Nataliya Tikhonova has published more than 150 works in Russia, the USA, Germany and the UK (*Social Stratification Factors during Transition to the Market Economy*, 1999; *The Middle Class in Contemporary Russia*, 1999, with M. Gorshkov and A. Chepurenko; *Russlands Sozialstruktur nach acht Jahren Reformen*, 1999; Manning, N., Shkaratan, O., and N. Tikhonova (eds.) *Work and Welfare in the New Russia*, 2000; M. Gorshkov and N. Tikhonova (eds.) *Woman of New Russia: Who is She? By What Does She Live? To What Does She Aspire?*, 2002; *State Social Policy and Households Strategies of Survival*, 2003, with O. Shkaratan, T. Sidorina and N. Davidova; *The Phenomenon of Urban Poverty In Contemporary Russia*, 2003). She is interested in the social consequences of economic change, particularly for social structure, and the positions, actions and values of different social groups, such as the unemployed, the poor, the middle classes, women and young people. She has a PhD in philosophy from Moscow State University (1981), and a higher doctorate from the Institute of Sociology, Russian Academy of Sciences (1999). She has been Deputy Director of the Russian Independent Institute for Social and National Problems since 1992 till 2003. Her current position is Deputy Director of the Institute for Multidisciplinary Social Studies, Russian Academy of Sciences.

Artur Tsutsiev is Senior Researcher, Center for Ethnopolitical Studies, North Ossetian Institute of Humanities and Social Studies, Vladikavkaz and Lecturer on Sociology at the Vladikavkaz Institute of Management. He has a PhD in philosophy from Rostov-on-Don State University (1990). He studies Russian ethnic minorities, the issue of ethnic identity, regional autonomies and the situation with ethnic conflicts in Northern Caucasus. His main publications are *The Northern Caucasus 1774-1995: History and Conflicts (Atlas)*, Vladikavkaz, 1997; *The Ossetian-Ingush Conflict*, 1992; 'The Russians and the Caucasians: essay on modern stereotypes' *Vestnik Instituta Tsivilizatsii*, Nos. 1-2, 1998-1999.

John Veit-Wilson has been involved in poverty research since his postgraduate studies in Sweden in the 1950s, and was a member of the pioneering UK Poverty Survey team directed by Brian Abel-Smith and Peter Townsend, 1964-67. He has published extensively on the relations between the variety of ideas of poverty and need, the methods used to study and measure them, and their uses in government income maintenance policy-making, including a cross-national study of the ten governments around the world who operated official minimum income standards (*Setting Adequacy Standards: How governments define minimum incomes*, 1998). He has been adviser and consultant on these issues to parliamentary, governmental and NGO bodies as well as poverty research teams, in the UK and Europe, and has also been active in NGO management for many years. He is Emeritus Professor of Social Policy of Northumbria University, where he was head of sociology, and since 1992 he has been Visiting Professor at the University of Newcastle upon Tyne.

Andrei Zdravomyslov is Leading Researcher of the Institute for Multidisciplinary Social Studies, Russian Academy of Sciences and Professor of the Higher School of Economy, Moscow. He is ex-President of the Russian Professional Sociological Association, life-member of the International Sociological Association and member of the European Sociological Association. He has published more than 300 works in Russia and many countries all over the world including *Man and his Work. A Sociological Study*, with Professor V. Yadov, which was first published in Russian in 1969 and then translated into English in 1970, German in 1971, and Polish in 1971. In 2003 a new edition of the book has been issued in Moscow. He is interested in theoretical and methodological sociological approaches, the problems of social and ethnic conflicts, and national and ethnic self-consciousness. In recent years he has studied tension, conflict , and violence in Northern Caucasus. He has a PhD in philosophy from Leningrad State University (1960), and a higher doctorate and Professorial title from the Institute of Sociology, Russian Academy of Sciences (1970).

Preface

This project was conceived in 1998 as a follow-up to the previous project published in *Work and Welfare in the New Russia*, 2000. Another genuinely collaborative enterprise, the questionnaires, analysis and interpretation have been widely discussed between us. The study began in March 1999, with funding from the EU (INTAS), as before. Visits and workshops have taken place in Russia, the UK and Denmark at least once a year since 1999. Fieldwork was carried out in November 1999 and November 2000, including a total of 268 interviews with households in three cities in Russia: Moscow, Voronezh and Vladikavkaz.

The idea was suggested by Nataliya Tikhonova, and the methodological framework followed a similar pattern to the previous project, suggested by Nick Manning. The presentation of our findings in this book has been a genuinely collaborative piece of work, to which we have all contributed over months and years of discussion. Not all of the points made in it are supported with equal weight by all of us, but the general findings and conclusions are. Responsibility for the individual chapters and appendices is as indicated.

Acknowledgements

We would like to thank the many colleagues who have contributed to this project. The project was originally developed and submitted to INTAS for EU funding in 1998 (grant number INTAS 971-21439). International meetings were hosted by the Russian Independent Institute for Social and National Problems (Moscow), the University of Nottingham, the University of Helsinki, and the University of Copenhagen. We would like to acknowledge all of this support.

Part I

Background

1 Russia in Context

Nick Manning and Nataliya Tikhonova

Попытка не пытна, спрос не беда
Trying isn't torture, asking isn't misfortune

One of the classic questions that the collapse of State socialism has posed for the understanding of macro-change in European societies is that of how the societies of Central and Eastern Europe have diverged in their development since 1990, and why. So far as social policy is concerned there have been three phases. Initially there were some rapidly implemented policies put in place by the new governments in the anticipation of the social consequences of the emergence of market mechanisms in the post-communist era. Quintessential amongst these was the issue of the expected explosion of unemployment, and the related loss of income that this would mean for families who had traditionally been supported by large State subsidies to consumption, with few accumulated savings to rely on. Economists had argued that there was a large overhang of underemployed people who would be released quickly by enterprises facing the chill winds of the global economic marketplace (Ellman, 1989; Standing, 1991). New schemes for fairly generous unemployment benefits were enacted in most countries, including Russia. Otherwise little social policy changed prior to the round of new elections that had taken place by the early 1990s.

With the new governments, most of which were characterised more by their distance from the communist parties than internal coherence or social rootedness, new social policy debates began to emerge in phase two. Here, a more complex picture of change emerges. First, unemployment benefits were cut back, as an unsustainable expense. An extended debate emerged about what actually was developing in the region's labour markets, especially marked in relation to Russia, where predictions ranged from dangerous collapse, to sustained boom (Manning, Shkaratan, and Tikhonova, 2000). Second the key policy actors who were involved in thinking about policy changes were involved in rather different policy networks. For some, such as the *Visegrad* countries (named after the royal summit of the Kings of Poland, Bohemia and Hungary at the Castle of

Visegrad in 1335, and emulated in a meeting of the Heads of State in 1991), the prospect of emulating the EU, both in terms of living standards, and political and economic security, led to discussions about devising either social democratic or corporatist welfare systems. For others, and in particular Russia, the heavy hand of the International Monetary Fund made loans and credits dependent on following a liberal ideology in which an American style residual Welfare State was paramount. In the event the collapse of industrial production in the Russian case, together with a chaotic transition to the political management of routine domestic mechanisms such as the collection of taxes with which to fund social expenditures, meant that residualism in welfare was inevitable.

The third phase was marked in 1998 by two key turning points – the return of five Central European countries to levels of economic production that they had enjoyed in 1989, and, in marked contrast, the further lurching collapse of the Russian currency, with a related and sudden jump in rates of poverty, inequality, inflation and unemployment. Divergence was here revealed in all its clarity. However there are further divergences concealed beneath this major bifurcation. Within Russia regional inequality has grown to the point at which the most advantaged areas, such as Moscow and its environs, have *per capita* incomes four or five times those of the least advantaged areas, such as the Northern Caucasus, with very contrasting patterns of unemployment, poverty and social exclusion. Within Central Europe we find that for example Poland's spectacular economic recovery to 129 per cent of 1989 GDP contrasts with the Czech Republic's more modest 106 per cent. The cost is that Polish inequality is far higher (at a Gini of 0.34 compared to 0.24, and with double the rate of Czech unemployment) (2001 figures from UNICEF, 2003, pp.89-92).

To what extent are these patterns evidence of diversity from a common origin, or path dependency from diverse origins? Path dependency has been the subject of wide-ranging multi-disciplinary reflection (Goldstone, 1998), and is generally used to explain stability in systems where relatively unique initial conditions fix developments despite changing circumstances. The 19th Century 'querty' keyboard or the 20th Century IBM PC keyboard (with many redundant keys) are examples. However, typically path dependency posits some kind of institutional lock-in of actors' behaviours, for example through resource dependency, cultural habits, or costly alternatives. Korpi (2000) has explored these effects on West European social policy: the survival of the 'Scandinavian model', despite the pressures of global financial flows or EU membership, suggests such path constraints, as does the recent resistance of the German policy community to substantial changes in German welfare arrangements.

There is no doubt that the regions and countries of State socialist Europe contained long-standing variations that Russification, the Warsaw Pact and COMECON had been unable to eliminate. For example, Estonia had for years had the highest standard of living and the most advantageous social policies of the USSR (George and Manning, 1980), in marked contrast to the republics of the Northern Caucasus, or Central Asia. Czechoslovakia had been on the verge of West European economic and social compatibility in the 1930s. Slovenia had been the most liberal and comfortable of the regions in Yugoslavia. Poland had continued as a deeply Catholic country throughout the 20th Century. Examples could be multiplied. In a sense there were three path dependencies. On the one hand all of these countries were recognisably part of the same economic and social system, epitomised visually by the common pattern of State socialist urban development and infrastructure that developed in the middle of the 20th Century. However the policy constraints that operated from the USSR for 50 years were in the end too weak to contain the second path dependency, namely the desire by local elites for autonomy and freedom to take their own developmental paths.

This they have done, despite the existence of a third set of path constraints provided by two sources: the ambition of some to join the EU club, including its social dimension, on the one hand; and the neo-liberal policy solutions proffered and often formally required in return for help from the International Monetary Fund and the World Bank (Deacon, 2000). Evidence for a third potential source of path constraint, the economic pressures of global economic forces, independent of political forces, is not widely supported empirically or theoretically (Alber and Standing, 2000).

What are the models that are emerging in Eastern Europe? Quite a variety of typologies have emerged in the literature for grouping together the various paths that these 27 countries have begun to travel. Table 1.1 summarises a selection of them, as they have emerged over time.

Table 1.1   Typologies of social policy and reform in Central and Eastern Europe, 1995-2000

World Bank (World Bank, 1996)

Most reform:	Poland, Slovenia, Hungary, Croatia, Macedonia, Czech Republic, Slovakia
Some reform:	Estonia, Lithuania, Bulgaria, Latvia, Albania, Romania
Less reform:	Kyrgyzstan, Russia, Moldova, Armenia, Georgia, Kazakhstan
Laggards (no reform):	Uzbekistan, Ukraine, Belarus, Azerbaijan, Tajikistan, Turkistan

UN Development Programme (UNDP, 1999)

Liberal approach:	Poland, Czech Republic, Hungary, Baltics
Late reformers:	Bulgaria, Romania
Non-liberal:	Belarus
Conflict over whether to liberalise:	Russia, Ukraine, Slovakia
Political breakdown:	Armenia, Albania

European Bank for Reconstruction and Development (EBRD, 1999)
"Transition Indicator"

3.4	Central Europe
3.2	Baltics
2.4	Western CIS
2.2	Central Asia

Deacon (2000)

West European Welfare State:	*(mixed Bismarck Insurance (e.g., payroll taxes), and Scandinavian State finance)* Czech Republic, Hungary, Poland, Estonia, Slovenia
Conserve State and workplace benefits:	*(which may collapse and lead to residualisation)*: Russia, Bulgaria, Romania, Macedonia

How can we ourselves usefully group these countries? There is no doubt that their economic situation is highly varied. Nevertheless there is a clear pattern that has emerged (Manning, 2001). The EU accession group is marked by a return to growth, less poverty (although not necessarily low unemployment), lower rates of teenage pregnancy, and lower rates of infectious diseases. We might characterise this group as the *recovery group* in which economic growth has returned, governments have the capacity to tax and spend for social intervention, and social costs have been contained. At the other end of the scale are the Central Asian and Caucasus countries (and regions of Russia in Northern Caucasus). These are typically exhibiting very high rates of poverty, growing levels of infectious disease, extremely low levels of government expenditure as a proportion of GDP, a return to traditional patterns of marriage, and economies that for the most part have failed to return to a vigorous pattern of growth. This might be called the *disintegrating group*. In between these two extremes are a variety of countries struggling with different problems. We can separate two types. Those in which *conflict* has disrupted economic and social life to such an extent that it is difficult to identify a stable trend in terms of social costs and their amelioration. We might include the Balkans and Caucasus areas here. Finally there are those countries in which economic growth has only just materialised, where as a consequence a large section of the population is suffering, but in which there is every potential for a better future in terms of available raw materials and levels of education. This group is *struggling* and may or may not join the EU accession pattern in the future. The pre-eminent case is of course Russia, highly significant for the region as a whole because of its overwhelming size. Indeed this country is so big that it is more appropriate for us to remember the huge regional variations within it, and consider that some of its regions should perhaps more appropriately be classified with other groups: the Northern Caucasus with the rest of the Caucasus regions, for example; or Moscow with the EU accession group.

Where countries are large, internal regional differentiation is growing fast. This is most obvious in the case of the biggest country, Russia. For example the regional impact of the August 1998 financial crisis was quite varied: 30 per cent of the regions retained their industrial production levels, while 15 per cent suffered further industrial loss of around 20-30 per cent (UNDP, 1999a, p.6). It is misleading to think of social issues in relation to the country as a whole, since very sharp differences are manifest between the different regions. For example, *per capita* income varies between three typical levels. At the top is Moscow with seven times the income of most other regions. In between are a small number of areas, such as St. Petersburg, the North, Siberia, and the Far East that have *per capita* incomes which are double most of the other regions, but still only about one-third of Moscow levels. Unemployment is similarly varied – very low in Moscow at around 4 per cent, and St. Petersburg at 9 per cent, but between 10 and 20 per cent for the rest of the country (Manning, Shkaratan and Tikhonova, 2000, pp.65-66). This is compounded by the Russian government's manifest divestment of its social responsibilities from central to local government. This decentralisation was foreshadowed in the 1993 constitution, but has been driven by the inability and unwillingness of central government to raise funds and redistribute them in relation to the varying needs of the regions.

Methodological Issues

The difficulty with such general comparisons is whether they hold right across a society, or even across its welfare system. What are we comparing? To what extent does the particular welfare area that we examine affect the argument? Following the critiques that have been mounted against Esping-Andersen's 1990 regime classification, heavily based on the interests of working age men, by those who claim that it does not adequately capture the experiences of women (e.g., Lewis, 1992), it follows that it may also be unsuitable for ethnic minorities, older people, children, sick and disabled people, and so on: 'the discriminating properties of generalised models of welfare regimes are now being more and more questioned' (Lewis, 1998, p.20). Some of the interests of these groups may be located within the kind of services they need (for example health care), and some located within the characteristics of people themselves. For example Alber and Standing (2000) acknowledge that in assessing the range of national strategies that might have been influenced by 'social dumping', there are considerable differences between labour issues and social service issues. Similarly domestic politics surrounding the expansion or contraction of social provision we know is heavily affected by whether a service is widely used and supported such as health care, or targeted on a smaller section of the population, such as income support, with a smaller interest base. Antonnen and Sipilä (1996) found that in considering the social care of children and older people, welfare regime types were at variance with those derived for income support. Indeed Pestoff (1996) argued that it was better to classify social policy changes in Central Eastern Europe by service than by country, suggesting for example that it made more sense to distinguish between services where change had been rapid (unemployment) and those where it was slow (pensions), or severely deteriorated (health and housing).

A further issue in tackling these questions is that of the methods that we can use, and the kind of data that each can generate. The literature gives examples of the whole range of social science methods, from deep case studies using qualitative methods of observation and unstructured interviews, to large-scale representative longitudinal household (panel) surveys. Most methodological debates have now moved beyond the quantitative versus qualitative argument to agree that different methods are suitable for different questions; none is superior, but some may be more appropriate. Unfortunately there are sharply varied costs attached to different methods. Reanalysing published national data is one of the cheapest and most readily accessible forms of data. A typical example would be the data presented by Alber and Standing (2000) to examine the question of whether there was convergence amongst Welfare States, and if so to what extent this could be identified over time as related to economic growth. However, as they acknowledge, these data are themselves highly abstracted measures of the reality of different social policies, usually confined to social security expenditures; moreover there are a number of alternative and rival explanations as to any patterns found. With global competition, do States cut social expenditure to lower labour costs, or raise expenditure to protect the vulnerable? With international harmonisation do States learn new models and strive to raise social standards or to reduce the 'burden of government'? They conclude, 'social science has difficulty in arriving at a common interpretation of recent trends' (p.102).

The alternative is to collect original data for the purpose to hand. There are of course many case studies in the literature covering one or two countries or one or two services. Many are commissioned by international agencies such as one of the UN bodies. These are valuable in generating hypotheses, but are very difficult to generalise from by way of an aggregated picture. Systematic comparative case studies of a small group of countries, regions or cities have become more common, and are much better at identifying unique and common dynamics and mechanisms of the way in which social policies are evolving across the region. The only alternative beyond this is to undertake systematic surveys of one kind or another. Here are a few examples.

Panel surveys, in which the same households are asked questions year after year, are extremely good at identifying change. Western Europe now has a household panel survey working for quite a wide range of countries. Unfortunately this is not the case in Central and Eastern Europe. However there are two panel surveys for Russia, one of which (the Russian Longitudinal Monitoring Survey) has had ten survey rounds since the early 1990s, the data from which are publicly available from the University of North Carolina at Chapel Hill. It is now in some financial difficulties however – this kind of research effort is expensive, and the focus has been on a range of rather general social issues. A second example is the series of studies reported in Appendix 2 in this book using four rounds of semi-qualitative interviews with the same Russian households since 1996, designed to identify changing social needs and household survival strategies. Again finance is dependent on repeated grant funding.

Most countries support a range of repeated omnibus surveys, with a large and representative sample of the population. The questions tend to vary, depending on the interests of those paying for them, although where they remain constant, quasi panel data can be constructed. Again these surveys tend to be rather general, and are difficult to use to address very specific issues. However Richard Rose, at the Strathclyde Centre for the Study of Public Policy, has made creative use of a number of these in his series of studies in Central and Eastern Europe.

One final, and in the context of Central and Eastern Europe, probably the most significant data source, has been the 'UNICEF monitoring project'. This is funded by the World Bank, and managed by the Innocenti Research Centre in Florence. Since 1993 the project has monitored the social needs of children and families throughout the 27 countries of the region, to identify social policy developments, and to gather a consistent and publicly available data source for further use. Each annual report has contained a mixture of regular data and special in-depth studies of particular social groups of social needs, or policy developments. The annual data sources include: an expert social policy survey in each of the 27 countries carried out by UNICEF field officers; UN (e.g., WHO), World Bank, OECD, and official government published data; and guest expert summaries of case studies and other independently published research material. A summary of the numerical data is provided on-line as the TransMONEE data base, the latest of which appeared in 2001, and some of which is reproduced later in this chapter.

It is axiomatic for any research that the questions posed, and the methods chosen, should be compatible. The questions posed in the search for patterns and causes of Welfare State change, and the consequences of global economic forces, are often given a theoretical context which makes them almost impossible to answer effectively within the cost and feasibility constraints that face social science research in this area. Each approach has its strengths and weaknesses. Whether together they can offer a multi-method basis for identifying the main contours of welfare change, and the social issues with which they have to grapple is a disputed issue, to which this book will hope to make some contribution.

A fundamental question here is whether we are witnessing the effects of Europeanisation or globalisation. Market imperatives, and the way they are filtered through institutional structures and networks, combined with the advice of international agencies, such as the International Monetary Fund and World Bank, have resulted in a variety of studies and a complex debate which is to a certain extent shaped by different concepts, methods, and foci. In a recent special edition of *Global Social Policy*, focused on Europeanisation, globalisation and social policy, Michelle Beyeler (2003) separates economic from political pressures and logics, and also the rational actor viewpoint from that of institutional cultures and traditions. We have already mentioned path dependency. It is not always easy to know what is rational in any particular circumstance. Alber and Standing (2000) observe that it may be as rational for a country to lower labour and social costs in a 'race to the bottom' in the face of economic competition, as it is for them to raise social and labour standards in a 'race to the top' in the face of political competition.

Russia in the 21st Century

In our previous book (Manning, Shkaratan and Tikhonova, 2000) we observed that a 'human crisis' was unfolding in Russia. It had been ten years since State socialist societies had embarked on an era of extraordinary change. Hopes for personal freedom, democratic involvement, and greater prosperity were for most people a distant dream, and the United Nations Development Programme announced on 29th July 1999 that 'A human crisis of monumental proportions is emerging in the former Soviet Union. The transition years have literally been lethal for many people. The hardest hit are the men of the region, who are living shorter, more unhealthy lives' (UNDP, 1999a). A variety of social indicators showed that despite a barrage of international policy advice, the economy had dropped into free-fall, and life expectancy, ill-health and poverty had changed alarmingly.

How has this changed since 1999? Have these trends continued? If so, what have been the consequences for ordinary Russians? In this book we report on a new study focused more directly on the development of poverty and social exclusion in Russia. We begin with a broad review of recent changes in the political, economic and social context before introducing the study design itself.

The Chechen conflict arrived in Moscow on 31st August 1999 with the first of a series of explosions near the Kremlin. Subsequently on 8th-9th September an apartment block in south-east Moscow was demolished, killing 94 people, and then on 13th September another apartment block was demolished, killing 60. Russians felt that they needed a strong man to deal with this frightening new development. He was to be Vladimir Putin, the man chosen to succeed Yeltsin, and previously Head of the FSB (the KGB's successor). Yeltsin had already nominated Putin as his chosen successor at some future date, but surprised everyone with his eve of millennium announcement on 31st December 1999, that he was to step down, and called for Presidential elections. Elections to the State Duma in December had indicated that Putin's favoured party, Edinstvo, was a strong contender, coming close to the Communist Party, each taking nearly a quarter of the votes.

Yeltsin negotiated immunity from any subsequent criminal prosecution, and Putin was duly elected President 26th March 2000, taking 40 million votes (53 per cent of the total, on a 69 per cent turnout). He had clearly taken many votes from the communists, which gave him an unprecedented and clear command of government. He felt the way was clear to move to a new, post-Yeltsin, phase in Russia's development, and he moved swiftly to centralise State power. Growing regional autonomy was reversed by dividing Russia into seven areas, each with an appointed rather than elected governor. He set about reasserting military self-confidence, challenging the power of the oil and banking based economic oligarchs who had supported his election on the assumption they could control him, and moving the economy back into growth (Macauley, 2003).

Our previous project was completed against the backdrop of the August 1998 collapse in the Russian currency, and an abrupt levelling of income dispersal which had begun to mark out a nascent middle class. The prospects for the Russian economy looked bleak in comparison to the fragile but continuous improvement that had developed over the preceding three years. Yet by the middle of 2003 the economy had experienced five years of sustained growth, averaging a rate of nearly 6 per cent. This is a level of economic performance that few would have predicted. The debate now is more about the conditions necessary for this recovery to continue than the question of whether the Russian economy can turn round – it has done.

The issues that have gone right for the economy are widely agreed: rouble devaluation; inflation under control; buoyant oil prices; and political certainty after the unpredictability of the Yeltsin years. Domestic investment has grown strongly, while the flight of capital abroad remains tolerable. Taxation has been increasingly effective, while government expenditure has been contained, resulting in several years of budget surpluses with which the government has been able to pay off debts. Yet there is still a lingering concern that the 'underlying structural' weaknesses remain. For example, the oil and gas industries contribute 25 per cent of GDP, and thus the economy is heavily dependent on international prices. This in turn may crowd out other forms of economic investment and growth. Moreover, while Putin has made clear his intention to control the 'economic oligarchs' and their regional hold over banking and industry, the outcome of this struggle between them and the State remains uncertain – after all a similar contest in the past led eventually to Khrushchev's abrupt departure from power. Nevertheless business confidence is growing, as is the recognition that the alignment of informal business practice with the formal regulatory environment may be in the interests of both State and business (Hanson, 2003).

Social Issues Remain

With the election of Putin as President in 2000, social policy issues have been more widely and seriously discussed than before. There has been a new 'social charter' declared, in which the State proposes to keep away from business planning, and in return asks citizens to obey the law (particularly to pay their taxes). Public commitment has been made to a reduction of the very high existing incomes inequalities through better pensions, the elimination of wages and benefits arrears, and the targeting of benefits on the poorest rather than the middle sectors. Similarly there has been a recognition that regional inequalities have grown rapidly, and should be reduced. The post-1998 financial collapse, which had reduced money incomes at a stroke, no longer casts such a shadow. With the steady growth of GNP and real personal incomes since he was elected, and the re-emergence of a burgeoning middle class, Putin has had the room to move on from what he has called the 'survival strategy' of the first ten years, and not surprisingly he retains widespread political support.

But realism does not mean that the implied massive shift in priorities towards the poor can actually be achieved. The barriers to this shift are the ones that have distorted social policy in the first place. The continued delivery of social policies through the enterprise as 'occupational welfare' means that enterprises are a major multiplier of disadvantage, since they channel social support to those who are relatively better off. Just as the retention of surplus labour in these very large organisations has kept unemployment under control, and, importantly, suppressed the potential for political disaffection, it has also contributed to the sharp rise in inequality in Russia in recent years.

The continuities of enterprise welfare activities are compounded by a second barrier to changing social policy priorities on the ground, the *de facto* regionalisation that has developed surprisingly quickly in the 1990s. Regional inequality has arisen out of the differential effects of rapid inflation, and the adjustment in economic restructuring that has been possible in some areas but not others. This has been compounded for some regions by local political élites which have tried hard to resist the economic changes, for example by blocking the development of new small- and medium-sized enterprises in the private sector. Regional differences are now so large that there would have to be an enormous re-centralisation of government services to even them out. It is difficult to see how the Federal Government will be able to slow down, let alone halt or reverse these regional inequalities, which have had such a marked impact on social policy (Manning, 2003).

Although the economy shows clear signs of recovery, and Putin has committed himself to domestic political reform of both business and social policy issues, this may not be reflected in the social circumstances of individuals and families. We know from UK experience that steady economic growth can be accompanied by growing inequality and poverty, such that even the OECD has expressed concern (Manning, 2004). The majority of this book is taken up with presenting a multidimensional view of poverty and social exclusion in Russia. By way of setting the scene for the more detailed study, we can take a look at a number of additional indicators of the social circumstances of ordinary Russians. Much of this data is drawn from the Unicef data bank, TransMONEE (Unicef, 2001).

There are several types of data presented here. Infectious disease and immunisation are indicators of both the general reach of health care throughout the population, and the possibility of excluded minorities where the poverty rate has multiplied. In Figures 1.1-1.3 we can observe that concerns in the early 1990s that a return to 19th Century patterns of disease was developing have been largely proved unfounded. Immunisation has improved, and the concern has now switched to the more modern (or even postmodern) disease of HIV infection.

Figure 1.1   Infectious disease rates, 1989-2000

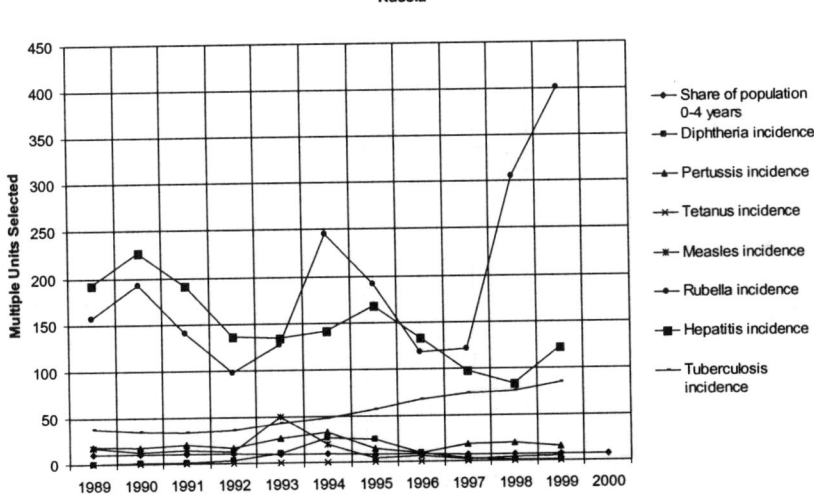

Figure 1.2   Sexually transmitted and HIV disease rates, 1989-1999

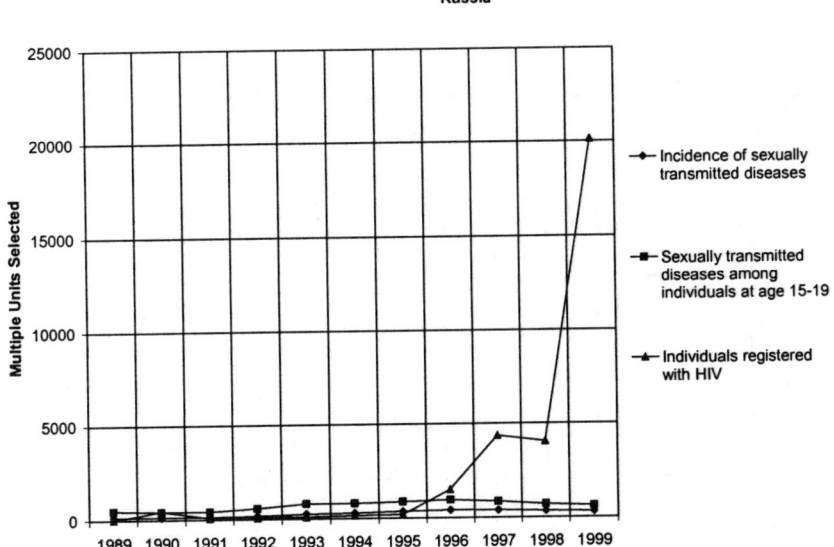

Figure 1.3   Immunisation rates, 1989-1999

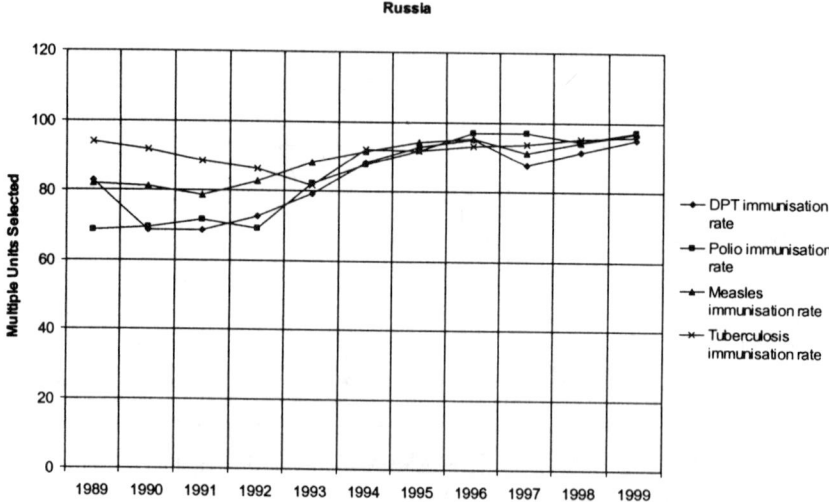

By contrast, mortality rates in Russia have become a widely observed indicator of the social tragedy that has overtaken different groups. Figure 1.4 shows the much commented upon dip in male life expectancy below 60 years – at a time when the equivalent for China was exactly ten years more. Figure 1.5 shows where the main change had taken place – mortality amongst middle aged men, generally assumed to be stress induced, and also the result of alcohol abuse.

Figure 1.4   Life expectancy of men and women, 1989-1999

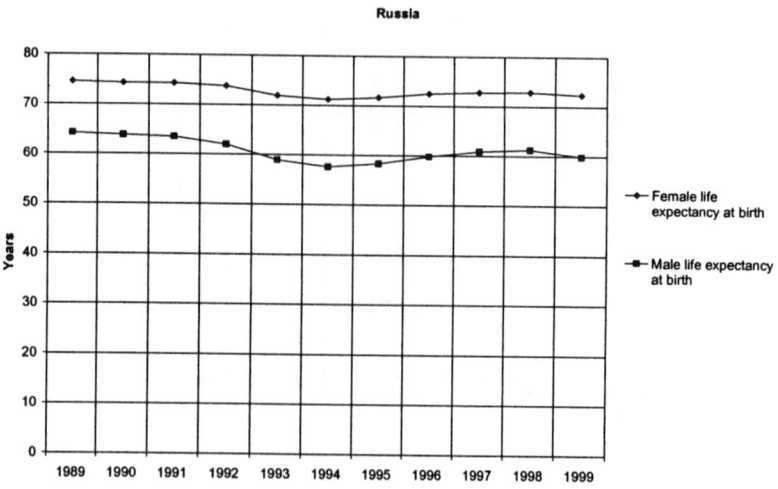

Figure 1.5 Mortality rates for middle-aged men and women, 1989-1999

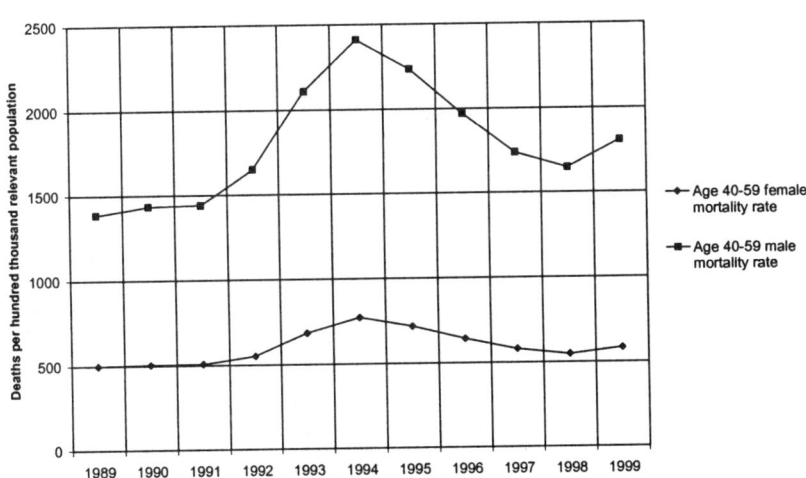

Further indicators of the social stresses in a society undergoing rapid change can be seen in the effects on children. Here we show the rapid jump in divorce rates, and the steady climb in the number of children who are not living with their natural families.

Figure 1.6 Divorce rates, 1989-1999

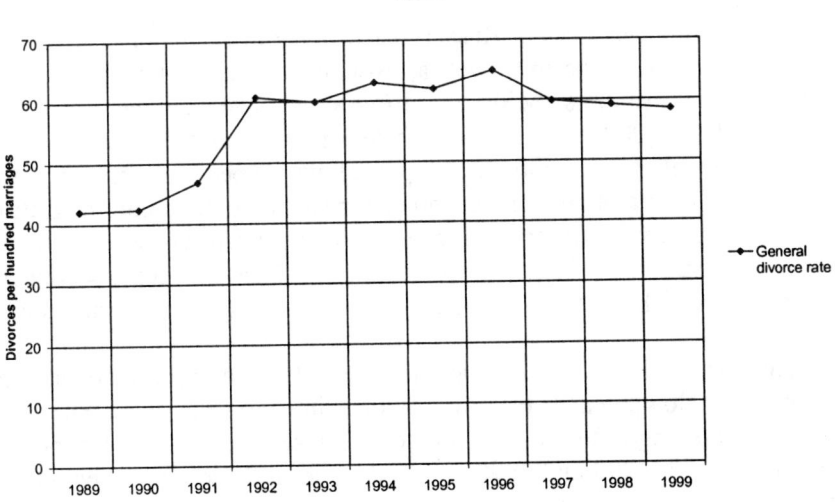

Figure 1.7   Children in alternative care, 1989-1999

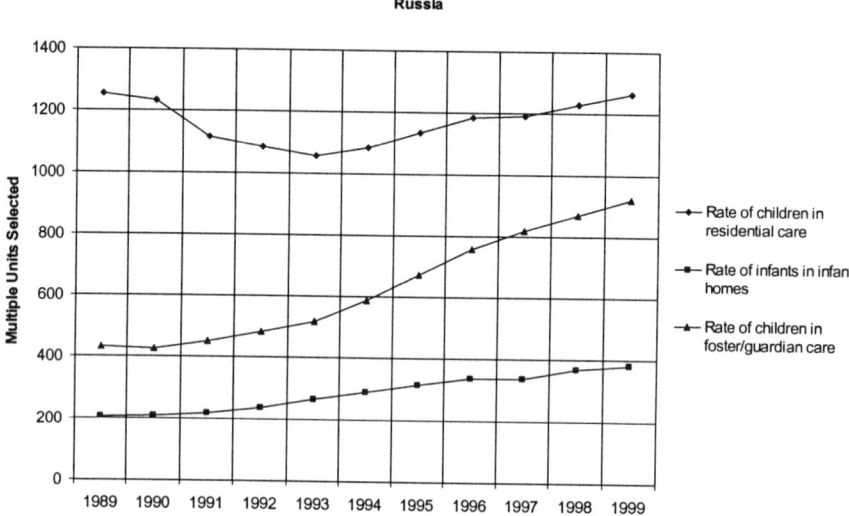

A final indicator of the impact of Russian social changes over the last dozen years is the rise in homelessness – a particularly severe problem in a region with such harsh winter weather. In all societies homelessness represents the loss of a secure and protected physical and social environment in which at least basic needs can be met. In Russia, homelessness particularly demonstrates the plight of the very poor, and at the same time indicates the acute needs that they must have by definition. The level of homelessness in Russia, particularly in its major cities is not known for certain. Charities such as Nochlezhka in St. Petersburg, and Medecins sans Frontiers (MSF) in Moscow estimate that there are now something like 8,000 and 15,000 homeless people on the street in these cities respectively (Stephenson, 2003, p.242), with a peak in numbers in the mid-1990s. The major reason for homelessness is the economic migration of men, particularly Russian citizens, moving from elsewhere in the Russian Federation or from CIS countries. Most have at least secondary education, and thus do not appear to be forming a separate social underclass.

Stephenson (2003) argues that the post-1998 economic recovery has resulted in a slowdown in the flow of men into homelessness. She cites MSF data showing a drop in the number of those homeless for six months or more between 1998 and 2000, and a decline in those citing begging as their main form of income from a half to a quarter of those surveyed.

However long-term homelessness appears to be growing, and qualitative studies suggest that there is a growing minority of homeless children graduating into an adult homeless 'career'.

The Study

It was against this background that the current project was undertaken. Our first project had highlighted that poverty was a new development, and a key consequence of the rapid changes that had taken place in the labour market in the 1990s. However the data collected then were not specifically designed to examine poverty, its dynamic change, and the causes and consequences for Russian households.

Although discussion about the nature and the causes of poverty has already been extant in Western Europe for many years, it has only recently begun in Russia. In the West European literature, there is active discussion of the nature of poverty. For example, is it the lack of money for simple physical survival, or the lack of resources to allow the social participation of those who are now poor? Or again, are budget based or sociological models of poverty thresholds more appropriate for evaluating poverty? The issue of poverty in Russia demands particularly urgent attention because, owing to a number of different circumstances, it is a particularly acute problem.

Firstly, in the course of its transformation, Russia has seen its former social protection mechanisms destroyed and no effective new social policy put in their place. This has resulted in a significant section of the population becoming 'dislocated' from former sources of its various means of support. Secondly, before the reforms there were relatively low numbers of poor people in Russia, and no particular way of life differentiated them from the majority of other people around them. Now, however, we are seeing a change in the nature of the reproduction of poverty, which is closely related to aspects of economic reforms within Russia's regional economic systems. A further factor is the absence – over many decades – of any stratification of the greater proportion of Russians, so that most people were not noticeably differentiated by their way of life or nature of consumption: this has led to public unwillingness to recognise a gap between the poor and other sections of society. As the population has polarised during the process of reform, this attitude has meant a sharp increase in the number of people who feel they are poor and has intensified their perception of social exclusion. Lastly, the conviction that Russia will continue to struggle for economic development, along with the feeling of personal injustice that this engenders, lowers the tolerance of the poorest section of the population towards their current situation. Thus, in general, the phenomenon of poverty in Russia has undergone qualitative changes, and the issue of what poverty is in Russia still remains open.

Using large-scale survey methods, VTSIOM and other academic Russian researchers, have begun to investigate different aspects of poverty, but the final goal of all researchers working on poverty issues in Russia – without exception – has been to attempt to determine the scale of poverty in Russian society. Thus, up to now, research into poverty in Russia has been dominated by the approach in which poverty has been understood first and foremost as quantitative, not qualitative in nature – as a particular level of income, or as low monetary income plus absence of other economic resources. In practice, these approaches have given a largely different picture of poverty, while estimated numbers of poor people have, correspondingly, fluctuated in the range 20-25 per cent to 80-85 per cent of the total Russian population. As a result, it has been impossible to give any kind of uniform assessment of the problem of poverty in Russia.

This uncertain understanding of the essential nature of poverty as a major form of social exclusion in contemporary Russia, not only creates confusion in any theoretical analysis of poverty and makes it impossible to estimate its scale (including by comparison with West European countries), but also militates against the development of any active, targeted social policy which might be called an anti-poverty strategy. Practically no research has been initiated into such very important aspects of the issue as: the concept of poverty in various regional, ethnic and socio-cultural settings; analysis of the lifestyles of the poor and their general and specific features in various types of social setting; the reproduction of poverty and the formation of a particular sub-culture among the poor, taking into account specific features of these processes in different regions of Russia, as well as looking at how they differ from analogous processes in Western Europe. At the same time, obtaining information about these issues, which is the aim of the project reported in this book, is a vital pre-requisite to devising effective social policy. Such information is made all the more important by growing differences between regional social policies, as differences between the separate regions of Russia intensify during the course of the reforms, as well as by the multi-ethnic nature of Russia's population and the status of national republics as distinct elements of the Russian Federation.

The initial hypothesis of the project was that poverty in different societies and social communities has both common and specific features, determined by different living standards and socio-cultural traditions in the social communities where individuals find themselves. Consequently the definition of poverty and the identification of both its common and its specific characteristics and boundaries, as well as the causes and mechanisms by which deprived conditions and lifestyles are created and transmitted, should be investigated by the use of comparative analysis of different types of societies. For the purposes of comparative research, the most promising approach to poverty is a multi-faceted assessment of the level of someone's welfare through a complex, integral criterion of the structure of consumption and way of life using not only quantitative but qualitative methods. We have therefore taken into account previous Russian and Western studies into social exclusion and poverty as constraints on social participation, including the research carried out by Chernina from Novosibirsk which, until recently, was almost the only exception to the conventional Russian quantitative approach to poverty.

The main strategy of the four teams which made up the project research group was to provide a comparative analysis of poverty in different countries (UK, Denmark and Russia), regions and types of settlement within one country (a huge capital city conurbation, a major provincial capital in southern Russia, and the capital of the national republic of Northern Caucasus), as well as ethnic and socio-cultural sub-cultures. Correspondingly, the research programme included four main objectives. (Details of the project methodology are presented in Appendix 1.)

Nature of poverty in the different regional, ethnic and socio-cultural communities

The basis for an analysis which enabled both the general features of poverty, and its specific characteristics in different social settings, to be distinguished was an inter-regional project, using a single method and a single set of research instruments. Undertaking the task required the solving of a number of separate sub-tasks:

- examination of differences in existing poverty perceptions, prevailing living standards, socially approved ideas of who are the poor and how the specific signs of poverty in particular types of society (community) should be defined
- self-identification of the poor and the main factors affecting it

- investigation of patterns of consumption structure, mode of life and social activities of poor people in different societies (communities), including forms of social participation, main values, motivations, commitments and the existence of poor individuals as a socially isolated group within the community
- analysing the general state of health and poverty correlation depending on the different types of societies.

The empirical section of the research was constructed as a panel survey, with repeat interviewing of respondents after a year in order to track the precise dynamics of their position and to separate the main fixed standards and markers of poverty from secondary and incidental ones. The survey took the form of in-depth, qualitative – but largely pre-coded – interviews. The interview subjects included not only heads of households but members of households. The total planned sample was 160 people and included various types of poor households (one-parent families, large families, single middle-aged/elderly women in poor health, and so on). The proposed distribution by city was: 40 people (from 25 households) in Moscow; 40 people (from 25 households) in Voronezh; and 80 people (from 50 households) in Vladikavkaz.

Given the relatively small sample, additional pan-Russian representative survey data were collected by integrating a relevant block of questions from the qualitative panel questionnaire into the questionnaire for the quarterly monitoring programme of the Russian Independent Institute for Social and National Problems, some of whose staff were members of the Russian team. The research group thereby had at its disposal material which was integrated with the qualitative interview data, offering a unique opportunity to identify poverty and its markers in Russian society in the context of regional, ethnic/national and socio-cultural factors.

Reproduction of poverty and the formation of specific poverty sub-cultures

Undertaking this task required an analysis of the types of poverty generation in Russia with regard to the heterogeneous character of poverty phenomena. These included:

- the separation of 'old' and 'new' poor[1]
- the dynamics of the material position of the poor and their main expectations for the future
- the survival strategies used by the 'old' and 'new' poor
- regional and ethnic effects of chosen survival strategies

- the formation of new mechanisms for social integration in contemporary Russia, including community integration and adaptation mechanisms used by the poor.

These first two main tasks are inextricably linked to each other, since only when integrated do they enable an understanding of the specific nature of poverty in various types of social setting in Russia. The method of the panel survey, with repeat interviewing of respondents after a year, was especially important in tackling the objective relating to the reproduction of poverty, and in assessing social and political tensions among the poor. In particular, interviewing young people aged 13 to 21 (where there are any in the family) was important for the research question related to reproduction of poverty.

Ethnic, national and political values of poor people, and their readiness for social protest

Forms of social protest as an answer to an individual's impoverishment and the ways of adaptation to poverty itself lay in different types of social mobilisation. In this part of the project the investigation included:

- the role of ethnic ideas and stereotypes about national cultures which influence the formation of different types of social mobilisation of those experiencing impoverishment
- the interrelationship (at different levels – individual, group, societal) between extreme nationalistic and/or ethno-centric views and some psychological aspects of poverty
- political values of poor people, including any correlation between ethno-centric beliefs and anti-democratic authoritarian orientations
- the extent of readiness for social protest displayed by poor people, and possible forms of protest in the state of different ethnic/national societies and cultures.

Meeting this objective depended not only on the results of the empirical research for the first two objectives, but also some additional empirical data. In addition, to ensure comparisons between ethnic, regional and socio-cultural characteristics in the Vladikavkaz (North Ossetia) interviews, 25 Russian households and 25 Ossetian households were surveyed. The analysis of political attitudes provided data which could be used to analyse Russian social and political issues (especially the prospects for political stability) and to develop proposals for improving social policy.

Russian results in the context of European concepts and data

In developing the instruments and selecting the methodologies for the project research, we made use of analogous research in Europe. This helped us to ensure the comparability of the research results, and to draw out both inter-regional and international comparisons. This entailed:

- clarifying general conceptions and theories of poverty and social exclusion
- analysing the specific use of concepts of poverty and social exclusion in the European Union
- comparing the Russian results with existing data from the United Kingdom, Denmark and the other Western European countries.

A Note on the Research Sites

Moscow needs little introduction. It lies in the centre of what is known as European Russia. Moscow's origins as a symbol of Russian spiritual and political power go back more than 850 years. Voronezh is situated approximately 250 miles south of Moscow. The city lies on the Voronezh River, both east and west banks, which flows into the nearby Don, which in turn leads to the Black Sea. Peter the Great decreed that Russia must have a navy, and that these ships should be built in Voronezh. Now the city has a population of about one million people and is situated in what is known as the 'Black Earth Region', a particularly fertile agricultural area. However, Voronezh itself is an industrial city, home to a large rubber and tyre plant and the Ilyushin Aircraft Company. Both Moscow and Voronezh were described in more detail in our previous book (Manning, Shkaratan and Tikhonova, 2000).

Vladikavkaz however is new to this study. Vladikavkaz is the capital of North Ossetia. North Ossetia is situated on the northern slopes of the central Caucasus between two of the highest mountain peaks in Europe, Elbrus (5613m) and Kasbek (5047m). The Great Silk Road passed through the Alan Kingdom, from which Ossetia inherited its ethnic and cultural traditions. It is one of the smallest, most densely populated and multi-cultural republics in the Russian Federation, with 700,000 inhabitants, representing about 100 nationalities living in an area of 8,000 square kilometres. Vladikavkaz is a city where some residents have been, in one way or another, affected by two armed conflicts on a regional scale. Chronologically, the first was the South Ossetian conflict of 1989-92, in the course of which about 30,000 to 35,000 Ossetian families were forced to leave Georgia and resettle in North Ossetia. The second was the Ossetian-Ingush conflict, which broke out in the autumn of 1992 in North Ossetia itself. Those who were direct victims of this conflict suffered the heaviest loss. In our sample, there were several Ossetian families who had become poor as a result of the unfolding of the conflict in South Ossetia, and also one Russian family whose fate had become linked to the circumstances of the Ossetian-Ingush conflict.

A Note on Poverty and Social Exclusion

Since minimum subsistence approaches were pioneered by Rowntree (1901) in the city of York, England, in 1899, a common approach to poverty measurement has been to base it on measures of the minimum income calculated by experts to be essential for basic necessities. A number of governments have adopted prescriptive methods of this kind as the basis of their social assistance benefit rates, though some have made allowances for social participation costs as well. Sen (1983) as well as Doyal and Gough (1984) have argued that there are irreducible 'basic individual needs' which have to be met for people to exist as persons in any sense: 'survival and personal identity are attributes which all persons need in order to be classified as persons at all' (Doyal and Gough 1984, p. 14). Thus minimum subsistence calculations concerned with mere survival fail to take into account the cost of maintaining personal identity in society.

Not surprisingly then, for social scientists relative notions of poverty have been predominant. Adam Smith in *The Wealth of Nations* (1776) observed in connection with poverty that 'by necessities I understand not only the commodities which are indispensably necessary for the support of life, but whatever the custom of the country renders it indecent for creditable people, even of the lowest order, to be without'. In the course of the 20th Century the weight of opinion has steadily shifted towards a consensus on this issue. We are all relativists now, it has been claimed, since it is impossible to extract the meaning of poverty, or particular manifestations of it from the social context in which it occurs: 'That poverty in economically advanced societies is to be defined relative to the standards of the society in question appears to be widely accepted' (Callan, *et al.*, 1993).

Nevertheless, for the industrial countries, the issue has become one of defining deprivation in a culturally relevant way. What does it mean to be deprived? The answer for Rowntree by 1936 was to include, in addition to the means of ensuring the maintenance of merely physical health, an allowance for newspapers, stamps, writing paper, radio, holidays, beer, tobacco and presents. And later for Townsend (1979), in a famous quote, people were in poverty 'when they lack the resources to obtain the type of diet, participate in the activities and have the living conditions and amenities which are customary, or at least widely encouraged, or approved, in the societies to which they belong' (p.31).

However a new issue has moved centre stage in discussions about poverty in the last ten years to rival the old debate on relativism: is poverty a matter of deprivation or income? With the rise of wage labour in the 19th Century, and the decline of household and community production, almost all of the needs and wants that individuals and households have are satisfied through the market, or so it is widely assumed.

Governments have understandably as a consequence conflated poverty with low income, on the assumption that below a certain income, individuals and households will be deprived of the goods and services that citizens should have. However this conflation is problematic on three counts. The definitions of income and deprivation are both contestable, and the relation between them is not straightforward. Income, or resources to buy goods and services, might be thought to be easily determined. But there can be considerable short term fluctuations in income. At what time should real income be measured? A second problem is that money and other resources often flow into a household rather than direct to individuals. The payment of financial benefits for children through their mother acknowledges this; children nevertheless do not get the income personally. Similarly, wages to men may not find their way fully into the household economy, an issue examined in detail for the Russian case in Chapter 6.

There are also difficulties in identifying deprivation. Lack of goods and services deemed customary, encouraged or approved, is culturally suffused. In post- or high-modern societies, characterised by cultural variety and difference, it can be difficult to know what 'customary' means, a point made with vigour by David Piachaud (1981) in criticising Townsend's definition, which was not rigorously derived from the population itself (but corrected in Mack and Lansley's subsequent and influential 1985 study). Moreover the relation between income and deprivation is not as close as might be expected at first sight. An important issue is the price of goods and services that vary not just regionally, but in the 'micro-economy' of even small cities, where purchase in small quantities can considerably raise unit prices. This can include energy, food, transport and clothes. Moreover the mix of goods purchased may not be the most efficient as a result of partial information or opportunity, for example in terms of diet. What is customary is of course also the target of energetic advertisers, who have every incentive to persuade poorer people, as everyone, to want things they may not really need.

A final point first raised by Stein Ringen (1988) is that those who are deprived may not lack income. They may either choose not to consume, or be constrained by other factors than lack of money (for example inability to access the money in the case of children or wives), or have high fixed costs, such as repayment obligations. Similarly, those who lack income may not be deprived, where for example the income is temporarily low, or there is access to other resources in kind – both common factors in rural or farming communities, and highly pertinent to Russia, as we shall see. For example, in a study of rural Ireland, Callan *et al.* (1993) found that only about half of income poor families experienced both deprivation and low income, and farmers were especially noticeable for constituting a quarter of the income poor, but only a little over 10 per cent of the income poor who were deprived (by his research standards).

In the Russian situation we would expect this mismatch to be worse for a number of reasons. With the hyperinflation of the early 1990s, the widespread delay in payment of wages and pensions, and the enforced leave experienced by a substantial minority of workers, households were using non-money strategies to survive. A great deal of mutual support through family and acquaintance networks has been revealed in a number of surveys, and in detail in a qualitative study by Lonkila (1997). Echoing the picture of late Soviet life painted by Shlapentokh (1989), Lonkila showed vividly the application of Granovetter's (1973) observation that the 'strength of weak ties' was that they put people in touch with a wider network of exchange, support, and obligation outside of the market. This was noticeably more extensive than in Finland, and a key survival mechanism from the socialist era that has been also functional for the new situation in which households find themselves.

Rose's annual surveys in the region identified the key non-monetary mechanism reported by households themselves as the growing of food. This ranks first, and slightly higher than waged income itself, as the key means of attaining resources for the household (Table 7, from Rose, 1996, p.24). Rose and McAllister (1996) have concluded, from a series of surveys across the whole of Eastern Europe including Russia, that 'money is not the measure of welfare in Russia'.

Where money income is available, it needs to be measured over longer than the normal period used in poverty surveys, and set against other resources in kind. This is neatly demonstrated by Ovcharova (1997).

Goskomstat survey data suggests that around 35 per cent of households fell below the official Subsistence Minimum where their income is measured over one month, but that this rate falls to 20 per cent when measured over three months. Secondly she shows, like Rose, that between 40 and 50 per cent of food products in Russia are currently produced outside the market. Even 50 per cent of Muscovites have vegetable plots (Rose and Tikhomirov, 1993). This is the single most important addition to money income, and judged by households to be of similar importance to money. Taking this into account, Ovcharova finds that the one month income poverty rate drops from 35 to 27 per cent, and the apparently high rate for rural households of 60 per cent drops to the urban, and overall, level of around 27 per cent.

A final reason we would expect this mismatch to be more severe for Russia is that with the change in the status of households so quickly, and the continued provision of extensive enterprise support in the form of non-market goods and services, there will be for many households a possession of goods and services at a higher level than their income would be able to sustain over the long term. A more detailed review of these issues and their pertinence to the Russian situation and the data presented in this book is presented in Chapter 2.

In comparison with the long history of both government intervention and social science writing about poverty, the idea of social exclusion is relatively new, at least in the form that it is defined and discussed now. Of course social differentiation has always occurred, and both the rich and poor have either voluntarily or involuntarily found themselves in separate worlds, both physical and social. However in modern times, the term has made its appearance through French social and policy debates in the 1960s. For some its attraction has been that it seems a less harsh way of describing poverty; for others it signals a significant shift away from a passive notion of deprivation to a more active conception of the multidimensional ways in which individuals and groups can become forcibly detached from the support and opportunities that normally flow through their immediate social environments, whether that of the family, of work, or of their local community.

In the EU, following French debates now echoed in recent years by the UK and other governments, a discussion has developed suggesting there should be a serious attempt to monitor and devise policies that will combat social exclusion. We wished to follow this argument in the study reported in this book. However our most challenging problem lay in trying to establish whether the concept of social exclusion can actually be applied to contemporary Russian society at all. Surely it is a concept created for and most effectively applied to other types of societies altogether? These are societies in which horizontal stratification has to some extent replaced vertical, where inequality is associated more with discriminations that exclude particular individuals or families from the main integration mechanisms than with belonging to poor classes or groups – and where, therefore, the solution to inequality lies in providing access to integration mechanisms rather than in income redistribution: societies, in other words, which are at a particular stage of modernisation.

In the light of this, we decided to test whether either or both of the concepts of poverty and social exclusion could be applied to the process of increasing social differentiation and the changes taking place in the structure of Russian society today. We were already aware that there is undoubtedly a specific group in Russia who are almost deliberately 'socially excluded'. These are people who do not have a 'permit' (in Russian, *propiska*) or – to use the more up-to-date term – 'residence registration'. Any Russian citizen without permanent registration is automatically excluded from generally accepted mechanisms of integration and social support. This is because social services in Russia are delivered through State bodies at the territorial level, and because the system whereby formal employment depends on having a permit for a given population centre remains unchanged since the Soviet period. So, a permit for a particular address functions as a marker dividing the formally successful section of Russia's population from the section that is deliberately placed in a position of social exclusion.

However, there are by definition many possible dimensions of social exclusion, and thus the study developed seven social exclusion scales: the right to secure, paid work (the Work scale); the right to essential medical assistance when needed (the Health scale); the right of access to education and culture (the Education and Culture scale); the right to significant relations of primary sociability and to inclusion in a community (the Relationships scale); the right to join social networks as one of the main ways to access resources (the Networks scale); the right of autonomy (the Autonomy scale); and the right to adequate housing (the Housing scale). More details on these, and on social exclusion are set out in Chapters 4 and 5.

Some Results from the Study

The results from this study are presented in detail in the remainder of the book, but we can introduce some of the key conclusions here.

Poverty

Processes of increasing material/property differentiation in Russia in the 1990s have left their mark, particularly on traditional practices of mutual support and on the quality of existing social networks as a survival resource. Poor households are gradually being deprived of access to a functioning network of relatives and friends, which forms the basis of social capital, and gradually excluded from active mutual exchange of connections, services and opportunities. They are falling out of the most significant social practices of traditional mutual exchanges. Other people involved in inter-family social networks with the poor are increasingly tending to give them simple assistance with resources and household support when they are in difficulties, but do not actively engage in helping them to find additional opportunities, guarantees or connections. This is something that should give politicians who are developing models of State support to the weakest and those most in need pause for thought.

The results of our project confirm that the behaviour of the poor in the process of tackling their problems does not differ qualitatively from the behaviour of most of the population, as has been observed in other European societies (Dean and Taylor-Gooby, 1991). However, the poorest groups of the population have far fewer material and social resources, or opportunities to exploit them. Even though they make no small efforts and undertake varied activities to try to get themselves out of difficulties, their possibilities are so limited that they are often incapable of overcoming poverty independently.

Our research shows that households in need place great value on alternative possibilities for survival: providing for oneself, and mutual assistance. However, the use of land to grow food, the exploitation of family property assets and the receipt of help from relatives and friends are often simply not available to such households, because of their lack of material and social resources. This leads us to caution politicians against the idealisation of the role of survival alternatives for Russian families, and we disagree with attempts to view them as a sufficient basis for refusing social assistance to the poor. The Russian phenomena of providing for oneself and mutual assistance require careful analysis if they are to be interpreted correctly.

Insufficient resources of the poorest intensify their deprivation, first sending them sliding over the 'threshold' and then helping to preserve the inescapable nature of their position. The voices of our interviewees resound, telling us of their degradation, dependency and lack of autonomy. Recently, following the well-known debates about the underclass, some sociologists have been trying to demonstrate evidence in Russia for 'culture of poverty' approaches, claiming that they apply to those strata of the population who have a weakened capacity for survival and have fallen to 'the social depths' in the course of the Russian reforms (Balabanova, 1999; Lokshin and Popkin, 1999). However, the issue is not whether the poor have particular 'subcultural' features, but whether there are trends towards ever broader social exclusion of the most vulnerable groups from the normal activities of life in society. Following this approach focuses the researcher's attention not on 'blaming the victim' (Ryan, 1971), but on analysis of a whole complex of social conditions and problems in which the person who is the object of research has to live and act. If the meagre resources of the poorest are further exhausted, then growing anomie, social tension and social exclusion in Russian society will be unavoidable. Opening access to channels for the reintegration, replenishment and growth of resources should be seen as one of the central issues in the struggle against poverty in Russia – a high-priority social policy objective for the State and a concern for society.

Social Exclusion

Where there is a prolonged process of growing deprivation over many years, poverty leads to social exclusion. In our research, we found a certain poverty threshold (usually coinciding with the boundary between being 'badly-off' and actually 'poor' on the deprivation scale), at which many markers of social exclusion start to appear and the household will enter the 'grey area'. Moreover, 'indigence' on the deprivation scale will undoubtedly mean that social exclusion objectively exists – although it may not always be recognisable. In cases of a slide into social exclusion over many years, where there is an unsophisticated structure of consumption or self-imposed restrictions, people may be unaware of their actual requirements, which they cannot satisfy because of their income level and their exclusion from alternative ways of tackling their problems (State support, network resources, and so on). These cases are very difficult to record quantitatively in empirical research. However, we demonstrate clearly that, where a particular level of poverty lasts for seven years or more, it is a definite predictor of the onset of profound social exclusion – leaving the 'grey area' for the 'black hole', adopting a new way of life and a new psychological state.

This time lag of several years – from the point when they fall into poverty to the point when the formation of social exclusion is complete – is a fairly long period, and the family may use it in different ways depending on their potential. Therefore, the individual features of the household situation and the probable nature of the influence of various risks predetermine not just the individual reactions of households to their new situation – but also how long they spend in the 'grey area', their prospects for return to the mainstream, whether they get stuck in the 'grey area' or slide into even more profound social exclusion.

The natural consequence of this may be a rethinking of social policy objectives, in order to try and take into account the 'individualisation of risks' – an approach that has already tentatively begun in the UK (Manning and Shaw, 2000). Unfortunately, in Russia today, neither public awareness nor wider academic circles nor policymakers seem ready to accept or even recognise the need for measures to neutralise the negative effects of social exclusion.

We did not in any way set out to throw light on all forms of social exclusion that exist in Russia today – and even less, on social exclusion in general. Our objective was much more modest: to determine whether there are excluded households within the poor sections of the population in large Russian cities, to attempt to define how their social exclusion manifests itself, what are the main risk factors that influence the onset of social exclusion, how the social exclusion process unfolds, and what its interrelationships with poverty may be. We see our results as information to be used for further reflection, rather than as a set of exhaustive answers to these questions. However, we are sure of one thing: we clearly detected a trend of qualitative change in the social structure of Russian society, with the establishing of a large section of excluded people and all the consequences that flow from this – far wider consequences than those of the large-scale poverty that Russians now simply experience as fairly common.

Ethnicity

While of course poverty is a difficult experience for any family, there were differences that we found between Ossetian and Russian families. Measured by money income per family member, Ossetian families in Vladikavkaz were more likely to be among the very poorest than were Russians, especially where there were a lot of children. On the other hand, they more often received significant – for them – support from relatives. Russian families were more active in their choice of life strategy, especially in seeking additional earnings, while Ossetian respondents were more optimistic in assessing their family's prospects. A key ethnically-related factor in the social exclusion of some of our Vladikavkaz households was the low level of primary informal connections, which have the potential to be converted into life chances and real moves towards greater prosperity. In this regard, poor Ossetian and Russian families in our sample were similar: both experienced – and reacted to – lack of such connections. However, such a lack was much more typical for the Russian than for the Ossetian families.

Thus a significant difference between our poor Russian and Ossetian families in Vladikavkaz was that the Russians displayed more initiative and attempted to change their material situation for the better in a variety of ways. In our sample, Russians were less likely than Ossetians to remain in a state of passive expectation. This also suggested that Russians cherished fewer illusions as to their level of connections: they have to rely on themselves to a greater extent. There were also significantly more unemployed people in the Ossetian sub-sample (7, 8, 13 and 18 per cent respectively for the Moscow, Voronezh, Russian Vladikavkaz and Ossetian Vladikavkaz sub-samples). In fact, as a result of having more children and more problems connected with health or inter-ethnic conflicts, the Ossetian families in our sample came close to the Russian families in terms of social exclusion. This similarity in levels of social exclusion had come about despite the *a priori* factor that the Ossetians had greater access to primary social connections: it became apparent that such connections do not provide an intrinsic defence mechanism that automatically comes into play to completely block a family's drift into a state of 'stagnant poverty'. These connections must be drawn on and actively reshaped in the context of strategies and support networks that are both more active and more efficient than those available to many of the families in our Ossetian sub-sample.

These characteristics of Russian and Ossetian poverty in Vladikavkaz reflect the position and feelings of Russians and Ossetians in the Republic as a whole. Ossetians dominate the representative and executive organs of power in the Republic – as well as the most prestigious and profitable occupations ('New Russians' in North Ossetia are almost all of Ossetian ethnic origin). The ethnic structure of migration shows this indirectly: according to Passport Office data, of the 16,500 people who left North Ossetia between 1995 and 2000, over 15,000 were Russians, while Russians represented no more than 5 per cent of those entering.

Gender

Our research group set out to clarify the issue of inequality in dependency and deprivation within the family, as experienced by husband and wife, and the differences that exist between the ways that men and women experience poverty and survival (depending on their differing everyday situation and type of family). In this respect it attempted to follow a longer tradition of UK studies of gender differences from this viewpoint (Goode, *et al.*, 1998). We also tried to take into account the critical comments that are often made of gender research with a mono-ethnic sample (Graham, 1992), and so we broadened the ethnic base of our in-depth interviews by including five Ossetian households and one Jewish household among the 22 surveyed in the sub-project on gender.

The results of a great deal of recent research (and ours was no exception here) provide evidence that the burden of the consequences of Russia's reforms of the 1990s has fallen most heavily on the shoulders of women. This is shown by – among other things – the predominance of female unemployment, women's limited access to the main institutions of integration (a good job, good-quality education, control, power) and the increasing dependency of families on the woman, when, in the face of a declining standard of living, responsibility for raising the next generation falls completely to her (Coudouel, *et al.*, 1999; Tikhonova, *et al.*, 2002). Moreover, Russian women's ability to choose between employment in the economy and working in the home is significantly restricted by their standard of living and the income needs of their families. In the absence of any real system of social support for the family, the majority of Russian households with children simply cannot survive without women's wages.

Thus in 1990 the function of breadwinner had been – in one way or another – fulfilled by a woman in only a third of the 105 households under study. However, by the year 2000, this function had shifted to practically half the women in the same households. What is more, this trend was evident among the Russian population in all the regions of our survey, and it was only among the ethnic Ossetians who took part that it was appreciably weaker.

At the same time, these changes do not always entail re-examination of existing stereotyped views of what being 'the head of the family' actually means. Over 90 per cent of the respondents whom we interviewed in the course of our household panel study were able to name one family member as head of their household. However, in defining the head of the family, they were guided by not one, but at least three, approaches: the traditional (patriarchal) approach, where the oldest member of the family (as a rule, a man) was designated as its head; the economic approach, where the head of the family was its main breadwinner and/or the person who controlled the family budget (in this case, the family might be headed by either a man or a woman); or the egalitarian (equal) approach, where the family did not clearly identify a head (Davidova, 2000).

Of the 105 households in the study, some were 'male' (headed and/or managed by a man), others were 'female' (headed and/or managed by a woman), with 55 household respondents of both sexes naming men as heads of household, 41 respondents of both sexes naming women and the other nine unable to single out one member as head of household (we referred to these as 'equal' households). However, the ratio of 'male' to 'female' households varied markedly between our different research regions. Moscow households were equally likely to be headed by a man or a woman. A particular feature of the Voronezh sub-sample was the preponderance of 'female' households, while in Vladikavkaz, in contrast, 'male' households predominated. Moreover, we encountered cases where the family member singled out as head was neither the breadwinner nor the person managing the family budget. That is, even when all the functions of head of the family were really being fulfilled by the woman, this role was not acknowledged, either by her husband or by the wife herself.

The main earner/breadwinner was designated by respondents as head of the family in only 60 per cent of cases: for example, in one out of five households with children under 18 where a man was head of the household, he was not the main breadwinner, having ceded that function to the woman. As far as making decisions about everyday budgeting was concerned, in the overwhelming majority of cases, this right (and often the additional duties that went with it) fell on the shoulders of the woman, even if she was not the acknowledged head of the family. In practice, only a third of men recognised as heads of families took part in the practical, everyday running of the home and the day-to-day planning of smaller family expenditure. Thus, the subjectively defined head of a Russian household was not automatically the person who made the main contribution to the family budget or carried responsibility for management within the family.

Conclusion

This project grew out of our previous work on the impact of changes in the Russian labour market on Russian households. It is unusual in having a qualitative approach to data gathering, alongside a panel element. Indeed included in the 105 households followed here over the span of a year, were 19 households retained from our earlier project that have now been interviewed four times since 1996. It may seem that this group is a fragile and insignificant sample from a population of 150 million people. However we have learned a great deal from their experiences without which we would be unable to identify the ways in which they have struggled with their circumstances over recent years. We hope that this book will be both a testament to their untold stories, and at the same time provide a basis for making a contribution to the understanding of poverty and social exclusion in a wider Europe, and to informing Russian policy makers.

Note

[1] The 'new' poor are a new phenomenon in post-Soviet Russia: there was nothing like them in the USSR. They consist of large sections of skilled specialists and blue-collar workers who have secondary vocational or even higher education, are middle-aged or elderly and, prior to the reforms, belonged to the best-off strata among the population (see Manning, Tikhonova and Shkaratan, 2000, p.264).

Part II

Poverty

2 Poverty, Incomes and Resources – Concepts and Measures

John Veit-Wilson

Голь на выдумки хитра.
The poor are resourceful in invention

Introduction

How can we understand what poverty, deprivation or social exclusion have meant in Russia during the political and economic upheavals of the past decade? The international debate reveals many disparate understandings of the poverties, deprivations and exclusions in societies around the world. This chapter aims to outline them to enable them to illuminate the findings of this study of Russia, in particular the way in which the social construction of 'poverty' depends on cultural history and social context.

The variety of national meanings of poverty cannot be read off from national statistics of income distributions or the like. Its social meanings and the specific resources needed to avoid it have to be studied and understood in their national or local context and manifestations. The research reported in this book suggests that historically Russian poverty may not be as susceptible to the same assumptions about its forms and meanings as those which drove the sociological or social policy analyses of poverty and influenced their dominant ideas and methods in Western European countries. There is an apparent contradiction between societies whose moral value systems traditionally endorsed economic independence, with its corollary of treating the economic dependence of poverty as a moral failing, and Russian society which, we are told here, traditionally condemned wealth and did not despise poverty. In Russia, poverty was perhaps not the moral issue attracting opprobrium and inducing shame to the same extent that it was in Western Europe, but rather a matter of 'getting by' materially. The focus on power over material resources which goes with individualistic approaches to poverty has to be complemented in the Russian context by greater attention to the social resources of mutual assistance and other forms of social capital which have long been more relevant there as resources to combat material deprivations and allow social participation. Only when these issues have been clarified can the next steps be taken, whether they are for quantitative statistics and qualitative data which can be meaningfully compared internationally, or for national policy measures to address the distinct national or local conditions.

The international literature on poverty, deprivation, social exclusion, and the scale and intensity of their complex consequences, as well as income and resources, is more than a century old and gigantic in scope and extent. The conceptualisations and definitions of poverty developed differently, often in dialectical modes, in different countries during the 20th Century according to the perspectives of the prevailing research pioneers who articulated them and the influences of the dominant ideological and policy concerns on which they were focused. The intellectual history of the variety of approaches remains to be written.[1] As a result, many different discourses, concepts and definitions, themselves associated with varying and often disparate purposes for seeking poverty measures (Veit-Wilson 1998; 2000), compete with each other globally without being distinguished according to their applicability to the issue in hand or taking account of the decisive contextual and cultural differences. Those purposes include the desire of social scientists for accurate and reliable social criteria with which to map the tolerable and intolerable in societies, and the demands of policy makers for politically credible tools with which to plan and operate income maintenance systems. These two disparate aims may be in conflict when scientists want measures which are reliable even if not precise while politicians want measures which are precise even though they may not be scientifically reliable. Different methods are needed to develop each of these kinds of measure, and they are judged by different criteria of acceptability and use.

This chapter focuses only on the issues raised by the study of poverty from a sociological perspective, and not those raised by the demands of social or economic policy. It can do no more than offer a condensed résumé of some issues pertinent to the research reported in this book, and to do so must start from first principles.

Needs, Deprivations and Poverties

In its broadest sense, we are concerned here with the poverty which the World Bank economist Martin Ravallion described as existing 'in a given society when one or more persons do not attain a level of material well-being deemed to constitute a reasonable minimum by the standards of that society' (Ravallion, 1992). If we are to confront the real issues here, the first thing to note is that this does no more than describe the phenomenon in a direct manner, following Stein Ringen (1988) – poor people are those who demonstrably do not attain a certain socially-prescribed level of well-being. The concept of poverty here lies in grasping the meaning of the abstraction 'well-being' and its absence, from which this definition can be derived. The concrete meanings of the abstraction can only be understood by examining the social and contextually-located construction of the reasonable minimum, in this case in Russia in the 1990s, including descriptions of the lifestyles below and above it and the factors which enable these lifestyles to be identified. The causes of the failure to attain the minimum are again another distinct matter.

These distinct aspects – concepts, definitions, identifiers, descriptions and causes – are very often confused with each other in common talk about poverty. Productive analysis is vitiated by failure to recognise and use the appropriate aspect. Further, Ravallion refers to *material* well-being and it aids clarity to try to distinguish this from looser approaches to poverty which extend even to individual intangibles such as alienation and anomie. David Byrne, in his valuable analysis of social exclusion (Byrne, 1999), quotes the distinction which Alan Walker makes:

> ... regarding *poverty* as a lack of the material resources, especially income, necessary to participate in British society and *social exclusion* as a more comprehensive formulation which refers to the dynamic process of being shut out, fully or partially, from any of the social, economic, political or cultural systems which determine the social integration of a person in society (Walker and Walker, 1997, p.8; original emphases).

This chapter focuses on the issues surrounding this approach to poverty and resources, in ways which allow application to any society, especially that of Russia, while subsequent chapters address the complex variety of forms of social exclusion and their consequences. The two subjects are clearly interconnected, in that similar resources may be relevant in both cases, but the focus of the first is on the distribution of necessary resources and their lack, while the second is concerned with wider issues of political and social forces and relations, and of individual and collective behaviour and integration, which may extend far beyond the ranks of the poor. To take an example, in largely marketised economies such as those of Western Europe and USA, lack of money is the chief cause and identifier of the condition of poverty; indeed, some usages treat the expressions as synonymous. On the other hand, a person may be rich but nevertheless socially excluded if they belong to certain categories discriminated against because of ethnicity, religion or gender. Contrary to common assertion, these conditions are not causes of poverty in themselves, nor are categories such as unemployment, old age, single parenthood or lack of education or occupational training, which are often simplistically asserted to be 'causes of poverty' or even as indicators of social exclusion. The fallacy of assuming they cause poverty can be exposed by noting that they are often found among the rich,[2] but they may empirically be found to be causes of social exclusion when other countervailing factors fail to compensate as wealth often does. The reason for the simplistic assertion is no doubt the reluctance of politicians to address the policy implications of the lack of income flows which are commonly associated with these characteristics – rich unemployed people have stocks of convertible assets and resources besides flows of earnings or pensions. The cause of poverty, as well as a way of defining it, is simply a lack of appropriate resources to gain access to participation in society according to prevailing standards; the condition of poverty is 'an enforced lack of socially perceived necessities' (Mack and Lansley, 1985, p.39). The lack of the specified resources may identify those in poverty, either directly (deprivation indicators) or indirectly, by proxy (incomes demonstrably too low for participation). The consequence is then Ravallion's description above. Nevertheless, those who continue to identify concepts of poverty with the idea of social exclusion, whether in the weak sense of being unable to participate or the strong sense of being prevented from doing so by the forces which 'shut people out', may find it useful to think of poverty narrowly as 'market-based exclusion'. The reasons why money and similar fungible resources are lacking may include the discriminations which are the material of the analysis of social exclusion.

Causes and Conditions – The Chain of Human Needs and Resources

Resources for what? Observing the unproductive discussion in the poverty debate, Hans-Jürgen Andreß expressed astonishment at the common omission of an answer and, after distinguishing between the individual and the collective aspects of poverty, quoted Georg Simmel who, writing a century ago, correctly identified the indispensability of an objective in the definition. Andreß concluded that 'Poor is that person whose resources do not satisfy their needs' (Andreß, 1998, p.1) and observed (p.4) that 'Resources per sé do not have an intrinsic value. Only if one uses them for certain purposes that have a certain value are they useful'. As S. Dubnoff pointed out (Dubnoff, 1985), the question of how much income is enough can only be answered in terms of enough for what, for whom, and who says, and to these three questions one must add, for how long? The same four questions must be asked of every assertion about needs, the resources to meet them and their adequacy, noting especially the critical role of the observer's perspective in affecting the answers to the questions.[3]

The nature of the needs which the resources are intended to satisfy may be as broad or narrow as the context of the debate sets, and Andreß discusses, for whatever reason, a rather limited and static view of needs which implies closure on others or on temporal change. A prerequisite for a more informed analysis is clarity about the totality of human needs over time and the range of resources which are required to meet them. We can then narrow down and distinguish which of these resources are the focus for analysis and action. I shall therefore omit rehearsing the volume of previous argument about human needs,[4] often framed on the basis of a specific social problem rather than a total social analysis, and instead offer the following brief but all-embracing definition of human needs based on a clear objective.

'Human needs' means the full range of intangible and material resources that are required over time to achieve *the production, maintenance and reproduction of the fully autonomous, fully participating adult human in the particular society to which he or she belongs*. The most basic needs every human has are the intangibles of having a society to be a recognised member of (which has its own collective needs for resources to sustain its continuity), and meaningful and supportive social and individual relationships throughout life within it. Material resources may support the physical organism but it is the full range of social and psychological resources which are required for the experience of humanity.[5]

This statement about human needs is not a matter of dogmatic belief. If contested, the argument must be in terms of what is empirically verifiable about all human societies and the resources required for societies to exist and continue, and for individual humans to grow and flourish in them. It must not be about what someone elsewhere (whether in space, time or social status) thinks is necessary or redundant among those resources (the political fallacy). There is an important distinction, often overlooked, between the social scientific approach of *discovering* empirically the full range of what is needed, and people's ordinary approach of *prescribing* normatively what ought to be needed (from some subjective point of view and usually drawing on a far more limited knowledge of the range in answer to a specific problem). Social science provides findings which are reliable but not precise (they fall within ranges of reliability), while policy makers want answers that are precise even if they are not reliable. This confusion between the empirical and the normative has seriously hampered the proper discussion of the subject of human needs, whether collective or individual.

The list of all the tangible and intangible resources required over a life span or even longer to enable a human being to become and remain a fully autonomous and participating adult member of his or her specified society would be a long and detailed one. It would be made even more complex if one includes what is required to provide and maintain the spatial and economic context in which that society continues and reproduces itself.[6] The numerous human societies exist under widely differing geographical, environmental and ecological conditions and have always each defined what they mean by full adult social participation in different ways. Abstract definitions of needs are therefore no guide to what is required in specific social contexts. This is what is meant by saying that, in concrete reality, human needs are always relative to the society, time and place in which they are expressed, and depend crucially on the observer who expresses them.[7] The specific resources required to meet needs inevitably vary by social context, time and feasibility. It is an empirical question whether what western sociologists have discovered or specified as household and personal needs are the same or different in Russia. What may be included in the inventory of necessary resources is discussed later in this chapter.

Where the resources are lacking or are withheld, then the needs may not be met and the individual or group can be described as deprived, in poverty, in terms of that society and its definitions of needs. This is similar to Peter Townsend's classic definition of poverty:

People are relatively deprived if they cannot obtain, at all or sufficiently, the conditions of life – that is, the diets, amenities, standards and services – which allow them to play the roles, participate in the relationships and follow the customary behaviour which is expected of them by virtue of their membership of society. *If they lack or are denied resources to obtain access to these conditions of life and so fulfil membership of society they may be said to be in poverty.* People may be deprived in any or all of the major spheres of life – at work where the means largely determining position in other spheres are earned; at home, in neighbourhood and family; in travel; in a range of social and individual activities outside work and home or neighbourhood in performing a variety of roles in fulfilment of social obligations (Townsend, 1993, p.36; emphasis added).

This is not the same wording as Townsend's earlier and widely quoted definition of poverty, which referred to resources being so seriously below those of the average that the poor 'are, in effect, excluded from' participatory lifestyles (Townsend, 1979, p.31). This exclusion is a *consequence* of lack of resources. The European Commission version of 1984 defines the poor as persons whose resources are so limited as to exclude them from participation, and here exclusion is again a consequence of lack of resources. Later uses of the term 'exclusion' seem to imply that it is a *causal* condition in which people possess negatively evaluated behavioural characteristics which exclude them from participation (the weak version, which Ruth Levitas (1998) sees as a moral underclass discourse) or lead them to be excluded by those with power to do so (the strong version). It matters whether exclusion is a cause or a consequence since it affects the policies which may be adopted to combat it, such as augmenting the resources lacked in the case of poverty (what Levitas sees as a redistributive discourse), or altering the characteristics in the case of those perceived as being deviant. Integrating the excluded (Levitas's third discourse of exclusion) could in theory be just as much a matter of distributing resources as of altering behaviour, but governments reluctant to do the former focus policies on the latter instead. It remains an empirical and contextual question which would be more effective. Townsend later reformulated the earlier wording to that quoted above, perhaps to remove the ambiguity about the use of the word 'exclusion'.

While the concepts of poverty and social exclusion may be distinct, there is much overlap, and research findings are equivocal on whether people in poverty are socially excluded in the sense of being different from those not in poverty. Van den Bosch's review of international poverty research in Europe came to a similar conclusion to that reported in this book about Russia, that:

> In my view the defining characteristic of the poor is that they have a material standard of living that is socially regarded as unacceptable; the poor do not share any other characteristic or combination of characteristics that distinguishes them from the non-poor. The poor are not necessarily excluded in the sense of having low status or being restricted in their social contacts. They cannot be identified on the basis of behaviour, or any other observable characteristic only (Van den Bosch, 2001, p.412).[8]

Townsend uses both 'conditions of life' and 'resources' as requirements to meet needs, but we must note that meeting needs is a sequential process, a chain, in which a specified resource enables people to achieve a condition of life which is itself a resource to meet another need, and so on to the total life experience. Is an adequate diet (or an education or good health, or any other examples like them) a need, a resource or a condition of life? It is commonly used as all of these, and whether it is perceived as one or another depends on its position in the analytical chain in which the usage arises and not on any inherent quality in the concept as such. Arguments about needs frequently confuse concrete examples with abstract categories. If we try to analyse statements about individual needs, we find that the abstract needs underlying them can all be classified into either physical or psychological domains, and each of these can be divided into two – the nutrition and environment of the physical organism, and the two domains of psychological needs which have been variously called identity and community, or being and belonging.[9] But the concrete examples always and inevitably relate to how such needs are experienced in culture, time and place, and usually draw on more than one classificatory domain. To take two simple examples, in most human societies, eating (nutrition) is carried out according to cultural conventions involving relationships (belonging),[10] while clothing, which provides the personal portable environment appropriate to climate and the community's culture, expresses identity needs and endorses status. If the 'right' clothing helps someone to get a job, is it a physical need or a cultural resource?

Analysis therefore requires specification of the objective and of the chain of intermediary resources by which that objective may be met. Relationships are invariably among the resources humans need to meet the end objective suggested above (starting with parents or their adequate substitutes to provide physical nurture and primary socialisation to every child born), but as this chapter focuses on poverty in the distributional rather than relational sense (which can be social exclusion), they will be referred to only as relevant in that context. Relationships are also important because in societies the needs and goals, even if unconscious and unvoiced, are inevitably collective, and thus the resources individuals need have to be collective as well as individual.[11] The dynamic chain is apparent in all analyses of human needs and the resources which meet them, whether the resources are individual or collective, interpersonal or intrapersonal, material or mental (or tangible or intangible). Against this background, the arguments about the social policy tactics of meeting certain needs in cash or in kind, or about the value of human or social capital in meeting collective or individual needs, are, at an analytical level, merely abstracted reflections of the social realities; they are not substantive factors in themselves. To treat them as 'real' isolates them statically and risks closing off the possibility of dynamic lateral thought about alternative solutions in social practice or policy to the problems of unmet needs. The scholars' aspiration to achieve valid abstract generalisations has been the curse preventing their insights from adoption by politicians who want contextually concrete answers to currently salient problems.

However fatuous it may be to try to impose consistency on the multiplicity of uses of the terms in the poverty debates, we could nevertheless describe the condition of all unmet need as deprivation, and the cause of this condition as the lack of relevant resources. A narrow, policy-oriented meaning of poverty then treats it as the special condition of lack of appropriate distributed money resources in marketised economies. A broader approach to poverty which overlaps with the meanings attached to the term social exclusion would see it in one of two ways. The strong approach sees it as the condition of lack of social integration (unmet needs for belonging and – as some would argue – behaving socially), whose cause, as Townsend pointed out (quoted above) is denial of the resources by power holders. The weak approach sees it as the individual's lack of their own functional resources such as personality characteristics, personal claims on others in networks of relationships (social capital) or impersonal purchasing power to gain participation in and recognition of community membership. At each step a condition of met or unmet need is also a cause of the next condition, and such analytical chains weave, dividing and merging over time, longer than the individual life-span if a viable society is to be maintained. The common social policy-oriented analyses chop such chains into short lengths concerned only with some politically significant events within which some section of the population suffers unmet need – which can of course include majorities of the population, not just minorities, suffering unmet needs according to the majority's own standards.[12] Nor are these matters as simple as common presentations imply. The majority's unmet needs may include the psychological need for security against perceived threats from minorities. But these same minorities may themselves also have unmet needs, both material and cultural, some of which they interpret as requiring threatening behaviours to acquire from others or to retain the resources to meet them. Examples in Western Europe include not only the high profile but low risk of crime or terrorism, but also the low profile and high probability of unmet collective needs for social security which are threatened by the refusal of rich minorities, usually corporations but including individuals, to share resources to increase collective well-being. No element of social analysis of the distribution of resources to meet anyone's needs or of the relationship of any sections of a population to the whole can fail to raise political questions about their counterfactuals.

Poverty Types and Discourses

The ways in which the whole subject of poverty is discussed powerfully affects the ways in which it is conceptualised, defined and measured, and the policies which are posited as combating it. This goes beyond mere clashes of scientific paradigm to deep-seated and long-lasting modes of thought, articulation and action. Paul Spicker elaborated eleven clusters of meaning surrounding varying definitions of poverty (Gordon and Spicker, 1999, p.150), but such clusters may not be as good at capturing the complex dynamics of usage, with its overlaps and exclusivities, as the concept of discourses does, in the sense of discourses which Michel Foucault developed to explain the history of thought about sexuality, madness or crime. Research into the ways in which the governments of ten countries conceptualised and dealt with the ideas of poverty and need in their income maintenance policies suggested that some seven distinct discourses of poverty were in use in the 1990s (Veit-Wilson, 1998; 2000). Four discourses might be called humanistic in that they addressed human behaviour and what structured it. These were approaches embodying assumptions about (1) social and political structures and systems, (2) behaviours, (3) social exclusion, and (4) inequalities. Three discourses were asocial in that they were not concerned with empirical evidence about human behaviour and the distribution of resources but with addressing poverty in formal and abstracted modes of definition or measurement, (5) by statistical distribution, (6) by theoretical economistic models, and (7) by legal status. In the field of cross-national comparisons of poverty, these three asocial discourses currently reign supreme in articulating measures, in the form (5) of household incomes below some decile of the median, (6) of GDP per head, and (7) of social assistance benefits and recipients. But none of these explain anything about the meaning of poverty in any country, which is perhaps their attraction to politicians and global officials.

This chapter refers to the complex question of disparate discourses only because agreement on the identification of resources appropriate to meeting human needs depends on prior agreement on the discourse appropriate to the analysis of the unmet need, the poverty, deprivation or social exclusion in question. Thus in a world in which all and every definition of poverty is inevitably relative, the traditional demand for 'absolute' definitions and measures is found only among those using the economistic discourse, which believes that 'man lives by bread alone', or at any rate that minimal material resources are all the poor need. They assume that meeting the economic need for the reproduction of human labour power requires no more than what Seebohm Rowntree described as an income sufficient for 'merely physical efficiency' (Rowntree, 1901), his Primary Poverty measure, which was in fact devised to show the public that many full time working class earnings were too low even for physical needs. A century later, such discourse users still compose dietaries and household budgets for this wholly asocial level of living – asocial because the great many studies of real people in poverty show that at such income levels they put as great or greater priority on maintaining their social and psychological need-meeting activities (spending on belonging and being) than on their physical needs. As Townsend put it, reviewing the evidence from decades of research, '... a lot of people, when their incomes are halved, do not surrender some of their social obligations to their families, to their workplaces, to their neighbours and so on' (in Yeates and McLaughlin, 2000, p.61). Modern minimum subsistence budgets of this kind tell us nothing about a society and its standards of minimum welfare, still less about what it really costs to take part in society at a minimum level of decency, but they do say a lot about the stratified and asocial beliefs of those who compose them. Examination of who continues to use subsistence approaches shows that it is chiefly governments who wish to massage their poverty rates downwards and the economists who serve such governments in their attempts to set minimum incomes at the lowest plausible limits.[13] The same is true in the UK, at least for the use of statistical definitions of poverty, since what little and dated empirical evidence there was suggested that household incomes needed for minimally adequate participation were at higher levels than the 60 per cent of median household incomes (adjusted for household size, composition and equivalences) taken as a statistical poverty measure (Townsend, 1979; Waldegrave and Frater, 1996).

The term 'absolute' poverty nevertheless has such lasting rhetorical power, as shown by the support which Amartya Sen gave it (Sen, 1983), that it was adopted by the United Nations Development Programme in the 1995 Copenhagen Declaration, and even relativist pioneers such as Townsend have become persuaded to use it on expedient and pragmatic grounds. The UNDP agreed statements which set out the whole of poverty, described later as 'overall' poverty, and within that a more limited subset of conditions which it labelled 'absolute':

> Absolute poverty is a condition characterised by severe deprivation of basic human needs, including food, safe drinking water, sanitation facilities, health, shelter, education and information. It depends not only on income but also on access to social services (UN, 1995, para 19).

Some of the abstract categories here would be included in traditional definitions of absolute poverty, although supporters of minimum subsistence budgets would rarely agree on how much money was needed in modern industrial states with marketised economies to pay for the necessary minimum of health or education. It is notable that there was international agreement that access to information (part of belonging) was a human need, and that social services were an essential resource to meet some of these needs, implying collective government action rather than merely individualised charitable or marketised solutions. These assumptions would not have been included in any discourse of absolute needs in the past.

The UN's description of poverty overall, which precedes the description of absolute poverty quoted above, is very broad, starting with the statement that poverty has many manifestations. Those mentioned include all the usual physical and social deprivations and pathological conditions which individuals suffer from, but extend to 'unsafe environments and social discrimination and exclusion'. It makes a salutary point to rich nations that poverty:

> occurs in all countries: as mass poverty in many developing countries, pockets of poverty amid wealth in developed countries, loss of livelihoods as a result of economic recession, sudden poverty as a result of disaster or conflict, the poverty of low-wage workers, and the utter destitution of people who fall outside family support systems, institutions or safety nets (UN, 1995, para 19).

It goes on to describe many of the groups who are especially vulnerable to poverty and exclusion, though, as suggested above, vulnerability must not be confused with causation. Research at the Townsend Centre for International Poverty Research at the University of Bristol showed that if poverty is defined in the UN terms, then not only this broad picture of poverty but even such 'absolute' poverty can be found in the UK (Townsend, *et al.*, 1997; Gordon, 2000a). The value of the UN approach is that it proclaims international agreement on the scope and variety – and social relativity – of the subject, but by conflating the individual with the collective, the deprivations with the conditions and the characteristics, the lack of resources with political acts, it offers little more than a conceptual palette from which any kinds and colours of pictures can be painted. It tries to encompass everything within one term but thereby prevents it from having any explanatory power or policy orientation. If we want clear diagnosis of social problems to allow effective policy formation to combat them, we need a coherent analysis, not a list of everything that could be understood by the term.

If there is to be progress in this large and diffuse subject, we must delimit the field in which we aim to work. To restrict the meaning of poverty to the material deprivations which have the consequence of hindering if not preventing people from meeting their human needs as specified above (for healthy individual development and social participation in the full expected range of social activities and personal developments over the life-span), will allow us to concentrate on the battery of different kinds of resources which can then be seen to be necessary to combat those deprivations.

Resources to Meet Material Needs

'Material needs' is a simple phrase but covers a complex field. The problem of specifying them is exacerbated by the absence of a clear boundary between poverty meaning the lack of material resources necessary to participate in society, which is a social matter, and the social exclusion to which lack of material resources may contribute. 'Material needs' is not a matter of the 'merely physical efficiency' which Rowntree described in order to show incomes were too low for social participation. We are inevitably talking about the individual's power over resources required to participate at what society defines as minimally decent levels, and this must include the social and psychological aspects of being and belonging as well as of the physiological aspects of nutrition and environment. The further complication is that the resources themselves, in the chain of cause and condition, may be social and psychological, as shown by the Russian research findings reported here. Personal characteristics and social networks (social capital) are both indispensable in the chain of acquiring economic resources even to meet physical needs.

The long-standing focus on money incomes in poverty research has hampered the search for and an understanding of the very wide range of other resources needed in the chain towards meeting human needs. This narrow focus had good reason: it reflected political not scientific concerns. The impetus for the research into what is the minimum necessary level of personal disposable incomes came from policy concerns about the levels of wages, taxable capacity, and social security and social assistance benefits in largely marketised modern industrial states. This research continues to be required, especially against the claims of politicians over more than a hundred years that it is behavioural failure and not lack of money which causes the problems of deprivation. Finding out what is the need for money when all else is held constant has driven the policy-dominated poverty research agenda. It could be argued that in poverty debates the development of the broader discourse of social exclusion in the last two decades of the 20th Century was a response to political resistance to this preoccupation with cash incomes alone as much as to its narrowness.

A step towards a broader scientific analysis of the underlying deprivation problems in order to identify the range of required resources was suggested not only by Peter Townsend and his research team's work in the 1960s (Townsend, 1979) but also by Sen's development of the concept of capabilities (Sen, 1983). Both of these emphasised the role of social objectives in the identification and analysis of relevant resources in social context. For instance, implementing the abstract capability of 'mobility' may need a great many different kinds of individual and collective resources depending on where it occurs on the globe and the capacities of the individual concerned. The capability of 'access to clean drinking water' could be met by individual purchasing power if a supply is available in bottles or by payment (or tax) for piped water, but only if the collective capitalised resources of collecting and purifying it, as well as bottling or piping, are already available *in situ*. The focus on capabilities as intermediary objectives on the chain is important but does not avoid the continuing need to identify the resources which are required to achieve each stage in the chain. In each social context, analysis has to consider what are the relevant and appropriate resources and, in largely marketised economies where many needs can be met by spending money, sufficient money in the form of personal disposable incomes continues to be crucial.

In the broader connection, the University of Bristol team has developed methods by which the generalisations of the UNDP's approach to absolute poverty can be operationalised, that is, turned into a check list of seven situations and experiences, scaled over a four-level range (mild; moderate; severe; extreme), against which specific social conditions can be measured (Gordon, *et al.*, 2003, p.8, Table 2.1). These seven factors are food, safe drinking water, health, shelter, education, information and basic social services. The form which the 'food' category takes refers to the nutritional adequacy of the available diet, in quantity and content, but not to costs and affordability. 'Water' refers both to the cash costs and to access, while sanitation refers only to access. 'Health' means treatment for ill-health and covers both costs and access. 'Shelter' covers condition, amenities and overcrowding but not cost to households. 'Education' brings in 'lack of resources', which might mean parents' or communities' ability to pay fees or collectively to make provision, as well as exclusion because of discrimination. 'Information' is partly a matter of affordability and partly of political control. Finally, 'social services' is taken to mean health and education provision and involves questions of access and of standards, rather than the availability and cost of treatment or schooling.

This simple list shows that a wide range of resources would be required to escape from absolute poverty. It is the product of one approach, and others might take a different view but, as it is a pioneering attempt to concretise the UN's abstract idea of absolute poverty, it is important as a starting point. Simply in this formulation, the necessary resources include government provision of appropriate education and health facilities in accessible places, and collective provision of clean water and sanitation facilities. Shelter implies either collective provision of housing or the household disposable income to pay for it, and information is mainly a matter of paying for equipment, except when governments curtail access to it or the printed media. But in general the resource chain here treats indirect cash resources as secondary to the question of whether the direct primary resources are available at all in the places where they are needed. This is an important reminder that personal disposable cash incomes are merely proxies giving access to marketed goods, services and experiences which meet needs, and if the resources are not marketed then cash is useless. Indeed, on the human needs scale there are many psychological resources (such as intimate personal attachments) which European values emphasise should not be marketed, or where ideology and political contingency create arguments about where the boundaries between commercial and kinship responsibilities lie. A topical example in many countries is personal care for those with dependency needs, whether the normal dependencies of childhood or the abnormal dependencies of disability (often wrongly described as being the dependencies of old age, where that is not the cause but the occasion of the disability).

Whatever the breadth of the field of resources which social science can illuminate, social policy concerns are generally much narrower. Though they are not the chief focus here, we have to consider their insights because they have driven much of the debate over what material resources are relevant and need to be measured. For example, in reporting on its aim of determining the taxable capacity of individuals in the UK, a minority of members of the Royal Commission on the Taxation of Profits and Incomes wrote in 1955:

> In fact no concept of income can really be equitable that stops short of the comprehensive definition which embraces all receipts which increase an individual's command over the use of society's scarce resources – in other words, his "net accretion of economic power between two points of time" (RCTPI, 1955, p.8).

This is similar to Richard Titmuss's formulation of income as 'power over resources through time'. Townsend's analysis of what aspects of income were involved in determining an individual's achieved level of living in the UK gave a list of resources (Townsend, 1970, pp.24-25) which, somewhat expanded, consisted of the following elements. All of these can be recognised in the Russian research findings reported here, though their relative values to the households surveyed may well differ substantially from those found in the UK or other countries.

Personal Income in Cash:
(a) current cash income from all sources, such as earnings, rents, dividends, interest, pensions, social security and social assistance payments, other cash benefits, fiscal (tax) allowances;
(b) ownership of stocks of assets which can become a source of flows of income in the present or future, and/or may be treated as security for loans giving income in the present. These include tangible assets such as land and property, bank deposits, stocks and shares, but note that they also include intangible but fungible assets such as educational and skill qualifications, knowledge and other forms of human and cultural capital – even personal characteristics may be fungible capital if there is a market for them.

Personal Income in Kind:
(c) occupational (employer- or enterprise-provided) benefits in kind having a cash value, such as pension rights, sick pay schemes, health insurance and care, stock options, transportation, housing, education and training, child care and allowances, meals;
(d) social welfare benefits in kind from both statutory and non-governmental sources but having a net cash value beyond any costs or charges, such as education and training, health services, housing, personal social services, transport;
(e) private income in kind, such as the value of all kinds of production and transfer of goods and services between people, kinsfolk, neighbours, friends and so on, which are not marketed but are similar to marketed resources, for example, foodstuffs and meals, personal care, gifts of all sorts, holidays.

Impersonal Income:
(f) environmental standards, meaning the value to individuals of the quality of locality and housing, as well as all other aspects of environmental conditions, transport services, safety and other aspects of working conditions, both material and social/psychological.

Social Capital

The resources listed in (e) above are a reminder that the concept of social capital is relevant to the sociological analysis of poverty, even if it is disregarded in policy formation for income maintenance. Like the subject of poverty, there is a vast literature on this concept, which has become more popular since it was taken up in the context of the ideological debate over the balance or substitution of civil institutions for those of the State (Puttnam, 2000). But the earlier use of the idea of social capital referred not to citizen involvement or the role of the State but to a productive resource, like economic and human capital, 'making possible the achievement of certain ends that in its absence would not be possible' (Coleman, 1988, p.98). This sociological account of social capital locates it in relationships of trustworthiness and trust in groups, and shows how it 'can be combined with other resources to produce different system-level behaviour or, in other cases, different outcomes for individuals', and further that it produces value '... for those actors who have this resource available and ... the value depends on social organisation' (ibid., p.101).

James Coleman's account of 'Social capital in the creation of human capital' contrasted it with what Mark Granovetter called '"the undersocialised concept of man" that characterises economists' analysis of economic activity' (quoted in Coleman, 1988, p.97) in a critique of individualistic and self-interested accounts of human behaviour typical of classical economics. However, as these economistic asocial discourses continue to dominate the globalised debate over poverty, it is salutary to be reminded that it is sociological concepts, not economic ones, which are at issue in analysing poverty here, even if the terminology of capital appears superficially similar. The concept in use is only as good as the evidence which supports it, and the research reported here suggests that Russian poverty is inexplicable without it. The capitalised asset is the potential for support or access to material resources offered by the network of trusting relationships, which in the Russian case seem at times to be crucial.

Nevertheless, the concept should be used with caution, since social capital may not be fungible in the absence of material capital. Help has to be repaid eventually in some form or another, and people who cannot reciprocate even favours may find that in certain situations the fund of social capital in their networks is not inexhaustible. Further, stocks of capital have to be built up, and this is no less true of human and social capital. Time is a key dimension: this research shows that settled residential communities are the implicit bank in which social capital can be invested and grow, for it is not an instantly liquid resource like cash. As reported here, social and political stability is a prerequisite for the establishment of these social networks over time, so that the social capital can be drawn on when needed later. Those people who are isolated socially or far from their natural networks, such as ethnic Russians in Ossetia, are therefore liable to be more deprived.

Time as a Resource

Having enough time for all the normally prescribed and desired activities is often noted as an essential resource in quality of life discussions. But, while it may not have received the attention it deserves as a relevant resource in the poverty literature, the sociological or economic treatment of time is far broader and equally relevant. Earning a living, cultivating a food plot, caring for children and other dependants, keeping social relationships intact, all need and take time, and in modern industrial societies such activities frequently demand more time than people have available, and the needs compete with each other. Marketised solutions relieve some problems if incomes are sufficient to pay for the services needed (for instance food or child care) and if they are available within affordable reach, but other aspects of these resources (such as personal relationships) are not interchangeable with services or treated as marketable. Like incomes, the social capital resource may provide alternative solutions to some shortages of the time resource. Time is thus an element in the chain of resources to meet needs to create conditions under which further needs can be met.

Such lists of need-meeting material and social resources can naturally be amplified and condensed according to the focal interests and objectives of the exercise, so there is nothing authoritative about them. The test of their validity is their ability to encompass what the empirical research finds to be the factors affecting real people's levels of living. Further, in real life they are often embedded in other social institutions and rituals, so that examining what is being mobilised or transferred for use or to meet needs over time can be a complicated and difficult activity. In this field, the international macro-measures of poverty are of little use to the sociological analysis of human poverty and are not discussed here. In considering resources some poverty analysts use narrowly economistic approaches but most would agree with Gordon that 'The concept of resources can be considered to encompass elements of human capital and therefore can be even wider than even a broad concept of income' (Gordon, 2000b, pp.39-40). In the meantime, Townsend's (augmented) list above is a useful summary list of the resources we should look for in marketised industrial societies including Russia, and an indicator of related other resources such as human and social capital which may be relevant in context.

Resources and Measures

Much poverty research has been carried out from the perspective of the social policy interest in better income maintenance and other social services to alleviate and prevent poverty. In general, this approach assumes that the focus must be on those aspects of poverty which can be directly affected by government policy, and not so much if at all on those which depend on traditional and informal social institutions less amenable to purposive change from outside. Thus it has often focused on measuring how much personal disposable income is needed not to be poor in a given society, using a variety of direct and indirect methods to arrive at what the adequate level of living is for which the income is needed. The chief measures have therefore been financial, rather than graded on the complex inventory of resources, which use of Townsend's model would suggest. Some methods have tended to assume that all other resources apart from money incomes are held constant, and this often includes both the nominal right to welfare benefits, rather than the actual value of benefits which have been available and obtained. Such assumptions seem to be problematic in the Russian context. Wages, self employed earnings and pensions may still be the most significant income source but their payment may be irregular, and the difficulty of estimating the value of the wide range of other resources complicates the picture as a whole (Mikhalev, 1998, p.363).

In the social policy approach it is not always clear whose normative standards of a minimally adequate level of living are taken as the poverty standards. Social assistance benefits, in those countries which have them, may have been set on the basis of what politicians think can be afforded and at levels below the lowest wage rates, neither of which may bear any relationship to evidence of what is needed to avoid poverty in those countries. If the idea of need has been raised at all, it may reflect ideological notions of the lowest level of living which politicians or their officials consider sufficient for poor people, rather than the views of those who have to live at such levels. There is therefore little point in examining social assistance benefits as such unless one wants to understand political conditions in a country. Similarly, statistical measures of inequality, measures based on formal constructs such as the food share of expenditure or other 's-curve' statistics of consumption,[14] tell us little about the realities of deprived and excluded lives, but a great deal about the ingenious methodologists who devise them and those who sponsor such efforts.

On the other hand, empirical sociological approaches can be divided into those which approach the question of the whole society's minimally acceptable level of living directly or by proxy (for a discussion of the meanings of direct and proxy, see Ringen, 1988 and Veit-Wilson, 1987). The direct methods are epitomised by the deprivation indicator approach originally developed by the Abel-Smith and Townsend research team (Townsend, 1979) and adapted by Joanna Mack and Stewart Lansley (1985) as well as by Björn Halleröd (1997). Essentially, the method hypothesises a list of culturally specific necessities, both goods, services and life-experiences or capabilities, and surveys the sample population to see what degree of assent there is to the proposition that these are necessities which nobody should be without. The survey population responds both about its views, whether or not it wants the items and whether or not it can afford them if it does want them, and gives details of its household incomes. The researchers then test statistically at what levels of enforced deprivation of socially-defined necessities there is a correlation with household income or with other sets of resources as well, or in some surveys with household expenditures. This direct method has been the basis of the methods used in the Russian poverty research reported here. The version of the method currently used by independent researchers in the UK is explained by Gordon and Townsend (2000a).

The indirect methods are those where attitudinal surveys into the subjective meanings of household income levels are taken as proxies for the adequacy of the levels of living which they can support. These methods are associated with the Universities of Leyden (where they were developed in the 1970s) and Antwerp where they were augmented (Van den Bosch, 2001). While politicians treat attitudinal research in general with great respect, for some reason they have great reservations about studies like these, perhaps because they may suggest that income maintenance levels are too low. This has not always been so – Dutch research in the 1970s and 1980s found the minimally acceptable household income levels below what the Dutch government was paying in social assistance (Goedhart, *et al.*, 1977; Muffels, *et al.*, 1990). Later researchers in Belgium who found considerable dissatisfaction refused to treat the survey responses as a 'true' poverty measure, preferring to use the social assistance level as 'real' poverty (Deleeck, *et al.*, 1992, pp.37-38). This exemplifies the fallacy of assuming the policy-oriented researcher knows best, since in such issues it is the population as a whole which sets the standards of acceptability of the levels of living and who therefore knows best if its incomes achieve them (Van den Bosch, 2001, p.406).

A hybrid of these approaches is that developed at the University of Loughborough (see Middleton, 2000) which uses 'focus groups', intense and iterative small-group qualitative discussions to establish the range of necessities for minimally acceptable levels of living for households of specified types, and their aggregate costs. In effect, this combines the deprivation indicator, attitudinal and budgeting methods in a productive but research-intensive manner to find and test minimally adequate income levels. Its findings are scientific in that they are empirical, testable, replicable and refutable. Against this, the traditional budget methods such as those used by the Family Budget Unit in the UK (Bradshaw, 1993) are based on evidence from the deprivation indicator surveys but augmented by expert normative judgement about the requirements of households containing individuals of varying age and sex. Such normative judgements are then converted into the conventional resources shown by standard household surveys so that they can be included in the budgets, but they must always be open to inspection and revision in the light of change in both scientific knowledge and conventional living patterns.

Taking account of time introduces a further dimension into these poverty measurements when used to count people in poverty. There are two problems. One is that, if there is movement into and out of poverty as measured by one or another of these methods, larger numbers of people experience such poverty over time than can be counted at one moment by cross-sectional statistics. Such differences can be very important not only to accounts of the experience of deprivation and poverty but also to the design of effective income maintenance systems. They also have implications for policy makers, in countering the stratified assumptions of a static 'them and us' social structure, in favour of the dynamic 'risks for all' situation. The other problem is that if resources are taken to be not only current flows of income but also stocks of tangible and intangible assets, then (as Gordon pointed out, 2000b) account must be taken of the situations in which people have low income flows but adequate asset stocks, or adequate income flows but low asset stocks. Such marginal situations are found in poverty research and reflect the dynamics of change, and they too can change as the assets deteriorate but cannot be replaced from the inadequate incomes, or as the adequate incomes complete the asset stocks. Sociological accounts of such dynamic situations are both a stimulus to better methodological development and a rich source for deeper understanding of the realities of deprived lives, to set beside the accounts in this book (Leisering and Leibfried, 1999; Walker, 1995).

These studies aimed to describe the dynamic experience of poverty in length as well as depth, quite apart from seeking the income boundaries between deprivation and minimal adequacy as the studies described them. Such 'poverty line' boundaries are more commonly found to be fuzzy indeterminate bands between high probabilities of correlation between multiple deprived levels of living and low incomes on one side, and little correlation between few if any deprivations and higher incomes on the other, rather than precise delimiting markers which are likely to be no more than averages found, not predictors of deprived outcomes.[15] These findings are therefore illuminating but sometimes frustrating for those trying to set income maintenance levels, even if much research has hoped to offer criteria by which to judge the adequacy of these systems. On the other hand, they are central to studies aiming to discover the range of resources and their levels over which people need to have power in order to avoid poverty and enable social participation as society identifies it. That is what the research reported in this book on the meaning and nature of poverty in Russia aims to do.

Conclusion

This chapter has set out some of the issues surrounding the idea of poverty and the resources which are needed to combat it. It has raised questions about studying the standards used to understand what poverty is in any given society at a stage in its development, and reported on methods of investigating the patterns of living in that society and what it sees as the features of the participatory lifestyle which would be the opposite of deprivation, exclusion or poverty. In discussing the nature of the resources needed over time to take part in society decently, it has distinguished between the narrow and immediate concerns of both governments and social scientists to identify and count people in poverty and to evaluate their income maintenance systems, and the much broader perception which people in the wider population hold of the resources necessary over time in their pursuit of dignified lives in their own communities. The research into the nature and extent of poverty and exclusion in Russia reported here shows that key resources lie in traditional and reliable community relationship ties and networks and not in ephemeral money alone, even while having a secure source of enough money income remains indispensable to avoid deprivations and market based exclusion – a 'both/and' and not an 'either/or' situation. The research illustrates the fragility and fluidity of the chains of resources needed to achieve desired ends, so that it becomes hard to see what is the cause, the condition or the consequence, each of which demands resources and risks deprivations, and where deficiencies in one may be compensated by another, or may not. The picture is far more complicated than the common political simplifications sometimes suggest. But if we keep the various separate factors clearly in mind, we can see in greater depth the realities of the struggle of people in Russia against the vicissitudes which the great changes of the 1990s forced on them, and understand better the changing meaning of poverty to them and the nature of the range of resources which they need to mobilise to fight against it, whoever and wherever they are.

Notes

[1] Some examples of historical discussion can be found in Aronson (1984), Fisher (1993), Himmelfarb (1984), Springborg (1981) and Townsend (1970).

[2] These characteristics are found even among the British Royal Family – the black swan disproving the hypothesis that all swans are white, to follow Karl Popper's view of science.

[3] This is why all questions about the meaning of poverty must include the answers of those who are experiencing it or have done so, as well as the answers of those who are not poor, about what they would consider poverty if it applied to themselves and not only to other people.

[4] For detailed scholarly discussions of issues surrounding the question of human needs, see for instance Doyal and Gough (1991), or Ware and Goodin (1990), as well as Springborg (1981).

[5] This fundamental point is often forgotten by those who try to specify human needs starting with material resources such as food or shelter, as if these were the most basic in defining and maintaining *humanity*. The subject is too large for debate here, but evidence can be drawn from the behaviour of humans under extreme conditions, where psychological needs (identity and community) are often treated as being at least as important as physical ones, and sometimes more so – see for instance the literature on the Soviet gulags, and also in the sociological literature (Allardt, 1975; Doyal and Gough, 1991, pp.35-36; Yeates and McLaughlin, 2000, p.61).

[6] On a global scale and over a global period of time, humans seem now to be acting in ways which obstruct their need for a supportive renewable environment, and human society is therefore at risk of eventual extermination. Before that happens, many individual generations will pass through their entire life-spans, so the discussion of fulfilling their needs can continue on that basis while the underlying conditions for future lives are being negated. To focus on one aspect of needs over time does not mean denying that there are others equally important on some other time-scale – the individual choice of what to do is based on temperament and ideology, as well as the contextual exigencies of the problem faced.

[7] This point is often misunderstood by those who think that 'relativity' means purely subjective opinions or distributive percentages. In fact, their assertions about 'absolute' needs are often nothing more than expressions of their own relative and subjective views. A scientific observer might discover that in a given social context a certain resource is an 'absolute' necessity to achieve the desired social objective, but over time and in other contexts the form of that specified resource might change, relatively.

[8] Chris Whelan remarked that his research in Ireland into the relationship between concepts of social exclusion and the evidence of the maintenance of social contacts (which the loose usage of exclusion assumes are at risk of loss) showed that there was 'almost no relationship, except that if you look at the unemployed you will find that they, if anything, have even more social contact than everyone else' (in Yeates and McLaughlin, 2000, p.69).

[9] Erik Allardt similarly classified needs into 'having' (the physical needs), 'being' and 'loving' (belonging) (Allardt, 1975). The failure over time to satisfy psychological needs for identity and belonging lead to many pathological conditions, including those labelled 'anomie' and 'alienation'.

[10] Note that what is socially needed is not the abstraction 'food' or chemical nutrients but the right kind of conventionally eaten dietary foodstuffs prepared and served in the right way, at the right time and eaten with the right people (see Charles and Kerr, 1986).

[11] Any impression to the contrary may arise where observers' and commentators' ideologies are individualistic, and/or the focus of attention or agenda for political action has been on dealing with deprived individuals rather than collective causes of their deprivations.

[12] The deplorably common confusion between the analytically normal (distributive positions related to a statistical mean or median), and the normatively acceptable, leads some commentators to believe, wrongly, that the majority of a population cannot suffer poverty according to the values of that society. But it is of course wholly possible that the majority's standards of what is tolerable are not achieved by that majority – the research in this book suggests that Russia in the 1990s may be a case in point, and also that populations may change their expectations and values in the direction of what is realistically feasible now rather than what used to be achieved (see also Macauley, 1996; Macauley, *et al.*, 1998; Mikhalev, 1998). These are exercises in the study of relative deprivation (Runciman, 1966), where the key issue is the status of the reference groups or ideas being used and not the objective situation as such.

[13] An example can be found in the briefings on poverty measures given by UN agencies (UNDP, 1999b).

[14] The food share or Engel approach takes, in typical examples, the proportion of average total household expenditure on food (or sometimes other essential utilities as well) as the basis for a calculation which multiplies the assumed cost of a minimum dietary (and essential utilities) by the same coefficient as the food share in the average household (allowing for size and composition). This method, which was used by Orshansky for the US 'poverty line' in 1965, has a certain political plausibility, but as Townsend pointed out there is no reason why the food share in a low income household should be the same as in an average one, and the dietary costed in this approach might not be socially acceptable. See Citro and Michael (1995) for a recent study of a modified version of these methods for US government use. The 's-curve' method examines statistics of elasticity of demand for 'basic' consumer goods and services and makes informed judgements about the income thresholds at which hypothesised basic needs seem to be satisfied. The aggregation and triangulation of such data is then taken as an indication of the minimum net incomes needed for a low level of living.

[15] In identifying poor households by appearance, Rowntree noted a similar point a century ago (1901, pp.116-117).

3 Poverty in Russia

Nadia Davidova

Голь на выдумки хитра

The poor are resourceful in invention

In approaching our research into the specific features of poverty in Russia, it was essential to define what poverty is considered to be and what its typological features are, in various communities. Poverty is actively studied all over the world – and it has many similar features all over the world. Theoretically (and in the opinion of most researchers), poverty is the inability to maintain a defined, acceptable standard of living. However, despite the accumulated experience of poverty studies, numerous attempts to assess how widespread poverty is in post-reform Russia have resulted in a fairly contradictory picture. This is because, in conditions where 'cash income ceases to be a reliable criterion of real consumption' (Economic Development Institute, 1998, pp.10-11), poverty can be interpreted in various ways – as a low level of income and expenditure, as the absence of necessary resources, as the impossibility of maintaining the desired standard of living, or as a certain sense of oneself in the social formation.

These important divergences in assessing poverty are linked to the use of different theoretical and methodological approaches to studying and measuring it. In Russia (as in most countries), the official and most widely used method of assessing need is the measurement of household income and expenditure, applied within the framework of an absolute concept of poverty. However, the weak point of quantitative evaluations of poverty (a weakness to which sociologists, unlike economists, often draw attention) is that they ignore a broad spectrum of other available resources that can help to maintain people's material welfare. So, researchers often resort to subjective approaches to evaluating the scale of poverty and the distinctions between poor groups in Russia (Bondarenko, 1997; Standing, 1998). But even subjective assessments of satisfaction with personal material welfare do not solve the problem of reliability of data, in so far as no direct relationship can be observed between subjective self-assessments and people's actual levels of welfare. Rather, the relationship is in the nature of a trend – one which Zaslavskaya in particular has noted (Zaslavskaya, 1996, pp.7-8). In the opinion of specialists from VTSIOM (the Pan-Russian Centre for the Study of Public Opinion), the subjective approach to evaluating poverty is more an indicator of the political robustness of reforms than a criterion of real material circumstances (Zubova and Kovaleva, 1998).

On the wave of criticism of traditional methods over the last ten years, interest has grown in Russia in the newest sociological approaches to the understanding and measurement of poverty. Here we are referring primarily to the concept of relative poverty pioneered by Peter Townsend (Townsend , 1979; 1993). This concept suggests that, in conditions where differing standards of consumption prevail in different communities, establishing a single 'threshold of poverty' is, at the very least, problematic. Within the framework of a relative approach, the situation of the poor does not correlate to indicators describing abstract minimum consumption, but to the average standard of living attained in a given country. There is a central understanding that assessing such a complex social phenomenon as poverty is impossible unless one first tries to gain the fullest possible picture of its specific features in a given community. Research programmes looking at relative poverty have covered different aspects of people's real lives, but have not revealed any one criterion that enables the poor to be differentiated from the non-poor. The well-known research into standards of living by Mozhina, who has dedicated more than 30 years to the study of poverty in Russia, has confirmed that poverty studies within this framework take on a 'wider social meaning' (Moscow Carnegie Centre, 1998, p.16).

In Russia, in this context, a typical set of deprivations characteristic of poverty has been defined (Macauley and Ovcharova, 1997), a qualitative analysis of non-élite strata of the population – differentiated by way of life and structure of consumption – has been carried out (Tikhonova, 1997) and an attempt has been made to articulate indicators of social exclusion (Chernina, 1994-8). However, research in this vein has not been extensive, and it is still the case that results more often raise questions than find answers. So, as a methodological basis for our project we chose the deprivation approach, based on the relative concept of poverty, because its main aim was to gain an understanding of the essence of the phenomenon, rather than to measure it precisely. However, the research group was convinced that we could not afford to reject any of today's existing methods for assessing poverty, despite their strengths and weaknesses. In the opinion of John Veit-Wilson, an authoritative British specialist in this field, each of these methods can frequently meet a number of objectives, and they are complementary rather than mutually exclusive (Veit-Wilson, 2000; also see Chapter 1).

Incomes of Poor Households in Russia

We realised that it would be fairly laborious to analyse poverty by identifying the types of social and personal participation generally accepted in a particular community, but this seemed much more informative than many traditional approaches, especially that based on the criterion of average *per capita* income. In the conditions generated by the current stage of market transformation in Russia, many sociologists have rejected the use of *per capita* income alone in assessing real poverty. Firstly, it is extremely difficult to verify the objectivity of declared *per capita* income in the Russian situation; secondly, *per capita* income alone is clearly not enough to give a full understanding of the resources that a family really has. Finally, against the background of a strongly differentiated picture of inter-regional and cultural differences, there is limited potential to apply this criterion to analysis of the issues.

However, we felt it was necessary to form an idea of the overall incomes of Russian families and of how strongly they differed by region. We had to analyse the particular features of the situations of poor households in Moscow, Voronezh and Vladikavkaz within their macroeconomic context, so we needed some notion of the extent and distribution of *per capita* cash income across Russia as a whole, as well as in the regions chosen for this in-depth study. In order to meet this objective, we used data from RIISNP's Pan-Russian Representative Survey of October 2000, in which social and economic differentiation between various population groups was assessed through median *per capita* income. The choice of this particular method was determined by the fact that there is a great deal of differentiation – both of incomes and of their purchasing power – between the various Russian regions:[1] consequently, more precise and reliable results could be obtained through the *correlation of respondents' per capita incomes with the regional median level*. Thus, despite objective variations in quantitative indicators of *per capita* income, it is possible to arrive at a fairly uniform indicator that takes into account the average standard of living in various regions of Russia (see Table 3.1).

Table 3.1   Incomes of Russian families (Pan-Russian Representative Survey, October 2000, n = 1751, in per cent)

Income Level	In Regions Studied in Depth			Average Across Russia
	Moscow	Central Black Earth Region (Voronezh)	Northern Caucasus (Vladikavkaz)	
Poor	12.4	24.0	23.2	18.6
Badly-off	32.7	32.0	37.0	35.1
Averagely well-off	34.5	38.0	27.5	33.9
Prosperous	20.4	6.0	12.3	12.4
TOTAL	100	100	100	100

The various income groups were divided on the following principle: those families who – at the time of the survey – had no more than 50 per cent of the regional median income were counted as *poor*; those whose *per capita* incomes were over 50 per cent but lower than the regional median were *badly-off*; those who had *per capita* incomes within the range of one to two times the regional median were *averagely well-off*; while those whose *per capita* incomes were more than twice the regional median were *prosperous*. The indicator was calculated separately for each region and then aggregated. This method allowed us to divide the poor from others in relative terms and also to represent the scales of insufficiency of their *per capita* incomes in each separate region. Data from the Pan-Russian Survey provide evidence that the inadequacy of *per capita* incomes in relation to median indicators was highest in Vladikavkaz and Voronezh, less marked in Moscow.

According to data from the Goskomstat of the Russian Federation, the *per capita* income of the statistically average poor Russian household was in the order of 500 roubles a month in the last quarter of 1999 (approximately $20) (Goskomstat, 2000a, p.174). The regional statistical indicators were as follows: in Moscow, the average *per capita* income of the poor in late 1999 had reached 924 roubles, while in Voronezh and Vladikavkaz it was 485 and 493 roubles respectively (ibid., p.223). In the first stage of our in-depth longitudinal survey (November-December 1999), we found that the average income of 105 poor households in Moscow, Voronezh and Vladikavkaz was 525 roubles: the Moscow households had an average of 783 roubles per family member per month and the Voronezh and

Vladikavkaz households 448 and 437 roubles respectively. In other words, our sample turned out to be less well-off than the statistically average poor family in these particular regions – and this was even more true for the Moscow families.

Our poor respondents themselves said that a family should be considered poor if its average monthly *per capita* income was less than 1,000 roubles in Moscow and less than 500 roubles in Voronezh or Vladikavkaz. Muscovites took the view that an average monthly *per capita* income of 1,500 roubles was needed to avoid poverty; respondents from Voronezh thought 900 roubles and those from Vladikavkaz, 1,000 roubles. In general, these figures reflected their views of what a real regional subsistence minimum would be. However, we should also note that, at that time (late 1999) – according to data from the regional subdivisions of the Goskomstat of the Russian Federation – the cost of a minimum basket of consumer goods (the official subsistence minimum, based on an assessment of need) was about 1,000 roubles per person in Moscow, about 700 roubles in Voronezh and about 600 roubles in North Ossetia (Goskomstat, 2000b, pp.157-8).

These absolute indicators of *per capita* income in the households we studied give only a general, very approximate picture of their degree of need. The depth of their poverty varies, while their resources differ substantially and range much more widely than the income amounts can convey. The research group started from the point of view that it was essential to analyse deprivation and restricted social participation in depth, in the aim of marking out the 'threshold' below which need swiftly grows to such an extent that it can place the household on the boundary of social exclusion – that is, *de facto* exclusion from the normal activities of life in a given community. It was precisely this that provided one of the key objectives of our longitudinal project: to evaluate the material situation of households in need, as well as their perceptions of poverty, in differing regional, ethnic, national and socio-cultural communities, within the framework of a relative concept of poverty.

The Poverty Threshold, Depth of Deprivation and Main Qualitative Characteristics of Different Levels of Need

As the basis of our research, we chose a multivariate approach to assessing the degree of deprivation and the dynamics of the situation in the Moscow,

Voronezh and Vladikavkaz households investigated. The application of this approach presupposed that *three main methodological objectives* would be tackled: 1) to define indicators of deprivation; 2) to determine how far they provided evidence of a reduction in the generally accepted standard of living for a given community; 3) to define, as applied to Russian conditions, qualitative 'thresholds' of deprivation, which would enable us to assess the living standards of a given family.

At the same time, we started from Peter Townsend's hypothesis, that, where the degree of deprivation in a household (measured by the presence of particular deprivations) remains above 'threshold' level, material circumstances deteriorate more slowly and less obviously – that is, the dynamic does not take on a distinctly negative, 'landslide' quality (Townsend, 1987). Within the framework of this approach, poverty presents simultaneously as process and as result: growth of deprivation and restrictions on a generally accepted set of essential goods and types of activity are linked with lack of resources and provide evidence of a falling standard of living, while poverty as a profound, self-generating state – from which, once you have fallen into it, it is extremely difficult or practically impossible to escape – relates more to the experience of crossing a certain qualitative threshold of deprivation.

The principle of distinguishing the poor on the basis of deprivation has met with approval among other researchers. For example, Mack and Lansley's work in the UK in the mid-1980s (Mack and Lansley, 1985) moved on from Townsend's 'expert definition' of a set of deprivation indicators, to ask the general population to specify markers of poverty and to name the goods and services that they viewed as necessities. Expert assessments were thus revised empirically. The same approach is currently used by the Statistical Monitoring Unit, which conducts research into poverty in the UK (Townsend, Gordon and Gosschack, 1996). In the Russian situation, the approach to measuring poverty through deprivations was first developed and applied by Macauley, Mozhina and Ovcharova,[2] who attempted to define the 16 most significant indicators of deprivation that separate poor Russians from the non-poor (Moscow Carnegie Centre, 1998).

The empirical results of previous poverty research in Russia based on the deprivation approach raised the following questions for our research group – which deprivations are markers not so much of poverty as of need, of being badly-off? What 'threshold' of consumption and social participation divides the poor from the badly-off, or those in need from those who have managed to keep up an average standard of living? Finally, which qualitative deprivations do the poor themselves find tolerable, and which more painful? What do they see as determinants of whether someone is poor? Which particular types of deprivation did our poor households actually have to endure? What is the qualitative structure of deprivation? What are the relative 'weights' of the various deprivations and restrictions in people's eyes? What does it really mean to be poor?

To assess the households under study, a list was drawn up that included the 26 most significant restrictions on a generally accepted way of life, structure of consumption and social participation.[3] The main objective was to understand the depth of deprivation experienced by the households, guided by how distinctly these people in need themselves connected a particular suggested marker with poverty. Our analysis of the subjective perception of markers of poverty showed that the less widespread a particular deprivation in everyday life, the greater its weight as 'actual proof' of poverty as a state of noticeable deviation from generally accepted current living standards.

Some indicators were seen by all respondents as undoubted signs of poverty and, therefore, their presence meant extreme need – such families had 'crossed the threshold'. Other indicators were less clearly associated with (especially, extreme) poverty; there was then a gradation towards those that reflected some restrictions on an average way of life in the given community, rather than poverty. Deprivations at the end of the scale furthest from poverty tended to be social, rather than material. Thus, we confirmed that a qualitative 'welfare threshold' really exists, and this in turn led to one of our project's most important conclusions: *in any deprivation-based approach to assessing poverty, it is essential to delimit the quantitative and the qualitative aspects of deprivation.*

The picture of qualitative deprivation given by members of poor households related the indicators to poverty in general and to extreme poverty in particular. It can be divided into four 'bands'.

Band IV deprivation – indigence, when there are not enough resources for normal food (some of the family go hungry; there is almost no fresh meat or fish); the family has cut down on hygiene products, does not replace children's clothing as they grow, does not buy fruit or juice and does not own consumer durables such as a TV or fridge. *All these items were linked with poverty by at least 90 per cent of respondents, and with extreme poverty by around 50 per cent.*

Band III deprivation – severe need (poverty), when there are further deprivations related to the quality of food (restrictions on treats, chocolate, sweets for children, fresh fruit and vegetables for adults), and to lack of clothing and shoes (adult family members cannot afford new); it is difficult to keep the home in good repair, or acquire enough simple everyday furniture; there is difficulty organising ceremonies such as wakes or funerals when necessary; difficulty purchasing vital medicines and medical appliances; there are limited possibilities of inviting people round or visiting. *All these items were linked with poverty by 80-90 per cent of respondents, and with extreme poverty by 30-40 per cent.*

Band II deprivation – constrained circumstances (being badly-off), when there are insufficient means for anyone in the family to have delicatessen foods, or to buy presents, newspapers, magazines and books; the quality of leisure is diminished for both adults and children; the family cannot afford a washing machine, or to visit relatives who live at a distance; they cannot afford fee-paying services – in particular, essential medical services. *All these items were linked with poverty by 60-80 per cent of respondents, and with extreme poverty by 20-30 per cent.*

Band I deprivation – borderline, is characterised by living standards that are close to the average, implying no significant deviations from the way of life generally accepted in Russian society. These families need better housing conditions (because theirs are substandard in some way); they have cut back on expensive, up-to-date consumer durables, fee-paying educational and recreational services, family holidays and entertainment. *All these items were linked with poverty by fewer than 60 per cent of respondents, and with extreme poverty by only 10-20 per cent.*

According to our preliminary research hypothesis, the qualitative 'threshold' deprivation experiences that divide the strictly poor from the badly-off should have lain between Bands II and III. On crossing this 'threshold', those of the households under study that were most in need had been forced to cut back on the most necessary expenditure (on food, clothes, medicines) and were often going entirely without other things – fee-paying services, social participation, maintaining their home in good repair, and so on. Moreover, the aspirations of the most deprived were falling so abruptly that we were left with the impression they had never been through an interim stage where they merely cut back on – for example

– holidays or leisure. In fact, the situation provided evidence that they had become used to poverty and completely lost any hope of restoring a normal way of life. It was especially disturbing that, in the households in the most unfortunate material circumstances, we found a distinct tendency to cut back on things for the children (consumption, clothing, education). On the other hand, the households whose deprivation was primarily concentrated in Band I can hardly be viewed as representing a position of need[4] (the first stage sample of our longitudinal survey included about 10 per cent of such families). The concentration of deprivations in Band II (being badly-off) was characterised by its own distinctive situation, on the borderline between deep poverty and average Russian living standards.

Understanding Poverty in Different Regional and Ethnic Communities in Russia

Our research showed that poverty and the various degrees of qualitative deprivation have their own specific features in different regional and ethnic communities.[5] One distinct feature of extreme deprivation in North Ossetia (Vladikavkaz) was the state of housing: cramped, overcrowded and impossible to maintain in good repair. In the Northern Caucasus, another fairly important criterion of poverty – a marker of having 'crossed the threshold' – related to traditions of ritual and ceremony: someone who cannot afford to organise these when they have a duty to do so is often considered indigent. Lack of money for meat, household appliances or – especially – holidays was perceived in the Vladikavkaz community as less painful than in Moscow and Voronezh: although these instances provided evidence of being in need, they were not markers of extreme poverty. If members of the Russian population of North Ossetia, surrounded by people of a different nationality, could rarely afford to visit relatives living at a distance, this implied that the family's standard of living was extremely low; in contrast, this type of deprivation was less significant for Ossetian families in Vladikavkaz.

Voronezh respondents felt restrictions on clothing much more keenly than they did problems with food or lack of certain household appliances. More significant in Voronezh communities were social contacts with friends and neighbours – a sense of being part of a community. Those who could not invite guests or visit others, because of poverty, were seen as excluded from the local community, and thus as extremely deprived.

Perceptions of need in Moscow related more clearly to issues of social participation and the corresponding quality of life: Muscovites often classed as 'poor' those who could not afford fee-paying leisure, medicine or education for themselves or their children. Muscovites were much more keenly aware of lack of money for high-quality foods (fresh meat, vitamins, delicatessen foods) and restrictions on buying newspapers, books and magazines: this obviously related to the respondents' perception that the higher standard of living enjoyed by most of the capital's population – by comparison with residents of the other regions we studied – was normal and generally accepted.

Assessing Living Standards According to Multivariate Deprivation Criteria

We must immediately stress that we met families at every level of need in all three of our cities. Some were existing at the level of indigence, while others were in straitened circumstances but trying to maintain acceptable living standards. Some were already 'over the threshold', while others were teetering on the brink but had not crossed it. Therefore, in the context of the research we were undertaking, we drew up a *Multivariate Deprivation Index (IMD)*[6] for the Moscow, Voronezh and Vladikavkaz households, to allow us to position each one at a glance. According to depth of impoverishment, *the scale ran from 'indigence' through 'poverty' and being 'badly-off' to being 'averagely well-off'*, based not only on the number of indicators, but also on their qualitative nature (the position of the particular restrictions in the four 'Deprivation Bands' above) and on perceptions of poverty in the regional and ethnic communities concerned.

Indigent households had an average of 16 points on the Multivariate Deprivation Index – from minimum 14 to maximum 21 – including no less than six of the most significant deprivations (those defined by respondents as linked to indigence and severe need). Our longitudinal survey results indicated that deprivation in these households was stagnant: it had taken an inexorable hold over all aspects of their lives and, in practice, it was unlikely they would ever escape it.

Twenty households were in this most difficult position of indigence. Most of them (15 families) were from Vladikavkaz. In many cases, their high IMD scores related to their large number of children or other dependants, especially as a result of traditional family structures among ethnic Ossetians. Twelve of the 15 had children: seven had between three and 11 children. Of the five remaining indigent households (in Moscow and Voronezh), four had children: one was a two-parent family with seven children; one, a lone mother with three children; and two were lone fathers, with one and two children respectively.

Although aspects of family structure, such as having a lot of children, are the most significant 'risk factors' for indigence in Russia, there are others: life events and family breakdown, especially loss of the breadwinner, sharp deterioration in health, forced move, and so on.

Apart from the 20 indigent households, another 32 families were – according to the IMD – living in poverty. Although they had not yet slid down into indigence, their standards of living differed strongly from the way of life accepted in communities in Russia. These *poor households* had an average of 13 points out of 26 on the IMD. In addition, their deprivations were concentrated at the levels of indigence and poverty, with these households experiencing no less than three of the most significant deprivations associated by respondents themselves with having 'crossed the threshold of poverty' (Band III and IV deprivation).

These 52 households – which were 'over the poverty threshold' according to the IMD – were fairly evenly represented in Moscow, Voronezh and the two ethnic sub-groups in Vladikavkaz: they formed about half the sample in each. Nevertheless, the highest level of deprivation (close to indigence) was more often seen in Vladikavkaz. It should be noted that a serious additional factor, which increased deprivation in some families, was alcohol abuse by the head of the household, leading to a drop in standard of living. This phenomenon, with the resultant slide into profound poverty, was observed in all our research regions. In total, respondents in a third of poor households faced this problem, as against a fifth of less deprived families.

In order to give a fuller picture of poverty in Russia, we felt it was necessary to use the 'social portrait' or 'ethnographic vignette' method. Our largely qualitative, in-depth research meant paying extra attention to various life stories that encapsulate the specific nature of being in – and surviving in – a situation of extreme poverty.

Here are some of the more instructive examples. (See also the detailed histories of 19 households followed four times between 1996 and 2000 in this and the previous project, given in Appendix 2.)

A *Moscow* couple, Vyacheslav and Tat'yana, with one child. Both the parents drank; they had sent their teenage daughter to boarding school. All the family's money went on alcohol. The wife worked as a hospital cleaner and brought home the patients' leftover food, which formed the basis of the couple's diet. The husband was not working, but did bits of work for neighbours from time to time in return for a drink. The family's IMD score was very high (16-17 points), and we noted a distinct deterioration in their situation over the year of observation, even despite the death of Tat'yana's mother, a paralysed pensioner whom the family had been supporting. The household bought no consumer durables, never did any repairs and left their child practically forgotten: no one even thought about the fact that the State was supporting her even though she had a parent living. When the head of the family was asked whether he was looking for a permanent job, he replied: 'there are no jobs at our level, and the only possible way of changing the family's situation would be if we were lucky enough to win the lottery'.

Alcohol abuse by Vladimir, a *Voronezh* respondent, was the reason for the breakdown of his family and the serious deterioration in his own situation: he slid down to the level of indigence literally over the course of the year of observation, although he had already been categorised as 'poor' before that. However, as a result of his divorce, not only he, but also his children, had suffered greatly. The mother had left one of them with Vladimir; the younger sons lived with her after the divorce, but one of them periodically came to his father's, because he was still at school nearby. Both the teenage sons, aged 13 and 15, were left without supervision when their father was drinking; both were known to the juvenile bureau, having been picked up by the police for various offences. Vladimir was not in a position to provide them with a normal diet, essential school supplies or money for school dinners. In addition, he was suffering a great deal because of the state of his accommodation: his ex-wife had taken the television and the fridge, and Vladimir had gradually sold all the remaining consumer durables. Everything was going to rack and ruin. According to neighbours and Vladimir's work colleagues (he worked as a tool-setter in an aircraft factory, but had recently been threatened with dismissal for absenteeism): 'he is a good chap – a warm-hearted person: it's a real shame'. The respondent himself described the degree of his impoverishment as follows: 'I have hardly anything to eat'. He asked us to pay him for the interview in groceries, 'because I can't hang on to money, I just drink it'. Vladimir pinned any hopes of changing his poor situation solely on professional assistance from a doctor. (Unfortunately, in Russia, treatment for alcoholism must be paid for privately and is fairly expensive – N.D.).

This Russian family from *Vladikavkaz* had had a fairly high standard of living in Soviet times – both spouses had worked in the defence industry, and the respondent's father had at one time been a deputy minister in the North Ossetian government. But they were now teetering on the edge of indigence.

The pensioner couple lived with their adult son and daughter; only the daughter was working – as an infant school teacher – and earning extra by giving private reading lessons to pre-school children. All the family's material problems fell on this woman's shoulders, since her father and brother both drank. She acknowledged that she could not get married, because there was no possibility of her having a dowry or saving anything to help her escape the situation (she was about 40 years old). Here are some extracts from her interview: 'we're in really unfortunate moral circumstances at home. My brother can just take anything he wants. Just as he likes, just like that – because he knows I won't do anything about it. There are things that I won't take home, because I'm not sure they won't disappear. I couldn't say we had these problems when everything was all right – I mean, with my brother. What if Dad was drinking? It wasn't like this ... Of course, it was unpleasant. But then everything was OK with my brother. It all began with him when he once almost got sent to prison ... and all the money we had went on rescuing him: he wasn't guilty, but it looked as if he was. And so these problems are still with us today. And my father, although he won't admit it, is of course to blame. I think my brother was just done for. It would have been better if he had gone away and left us ... You know, it puts you under constant subconscious pressure, it stops you from living normally ...'

The remaining 53 *badly-off families* under study in Moscow, Voronezh and Vladikavkaz were in varying degrees of need, but their level of deprivation led to their being classed as 'badly-off', rather than 'poor'. While the poor – those who had 'crossed the threshold' – suffered substantially reduced opportunities to consume basic necessities, the badly-off were not in such severe need: their deprivations related less to meeting physical needs than to more complex consumption and to full social participation.

As we go up the scale, problems related to consumption behaviour in badly-off families, such as cutting back on food, health care and – most importantly – on the children, become less severe. However, their means were still too restricted for them to afford the most widespread and generally accepted standard of living for their own community.

Thus, *badly-off households* were much less deprived: they had an average of seven or eight points of relative deprivation (from minimum five to maximum 11), and most of the restrictions that affected them were in Deprivation Bands II and I. The main difference between them and more deprived households was that – judging from the results of our year of observation – they had real opportunities to improve their position, or at least prevent its decline. The dynamics of the situation between 1999 and 2000 showed that 80 per cent of the core of the 'poor' and 'badly-off' group (on either side of the 'deprivation threshold') remained the same, but that the chances of getting back over the threshold from poverty were much lower than the chances of clinging to badly-off status. This confirmed our preliminary hypothesis, and allowed us to conclude that, in the Russian situation, the 'threshold' hypothesised by Townsend[7] actually straddles Deprivation Bands II and III on our proposed scale.

Typical 'badly-off' families would mostly be fairly small households (three to five people) with children, but no more than two. Some were two-parent, others one-parent families: being a lone parent in Russia does not by any means always lead to a sharp fall in living standards. It depends very much on the specific situation in a particular family, and on a number of other accompanying factors, including – most importantly – whether the parent and child/children live as a nuclear family or in a multi-generational family. The presence in the household of members of the older generation, whether employed or retired, represents an additional resource for the lone-parent family. In this situation, the older member of the family can directly place his or her own financial resources at the disposal of the household as a whole, or – if a pensioner – can take on the greater part of the household duties (this practically always means responsibility for child care), enabling those of working age to save time and find additional sources of income. We should point out that the findings of some researchers that lone parenthood is a high-risk factor for poverty in Russia (especially for women) (World Bank Group, 2000) need to be re-examined in the light of the socio-demographic and economic structures of various types of household. The results of our research suggest that the risks of nuclear and of multi-generational lone-parent families in Russia differ, from the point of view of both depth and degree of impoverishment.

Let us look at the living situations of two lone-parent families in Moscow.

> In both cases, the woman was bringing up one child on her own, following divorce, and in neither case was the family receiving maintenance payments from the ex-husband. However, Alla was living alone with her daughter, while Irina was still living with her parents and her younger sister: her father was working and her mother was a pensioner. Both women were working in the social services sector, with disadvantaged people: Alla was a home care assistant for the disabled and Irina worked as administrator of a hostel for homeless people.

> Alla's household demonstrated fairly high indicators of deprivation, placing her 'over the threshold of poverty': there were many foods she could not

afford, including fresh meat and fruit; she was wearing old clothes and shoes; she had to economise on her teenage daughter's leisure and educational consumption and could not give her any pocket money or let her take part in any activities that required additional expenditure. However, in Irina's family there was practically no trace of deprivation: across the whole year of observation, it was difficult to recognise that her household was in need, other than in the most notional sense. The only small economies she had to make were on fee-paying entertainments and full-price holidays. Irina would have liked to buy somewhere to live away from her parents, but could not do so: however, similar restrictions apply to the overwhelming majority of the Russian population, and this has nothing to do with poverty.

Why were there such differences in the living standards of these two lone-parent families? Firstly, because of the status and nature of Irina's father's employment: he had a secure, well-paid job and never refused Irina money. He provided for the family's main consumption. Secondly, because Irina could leave the child care to her mother and take on extra work: she told us that she did regular overtime at her job. Thirdly, because of Irina's parents' fairly high standard of living and accumulated resources – they had savings, a dacha and a car; they had never had any particular employment problems, and received their wages on time.

Alla, on the other hand, had been made redundant in the reorganisation of a scientific research establishment – a budget-funded organisation, where her low pay had prevented her from building up any kind of savings at all. This had adversely affected her health, leaving her under a great deal of psychological stress. As she said, 'I can only get moral support and advice from those around me': her parents were dead, her older son had left home and had his own problems. Overall, despite the fact that Alla – unlike Irina – was getting some support from the State (a housing subsidy), she was not in a position to provide for her own and her daughter's consumption needs and was sliding further and further into poverty. Over the year of observation, deprivation in Alla's household grew, pushing her still further 'over the threshold'.

Overall, the deprivation approach taken in our research provided a fairly reliable criterion for assessing the level of need in households in the three cities. At least, it was more reliable in recording real poverty than many traditional methods, and it allowed qualitative thresholds to be drawn within poverty itself. This conclusion was also confirmed by comparing the results of the multivariate deprivation analysis of our households to results gained from other approaches to assessing poverty – in particular, to objective facts about income distribution, to people's subjective assessments of their own material circumstances compared to others, and to people's own assessments of their standard of living on a 'poverty-sufficiency' scale. As we cannot dwell on this in more detail, we should emphasise that the research group paid special attention to this aspect of the issue, since we were initially convinced that the poor – as measured on the IMD – were those who suffered deprivations because they lacked the necessary level of resources and had low incomes (as those who take this view constantly stress – Holman, 1978, Veit-Wilson, 1999). Precisely because of this, it followed that an important objective of our research was to obtain a wider picture of the resource potential of Russian households in need, since this directly determines their potential to adapt to conditions that threaten a further reduction in their standard of living.

Specific Features of the Resource Potential of Poor Households in Russia

In our research project special attention was devoted to a detailed analysis of the resources that directly influence the life practices of various types of poor households in different local communities. As a research issue, this is directly related to current political debates about the search for a new model of Russian social policy in conditions where the complex system based on the Soviet model of welfare has practically receded into the past. A fairly clear picture of the adaptive potential of poor Russian households is crucial, if effective models of social support for those most in need are to be developed.

Sociological investigations of the socio-economic position of the Russian population have shown that, apart from current income in cash or in kind, Russian households have 'emergency rations' of various accumulated resources, on which they can draw when trying to survive (Rose, 1993; Kabalina and Clark, 1999). These can be *material assets* (belongings, savings, property), *social capital* (connections, contacts, mutual support) or *cultural and symbolic capital* (level of knowledge, skills or qualifications). The 1990s in Russia were characterised by uncertainty and instability of all kinds of income, including income from employment. Therefore, Russian households have diversified their activities as much as possible in order to acquire any independent source of existence – selling their labour power on the open market, claiming social transfers, actively using the potential of the household economy and help from their immediate circle, exploiting the family's accumulated resources. Pushing the boundaries between various means of survival, combining and diversifying them, allows many Russian households nowadays to avoid a situation where their overall level of material welfare is strictly dependent on their current cash income.

Such results provided a starting point for our analysis of specific features of the resource potential of Moscow, Voronezh and Vladikavkaz households. We wanted to develop this line of inquiry, asking: what sort of access to alternative means of existence do different households have when they become poor? What is the role of these alternatives in the practical survival of those most in need? Can they prevent a further fall in the family's standard of living? Despite much discussion of 'the informal economy', both in the academic community and in political circles, there have never been full answers to these questions about the issue of the Russian population's universal use of informal ways of organising their lives during Russia's transition to the market economy.

In addition, these questions are key to understanding the set of issues surrounding poverty and social exclusion in contemporary Russia. It is obvious that the resource potential of households significantly influences the survival strategies and life practices that they deploy in order to ward off a reduction in their standard of living or to escape poverty. In our research, we decided to focus especially on the most significant types of resources for Russian families: *material and social* resources. Despite the fact that our sample had been deliberately formed from poorer people (implying that their resource potential was, by definition, inadequate), we hypothesised that the resources they used to tackle their accumulated problems would vary in both size and nature.

It must be said that the resource potential currently used by Russian households in the process of tackling problems has not only an economic but also an underlying socio-cultural dimension. The issue of accumulated resources and of the significance of informal support networks in the everyday life of Russians is often seen from precisely this point of view by many researchers, working both in the West (Ledeneva, 1998; Rose, 1998; Shlyapentokh, 1989) and in Russia (Akhiezer, 1991; Kozlova, 1998; Yakubovich, 1999). On a theoretical level, it is debatable what the present-day social capital of Russian households represents: a product of the Soviet shortage economy (Shlyapentokh), the anti-bureaucratic, illegal tactics that people adopt in an 'anti-modern society' (Rose) or the consequence of the population's adherence to historical traditions of communality and an inculcated tendency towards collective activity (Akhiezer). However, serious researchers of socio-economic issues hardly doubt that the high adaptability of Russians to the negative consequences of market reforms arises, in many cases, from a residual foundation of fixed social connections and customary ways of behaving. It was this that we also set out to study, through an analysis of the survival potential of households in Moscow, Voronezh and Vladikavkaz.

To compile a fuller picture of the specific features of the resource potential of our households, we included in the questionnaire a block of questions intended to measure the presence in these families of various types of strategically significant property – a privatised flat or one's own house, dacha, land, car, garage and also different types of household articles. Another block of questions allowed us to build up a detailed picture of what kinds of support, goods or services the households received from informal mutual assistance networks. We therefore collected data that shed light on both their material and social activities.

Property Resources in the Households Studied

Accumulated property proved to be the most significant potential resource, acting as household 'stock'. Ownership of certain property resources (real estate, private plot of land, car, etc.) opened up possibilities for their deployment in maintaining material welfare and was often decisive in achieving this when the family's living standards fell. Property represented something inalienable, and was likely to lead to the adoption of more active survival strategies.

What property did the poor households in Moscow, Voronezh and Vladikavkaz own, and how did it relate to their degree of deprivation? See Figure 3.1.

Figure 3.1 Presence of strategically significant property (privatised flat, dacha, land, car, garage)[8] in households at various levels of deprivation, in per cent

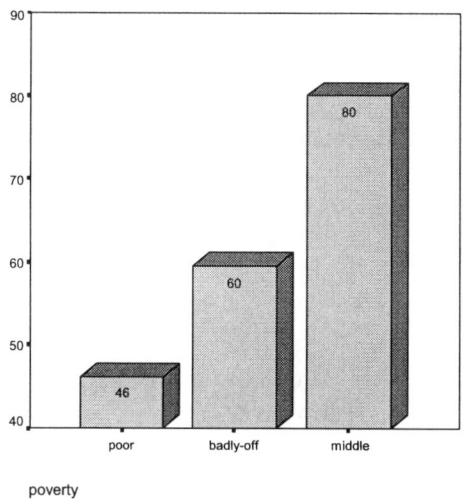

Figure 3.1 clearly shows that over half the most deprived families in our survey ('the poor') had absolutely no property of a type that could be deployed in the survival process. Thus, a whole range of elements for a strategy to overcome their difficulties successfully was unavailable to them right from the outset: they could not grow food at a dacha, sell surplus produce, use a private car to generate extra earnings, rent out any real property, and so on.

Voronezh respondents were worst-off in terms of strategically significant property resources, which were present in only one-third of poor households, while in Moscow far more – one poor family in two – had some such resources. But this did not alter the general trend: in all regions, households that had 'crossed the threshold of poverty' lagged behind the more fortunate (the badly-off and the averagely well-off) in ownership of strategically significant property.

This difference was most striking in the area of land use – and thus of the natural survival resource of growing one's own food. Families below the poverty threshold were much less likely to have access to land than those above: out of 52 poor households, only nine had land, and five of these were Muscovites. Among 'badly-off' families, at least one in four in

Voronezh and Vladikavkaz and two out of three in Moscow had some land.

This is an especially important area of discussion, because public – and political – opinion tends towards the belief that the Russian population is surviving through the use of individual smallholdings for growing food; and it is true that, if a family is in the situation where material circumstances are deteriorating, land could really become a serious aid to their survival. However, there is one big 'but': despite the fact that many Russians declare the dacha to be significant in their survival strategy (in the RIISNP Representative Survey for Autumn 2000, over half of Russians included a personal plot of land among their supplementary means of meeting the family's basic consumption needs[9]), the families most in need simply have no land – and this undoubtedly seems to be a serious factor in increasing their deprivation.

Informal Mutual Assistance Between Russian Households: The Significance of the Social Resource

In recent years, Russian and non-Russian researchers have consistently recorded the main exchanges between Russian families in social networks (Cox, Yezer and Himenez, 1998; Kabalina and Clark, 1999; Rose, 1998), showing that informal mutual assistance is a significant factor in overcoming difficult situations during the economic transition period. Thus, the extent and depth of social connections and the presence of social networks as a real and potential source of help from outside constitute a very important additional survival resource.

We set ourselves the task of discovering more about this fairly important aspect of practical, everyday life for Russian households. Unfortunately, there is as yet a distinct lack of in-depth comprehensive research into the social networks used by families in the survival process. There is practically no data on the full spectrum of the social contacts of households, since most large-scale research has, as a rule, looked at individuals, not families. We know little about the functions of social networks and how they change according to household situation; about the nature and conditions of the chief kinds of mutual exchange; above all, about *how changes in the living standards of various kinds of family are reflected in changes in the structure and types of help they receive.* In other words – what is the interdependence between a family's social network situation and their success in overcoming difficult situations in life?

Judging by data from large-scale surveys, many of these very important aspects of social exchanges frequently remain outside the framework of the picture that people draw of their own adaptive behaviour. The problem of finding answers to such questions through research clearly lies in the fact that the mutual exchange of resources and services by relatives, friends and colleagues is such an organic part of everyday life in Russia that it is hardly noticed: it is taken for granted, perceived as routine, naturally woven into the fabric of everyday life. This does not, of course, make it any less significant. We attempted to use the qualitative material from our research into poor households in three cities to gain an understanding of the real (rather than the declared) scale of involvement in informal support networks, to get a picture of the concrete help given and to understand what lay behind the simple response: 'We get help from others'.

It became apparent from our research that quantitative data on sources of income, based on what respondents themselves say, do not always adequately reflect the real volume and true role in people's everyday lives of support from relatives and friends. So, although 30 per cent of our poor households said that such help formed part of the structure of their total income, only 16.2 per cent of the population in the RIISNP Pan-Russian Survey (Autumn 2000) reported this.

Because we had some doubts about the reliability of these indicators, we carried out a special analysis of the types of support that had actually been received from informal networks over the previous year by the households under study. We first constructed an *index of help received by households from social networks*. We chose this method of organising the data obtained in the course of our qualitative interviews because research specifically into social networks has already established that their functional characteristics are many and varied, depending on the activities of those involved (Wills, 1985).

From this starting point, support received by households can be viewed as psychological, material, informational or instrumental. The psychological function often consists just of sympathy, sharing the family's experiences; the material function consists of the mutual exchange of financial help, food and other help in kind, as well as any other aspect of material existence; instrumental and – especially – informational support relate to the exchange of services and to the social capital of networks: connections, protection and advice, including in the areas of looking for jobs or extra work and of tackling household problems. As far as their impact on the material circumstances and prospects of the recipient household is concerned, the various types of support that characterise the functions of social networks fall into a definite hierarchy. For example, financial and informational/instrumental support are more significant, as well as more valuable in offering prospects for changing the situation, than sympathetic support or help with household activities and everyday matters. Access to complex, multi-functional assistance makes the survival process much easier and increases a household's chances of improving its material circumstances.

The different types of help do not always appear in 'pure form' in the real lives of Russian households: they are often interwoven in patterns that vary according to the particular situation and structure of the networks involved (relatives, friends, neighbours, etc.). Therefore, in constructing our index, we applied the hierarchical principle of expansion, by which the more significant types of help 'swallow up' those that have less impact on the family's circumstances, thus reaching a higher position in the index. For the purposes of our index, we ranked the main functions of social networks in the following hierarchy:

1. *simple instrumental (household) help*: support with everyday activities – running the house, looking after family members, sympathetic support, etc. – *and simple resourcing support*: resources in kind, such as foodstuffs and other items, including home-grown food;
2. *financial assistance*: direct cash support from others in the family's social networks;
3. *complex instrumental/material/informational support*: deploying social capital (exchange of services, recommendations and connections), not just cash or resources in kind. Chief activities relate to how to find jobs, extra work, educational advice or training opportunities. Others are complex instrumental services that require organisation, acquired knowledge and/or specific material/symbolic resources – help with repairs, building work, transport, organising expensive events and ceremonies, etc.

The use of this index to rank various items from 1 to 3 enabled us to gain a much more useful picture of the real degree of involvement in social support networks, as well as of the volume and interrelationship of different types of help received, both by statistically average Russian families and by poor households in the three cities we studied.

In fact, it turned out that half of Russian households received some kind of support from social networks, although they did not always recall this when answering direct questions about the structure of their total income. On average across Russia, 49.5 per cent of respondents said that their family had obtained some kind of help from their immediate circle in the course of the last year.[10] Thus, it is correct to refer to the *large-scale involvement of Russians in private informal support networks.*

Analysis of the conditions under which social networks provide help shows that involvement in inter-family support networks helped those at all levels of welfare to a similar extent: the pan-Russian data revealed that 50 per cent of the poorest households (those with incomes under half the regional median) and 53.9 per cent of the best-off (those with incomes over twice the median) had received no help from relatives or friends during the previous year. This is not surprising: social networks are complex resources, established over time, and a household either has them or does not, regardless of its circumstances at a given point in time.

However, more detailed analysis of the role of mutual social assistance in the survival process of Russian households shows that – although receiving support in itself depends very little on the extent to which the various families need it – there are particular features of social networks in better-off families that are qualitatively different from their functions in poorer circles. These relate, above all, to the volume and interrelationship of different types of help received. How did private informal support networks function in households with various levels of material welfare, and what specific types of help had they received? See Figure 3.2.

Figure 3.2 shows that, when the poorest families in Russia get help from social networks, it is primarily in the form of simple household or material support: their involvement in the exchange of social capital is substantially lower than that of better-off families. Thus, we came to one of the most important conclusions of our research: *the poor have less access to social capital – which is the most important aspect of social support and precisely the one that actively helps to overcome difficulties – than does any other group (even though they do get other kinds of assistance).*

Figure 3.2   Types of help received by Russian households at various income levels (data from Pan-Russian Survey, October 2000, n = 1751, in per cent)

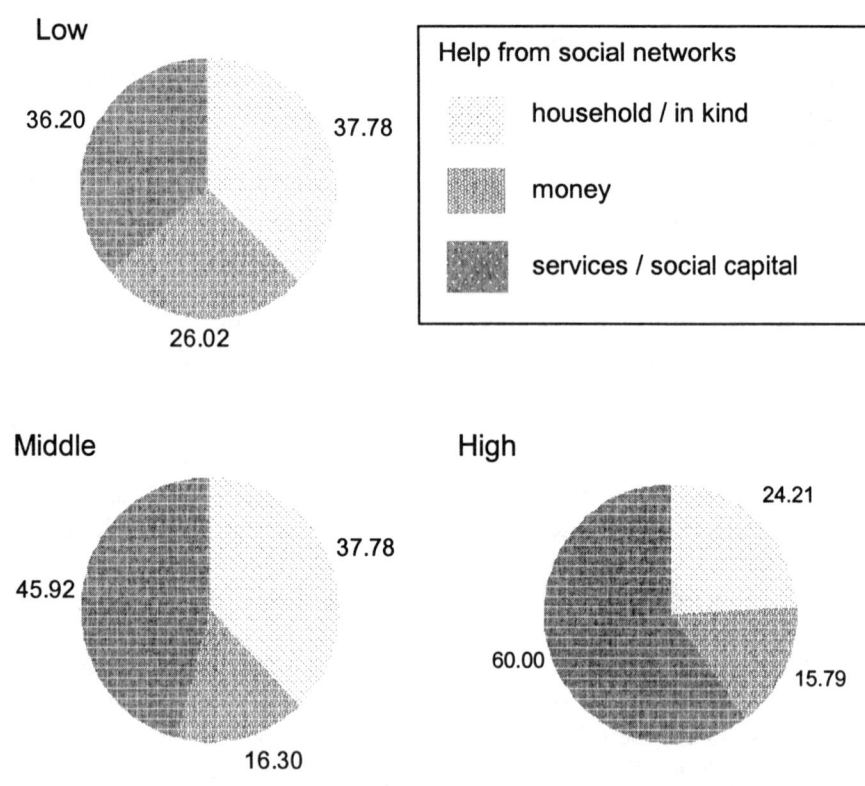

The results of our longitudinal project fully confirm those of the pan-Russian research: a trend towards gradual exclusion of the poorest households from the most significant, complex types of inter-family exchanges involving social capital and a shift in the way support networks function among the most deprived, towards the provision of simpler types of help. As Figure 3.3 shows, the picture of types of support for the poorest gained in both surveys was similar – although our data show that households in need in our three cities make active use of help from relatives, friends and neighbours more frequently than the statistical average for Russia: only 28 out of the 99 households taking part in Stage 2 of our survey said they received no such help, and there was little variation by level of need.

Figure 3.3 Help received by households at various levels of deprivation (data from Longitudinal Household Survey, 1999-2000, Moscow, Voronezh and Vladikavkaz, n = 105, in per cent)

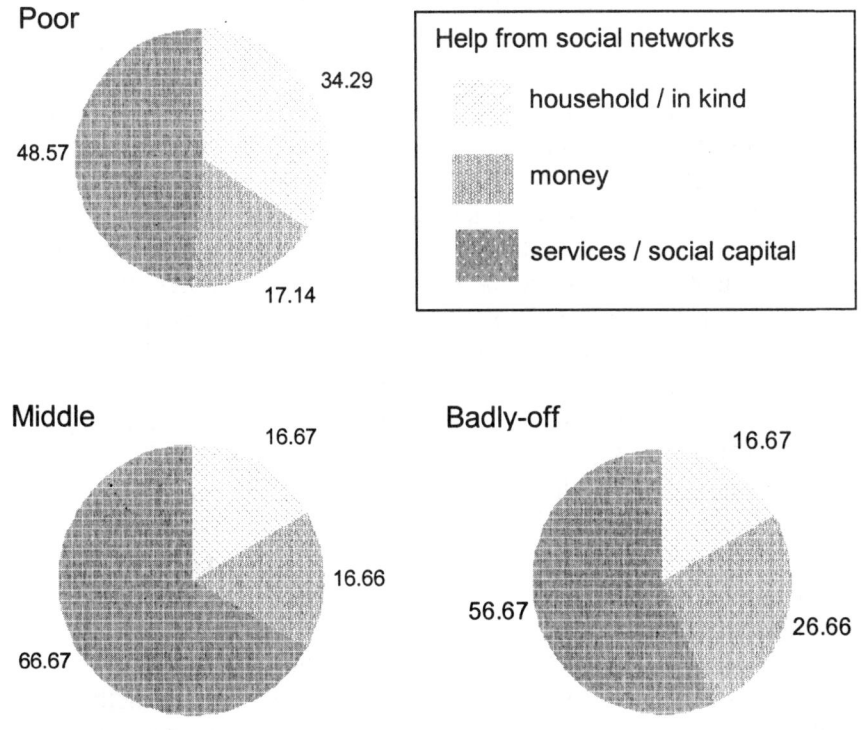

It should be said that the profiles of the individual regions chosen for in-depth investigation left their stamp on the overall results of the longitudinal project. Empirical data from many representative surveys confirm that social networks function more intensively where it is objectively harder to get by, including in poorer regions of southern Russia and in conflict zones in the Caucasus – thus, in Voronezh and Vladikavkaz.[11] Moreover, in poor regions, non-monetary exchanges and exchanges in kind are much more prevalent. In contrast, in better-off, more developed regions, social networks clearly tend to function more on the basis of connections, services or protection. In Moscow, for example, over half the households involved in networks characterised them as being of this type – one of the highest indicators for any part of Russia. It is not impossible that specific features of the way social networks function and of the reasons they become active are shaped not only in the economic sphere, but also by the traditions of the local community (Davidova, 1998): however, this is an area that requires more closely focused research.

Nevertheless, it is completely clear that the level of need and depth of deprivation of the families in our three cities had an impact on their potential to make use of their social resources. Moreover, our research demonstrates that 'poor' households asked for outside support more often than 'badly-off' households; this was why they were more likely to remember to mention it as a source income than other families – a likelihood that increased as their dependence on it grew. In more fortunate material situations, households do not perceive similar volumes of assistance (whether in money or resources) as anything special: such help is to some extent just a set of mutual – sometimes mutually advantageous – everyday practices.

This point may require some clarification. Russian sociologists have concluded that relations within informal private networks almost always exist on a mutual basis: although no one calculates the equivalence of such exchanges, equivalence does exist at an invisible level – symbolic rather than economic (Clark and Kabalina, 1999; Zaslavskaya and Kalugina, 1999). Active use of mutual social assistance resources often depends on the fact that certain social relations exist, as much as on any objective material necessity or specific life situation: helping is a by-product of such relations, not an aim in itself. That is, for a given survival method to be used, it is essential to have some established inter-family networks, not just to be experiencing some kind of difficulties. There is no guarantee, therefore, that the people most in need will have access to this significant social resource when they most require it. What is more, it is clear that part of the reason for mutuality in social networks is that stable material circumstances enable such networks to remain unchanged, while the networks themselves guarantee a certain level of welfare. Russian and Finnish sociologists, in particular, have come to this conclusion in their attempts to clarify the main differences between the state of social networks in Russia before and during the reform period (Poretskina and Jyrkinen-Pakkasvirta, 1995; Lonkila, 1997). We should add that, even in the Soviet period, Russian researchers engaged in serious study of the social behaviour of the individual were already suggesting that difficulties and setbacks in everyday life could lead to isolation, especially isolation from other people (Yadov, 1979): it is particularly important to take this into account in analysing the contribution of mutual social assistance to the practical survival of poor families in Russia today.

Poverty in Russia: The Challenge of New Social Policy

Poverty research in Russia today (including our own) demonstrates that households in need place greater value on alternative possibilities for survival: providing for oneself and mutual assistance. However, the use of land to grow one's own food, the exploitation of family property assets and the receipt of help from relatives and friends are often simply not available to such households, because of their lack of material and social resources. This leads academics, relying on empirical facts, to caution politicians against ill-considered idealisation of the role of survival alternatives for Russian families, and to oppose categorically any attempts to view them as sufficient basis for refusing social assistance to the poor. The Russian phenomena of providing for oneself and mutual assistance require further in-depth study if they are to be interpreted correctly.

Processes of increasing material/property differentiation in Russia in the 1990s have left their mark, particularly on traditional practices of mutual support and on the quality of existing social networks as a survival resource. Poor households are gradually being deprived of access to the symbolic component of functioning networks of relatives and friends, which forms the basis of social capital, and gradually excluded from active mutual exchange of connections, services and opportunities. The causes of these changes will have to form the object of serious specialist research; however, we are already observing empirical confirmation of the social exclusion of the poor, as they are falling out of the most significant social practices of traditional mutual exchanges. Other people involved in inter-family social networks with the poor are increasingly tending to give them simple assistance with resources and household support when they are in difficulties, but do not actively engage in helping them to find additional opportunities, guarantees or connections. This is something else to give the politicians, who are developing models of State support to the weakest and most needy, pause for thought.

The results of our project 'Poverty and social exclusion in Russia' do not unequivocally confirm that the behaviour of the poor in the process of tackling their problems differs qualitatively from the behaviour of most of the population. Similar results have been obtained in a number of other pieces of research, both in Russia (Commander, Tolstopiatenko and Yemtsov, 1997; Zaslavskaya and Kalugina, 1999) and in the West (Dean and Taylor-Gooby, 1991). However, it is obvious that the poorest groups of the population have far fewer material and social resources, or opportunities to exploit them. Even though they make no small efforts and undertake varied activities to try to get themselves out of difficulties, their possibilities are so limited that they are often incapable of overcoming poverty independently.

The insufficient resource potential of the poorest intensifies their deprivation, first sending them sliding over the 'threshold' and then helping to preserve the inescapable nature of their position. The voices of our interviewees resound, telling us of their degradation, dependency and lack of autonomy. Recently, in the turn of well-known debates about the underclass, certain sociologists have been trying to find approval in Russia for 'culture of poverty' approaches, claiming that they apply to those strata of the population who have low adaptive potential and have fallen to 'the social depths' in the course of the Russian reforms (Balabanova, 1999; Lokshin and Popkin, 1999). However, the issue is not whether the poor have particular 'subcultural' features, but whether there are trends towards ever broader social exclusion of the most vulnerable groups from the normal activities of life in society. Following this approach focuses the researcher's attention not on 'blaming the victim' (Ryan, 1971), but on analysis of a whole complex of social conditions and problems in which the person who is the object of research has to live and act. If the meagre resources of the poorest – without which they are not capable of providing independently for their own adaptation – are further exhausted, then growing anomie, social tension and social exclusion in Russian society will be unavoidable. Opening access to channels for the reintegration, replenishment and growth of resources should be seen as one of the central issues in the struggle against poverty in Russia – a high-priority social policy objective for the State and a concern for society.

Notes

[1] In fact, there is also significant variation between the officially established subsistence minima in different regions of Russia. At the same time, the level of the regional subsistence minimum is extremely controversial, since the Russian Federation's Subsistence Minimum Law, although it has been formally adopted, does not work in practice, because it does not compel the regions to use a uniform method of assessment.

[2] The research project 'Poverty in Russia: deprivation and social exclusion', 1997.

[3] For more details on deprivation indicators, see Appendix 1 on 'Project Methodology'.

[4] The various types of deprivation currently experienced by Russians affect the overwhelming majority of the population (a fact which is linked with the difference between the present standard of living in Russian society and that in developed Western countries). These deprivations relate primarily to the qualitative parameters of life: housing conditions, replacement of consumer durables, consumption of certain goods and services, social and cultural participation. So, in the context of our proposed research, which was based on the relative approach to poverty, it was necessary not to include an examination of all limitations on consumption in Russia when defining poverty in a given community.

[5] For more details about the ethnic dimension of this issue, see 'Ethnic and cultural aspects of poverty' in Chapter 6.

[6] For more details about the IMD, see Appendix 1 on 'Project Methodology'.

[7] 'People can experience one or more forms of deprivation without necessarily being in poverty. People with the same resources may display a different relationship to forms of deprivation. And people with fewer resources than others may be much more likely to experience forms of deprivation even when their resources remain considerably above the "poverty line". However, it is assumed in this conceptualisation that at a certain point in descending the scale of income or resources deprivation is likely to grow disproportionate to further loss of resources and that this "threshold" properly marks the beginning of a state of objective poverty' (Townsend, 1987, pp.130-1).

[8] At least one of the types of property listed.

[9] Data from the same survey provide evidence that residents of Southern and Central Black Earth regions of Russia (in our longitudinal research, Vladikavkaz and Voronezh belong to this group of regions) refer to the use of a dacha for survival purposes more often than on average across Russia. We should note that the importance of the dacha in supporting the level of family welfare is much more rarely mentioned by residents of the capital city megalopolises (12.7 per cent in St. Petersburg, 22.9 per cent in Moscow).

[10] The data quoted here are from the Pan-Russian Representative Survey carried out by the RIISNP in October 2000. According to data from the Russian Longitudinal Monitoring Survey in 1992, 39.7 per cent of Russian households were involved in informal mutual assistance networks; however, Kabalina and Clark's research in 1998 recorded more significant scales of the main kinds of mutual exchange – up to 65 per cent of the households they investigated (Clark and Kabalina, 1999, p.259).

[11] This is also true in regions with severe conditions of existence, such as the North, Siberia and the Far East.

Part III

Social Exclusion

4 Social Exclusion: Concepts and Debates

Peter Abrahamson

Не житьё, а каторга
Not living, but penal servitude

History and Origin

The phenomenon of social exclusion is nothing new. Within sociology society has always been defined precisely with reference to processes of integration and exclusion. The way a community defines itself is by making a distinction to those outside it; by drawing the boundary. Likewise within communities where certain groups or individuals are labelled non-members, in the extreme case as outcasts, outlaws or untouchables; but also very commonly as physically or mentally handicapped, or plainly poor people. These groups of people were assigned special quarters of town or special buildings such as asylums or workhouses, and until recently one might lose political citizenship when demanding social citizenship; i.e., those receiving poor relief could not vote or run for political office.

A distinction can be made between voluntary and enforced social exclusion. When the nobility in all practical matters of every day life isolated themselves from the life of the common people it can be defined as a process of social exclusion, but it was voluntary and led to privileged positions. Otherwise, when 'idiots' or widows no longer able to provide for themselves were placed in an almshouse it was the result of coercion. In contemporary late modern societies processes of voluntary social exclusion can be identified, e.g., as so-called 'gated communities' (Low, 2001) or what Giddens has labelled 'voluntary exclusion of the elites' or 'exclusion at the top' (1998, p.105). Likewise, enforced exclusion is currently found in more extreme cases when convicted criminals are confined to prisons or when undocumented immigrants are deported; and also when particular ethnic minorities in all practical terms are forced to live in separate parts of town not enjoying otherwise common service infrastructures, such as the

Roma population in Europe. Other examples include the denial of schooling to children of undocumented immigrants, as recently legislated in California or the situation regarding asylum seekers everywhere when they are denied access to the labour market, schools, normal housing, etc.

Following French sociology social exclusion is undesirable since it threatens the social fabric of society, the social bond (*lien social*) said to exist among citizens. Hence, from the perspective of Durkheim social exclusion expresses a lack of solidarity. Modern societies are supposed to develop an organic solidarity among the members of such a society because of their interdependence created by the division of labour (Durkheim, 1966). In French political thought – republicanism – the State is responsible for integration or social solidarity; for societal cohesion. This comes out very clearly from contemporary analysts like, for example, Pierre Strobel:

> The debate on exclusion puts to society as a whole the fundamental question of the social bond and the means that society has of holding together and ensuring solidarity among its members (Strobel, 1996, p.186).

Yet, historically it is clear that real integration was been reserved for the deserving poor, while the undeserving poor have been *de facto* excluded and confined to the above mentioned institutions (Procacci, 1993).

In these senses social exclusion is part and parcel of (any) society but when social exclusion has been a focal point for social scientists and policy makers during the last decades of the 20th Century it is in a more specific meaning, namely as a substitute for or complementary to poverty. This new discourse first arose in France, as Hilary Silver writes:

> Exclusion became the subject of debate in France during the 1960s. Politicians, activists, officials, journalists, and academics made vague and ideological references to the poor as *les exclus*. However, the exclusion discourse did not become widespread until the economic crisis. As successive social and political crisis erupted in France during the 1980s, exclusion came to be applied to more and more types of social disadvantage and the continual redefinition of the term to encompass new social groups and problems gave rise to its diffuse connotations ... The coining of the term is generally attributed to René Lenoir (1974), who was then Secretary of State for Social Action in the (Gaullist) Chirac government (Silver, 1994, p.532).

It was meant to cover what had emerged as the 'new poor' such as single parents, drug addicts, homeless people, etc. developing from new social problems such as unemployment, ghettoisation, and fundamental changes in family life (Cannan, 1997; de Haan, 1998).

Furthermore, social exclusion was often associated with the spatial dimension referring to deprived (urban) areas, the ghetto; neglected inner city neighbourhoods or suburban public housing estates such as the French *banlieues* (Byrne, 1999). So, not only were certain categories of people excluded from mainstream society, they were also viewed as allocated to certain spaces disintegrated from where regular folks worked, lived, shopped and spent their free time. Reflecting upon experiences from both Europe and North America Loïc Wacquant (1996) talks about *advanced* marginality when he discusses post-Fordist processes of social exclusion and impoverishment:

> Such new forms of exclusionary social closure and peripheralization have arisen, or intensified, in the post-Fordist metropolis as a result, not of backwardness, but of the uneven, disarticulating, mutations of the *most advanced sectors* of Western societies and economies, as these bear on the lower fractions of the working class and on dominated ethnoracial categories, a well as on the territories they occupy in the divided city (Wacquant, 1996, p.123).

He identifies what he calls some distinctive properties of this 'advanced marginality'. One is labelled *territorial fixation and stigmatisation*, where he discusses the popular images connected to urban deprived areas. Whether the ghettos are dangerous or not are overshadowed by the belief that they are horrible places which set off socially detrimental consequences. At the same time an obverse process is observed called territorial alienation and the dissolution of 'place'. The 'banlieu' and the 'ghettos' have changed from 'places' of shared feelings, joint meanings and practices and institutions of mutuality into indifferent 'spaces' of mere survival and contest. The neighbourhoods have lost their appeal as places which one identified with and was proud of. Another distinct property of advanced marginality observed by Wacquant is the loss of hinterland. Earlier, periodically redundant workers could fall back upon the social economy of their community of provenance, be it kin, clique, or church. Instead of these former networks of civil society, today's marginalised are forced to rely on what he calls 'individual strategies of "self provisioning", "shadow work", underground commerce and quasi-institutionalised "hustling" ... which do little to alleviate precariousness ...' (Wacquant, 1996, p.127). In this sense, social exclusion is a relatively recent and predominantly urban phenomenon.

The Substitution of Poverty by Social Exclusion

From France the discourse on social exclusion was spread to the rest of Western Europe by the adoption of the term by the EU-institutions, primarily the European Commission, but also the European Parliament and the Council of Ministers and finally by the European Council with its implementation of the so-called National Action Plans for Combatting Social Exclusion in 2000. Hence the EU started to promote heavily the concept of social exclusion, as when the Commission had the Council adopt a Resolution of 29th September 1989 which was about combating social exclusion. Here it was:

> emphasized that social exclusion is not simply a matter of inadequate [resources], and that combatting exclusion also involves access by individuals and families to decent living conditions by means of measures for social integration and integration into the labour market; accordingly request the Member States to implement or promote measures to enable everyone to have access to education, by acquiring proficiency in basic skills, training, employment, housing, community services, medical care (Quoted from Robbins, 1993).

With reference to this resolution the Council accepted a suggestion from the Commission to establish an Observatory on National Policies to Combat Social Exclusion. The Observatory's first coordinator, Graham Room (1990) coined the following definition of social exclusion:

> (Individuals) ... suffer social exclusion where a) they suffer generalised disadvantage in terms of education, training, employment, housing, financial resources, etc.; b) their chances of gaining access to the major social institutions which distribute these life chances are substantially less than those of the rest of the population; c) these disadvantages persist over time.

What has happened at the European level is the substitution of poverty with social exclusion as, for example, expressed by Martin Evans: 'European Union social policy has moved away from the concept of poverty towards social exclusion since the early 1990s' (Evans, 1998, p.42).

Social exclusion indicates that *processes* are taking place. Some segments of the population are being excluded; it is thus a dynamic concept. It is also a *multi-dimensional* concept making reference to different institutions and sectors. The first points to processes whereby some people are unable to participate in activities carried out within various institutions of integration such as labour markets, housing markets, schools, health care systems, local social networks of both formal and informal kinds, etc. Somehow they are being *discriminated* against; they are being denied access to these institutions of integration. In terms of citizenship the socially excluded are either not granted social rights or are not able to exercise such rights (Berghman, 1996; Atkinson and Davoudi, 2000). The multi-dimensional character of the concept indicates the necessity of complex policy responses; i.e., it is not enough to provide socially excluded people with just more money or with marriage counselling, for example, but an encompassing set of policies must be implemented if the excluded are to be brought back into (mainstream) society.

The, so far, most authoritative definition of social exclusion was coined by Room in 1999:

> ... to use the notion of social exclusion carries the implication that we are speaking of people who are suffering such a degree of multi-dimensional disadvantage, of such duration, and reinforced by such material and cultural degradation of the neighbourhoods in which they live, that their relational links with the wider society are ruptured to a degree which is to some considerable degree irreversible (Room, 1999, p.171).

Hence, the definition is reserved processes of a certain duration and severity and allocated certain spaces.

This was the backdrop for what he called a reconfiguration of the research debate over disadvantage and social exclusion. He identified five sets of changes (Room, 1999, p.167):

- from financial to multi-dimensional disadvantage;
- from a static to a dynamic analysis;
- from a focus on the resources of the individual or household to a concern also with those of the local community;
- from distributional to relational relations of stratification and disadvantage;
- from a continuum of inequality to catastrophic rupture.

So, whether labelled social exclusion or poverty, social science research is now more concerned with a dynamic perspective on multi-dimensional disadvantages in localities that are viewed as outside mainstream society.

Why this New Prominence of Social Exclusion?

A number of explanations have been offered as to why this shift from poverty to social exclusion has occurred. One is the political sensitivity of poverty (Room, 1994). In some countries the existence of poverty is simply politically incorrect, since a lot of resources are devoted to welfare arrangements. The recognition of poverty is then a critique of the existing policy measures. Social exclusion, on the other hand, may be a more feasible concept, since it locates the problems more on an individual level. Another explanation emphasises a semantic differentiation of the same phenomenon and identifies social exclusion as a Francophone concept with roots in continental European social science, while poverty is the Anglo-American concept for essentially the same processes and situations (Silver, 1994; Room, 1995). Still others see poverty as a condition or a situation, while social exclusion is emphasising the processes, i.e., as a more dynamic concept (da Costa, 1995). In this view poverty is strongly related to (long-term) unemployment, and has to do with lack of primarily economic resources following from the lack of paid employment. On the other hand social exclusion is the marginalisation process affiliated with denied access to societal institutions of integration. Yet, other explanations see social exclusion as the end result of extreme poverty; the socially excluded are the 'down and out' segments of our (urban) population (Castel, 1991). Finally, one explanation locates the two concepts in different historical times: poverty is a classic phenomenon which in modernity is related to (early) industrialisation, while social exclusion is its postmodern or postindustrial equivalent. Here, both poverty and social exclusion must be understood with reference to their opposites: wealth and integration. Poverty is a traditional condition for the majority of people (the working class) brought onto them because of the exploitation by the rich (the bourgeoisie). Social exclusion, on the contrary, is a postmodern condition for the minority of people who are marginalised from mainstream middle mass society (see further, Abrahamson, 1995). This last explanation is consistent with the new political emphasis on the development of a so-called *underclass*, and reflects profound changes in societal differentiation, as exemplified by Serge Paugam (1996, p.5) when he makes a distinction between integrated, marginal and disabling poverty. Regarding *integrated poverty* he writes:

> ... the "poor" form a broad social class, rather than a strictly defined "underclass", they are not heavily stigmatised. Their standard of living is low, but they remain part of the social networks which stem from family and the immediate neighbourhood.

This situation changed with the Welfare State, if not necessarily because of it. Being a worker or a pensioner no longer meant being poor; poverty had become *marginal*. Now, after the Welfare State, or at least after the golden years, we experience advanced marginality in the form of underclass and social exclusion. *Disabling poverty*, Paugam writes, '... is concerned more with the question of exclusion than that of actual poverty, although social actors continue to employ both terms' (1996, p.5).

These changes in focus for social scientists reflect changes in the problems addressed which, again, are connected to what has been labelled a postindustrial or postmodern condition: there is widespread agreement within the social sciences that modern society has developed into something different from early industrial society; but they label it very differently. The development has been related to changes in the social structure, especially the polarisation and the 'middle classization' of society; to changes in the political processes, a weakening of the labour movement and a strengthening of various new social movements; to changes in popular culture, exemplified by the mass media revolution; and to changes in family life, the increase in single parenthood and serial and same sex marriages. Social exclusion dynamics are at play within all four orders of society: the market, the State, the associations and the informal networks.

The development towards a postindustrial society has produced an altogether very different labour market, where people cannot expect to be employed throughout their life with the same local big employer; where service production dominates over manufacture, where vertical hierarchies are succeeded by a horizontal stratification into insiders and outsiders, core and periphery employees; where even the lowest paid jobs require numeracy and literacy skills and often language skills. Processes of discrimination and exclusion from labour markets feed into complex webs of potential social exclusion.

Within the social order comprised of the public sector, processes of marginalisation can also be identified, and the traditional view of the Welfare State as an institution of integration must be modified, as stated by Bill Jordan:

> There is an increasing evidence of an overall tendency within welfare states towards the formation of new and smaller clubs with more homogeneous memberships ... The exclusion of bad risks and the grouping together of narrower risk-pools in such systems reinforces the residential segregation of rich and poor. The "Americanization" of European welfare states consists mainly of a division into two clubs, a social-insurance club for those in secure

and adequately paid employment, and a social-assistance club for the rest ... (Jordan, 1996, p.68).

The club metaphor is also applicable to the social order of associations where the tendency is towards a more differentiated and complex set of 'belongings'. The all embracing organisations of the 19th and 20th Centuries, the political party and the trade union are now being gradually substituted by smaller *ad hoc*, one-issue movements which operate with more restricted forms of access and closure. These changes in publicity (*öffentlichkeit*) may also feed into processes of exclusion.

The final social order, that of informal networks, seems to be strengthened under postmodern conditions where, as Rose puts it:

> ... "the social" may be giving way to "the community" as a new territory for the administration of individual and collective existence, a new place or surface upon which micro-moral relations among persons are conceptualised and administered (Rose, 1996, p.331).

Furthermore, the reconfiguration:

> ... of ethical vectors is re-organised under the sign of community. The subject is addressed as a moral individual with bonds of obligation and responsibilities for conduct that are assembled in a new way – the individual in his or her community is both self-responsible and subject to certain emotional bonds of affinity to a circumscribed "network" of other individuals – unified by family ties, by locality, by moral commitment to environmental protection or animal welfare (Rose, 1996, pp.333-334).

The combined effects of changes within these four social orders result in a change in the overall social structure of late modern societies as pronounced within French sociology by scholars such as Castel and Touraine. Alain Touraine gave the following indication of change (1991, p.8):

> At this moment we live in a change from a vertical society, which we have grown used to name a class society with people on top and people at the bottom, to a horizontal society, where the important thing is to know whether one is at the centre or at the periphery ... Today it is not about being "up or down", but "in or out" (my translation, P.A.).

Robert Castel views the social structure of contemporary postmodern society as an uneasy unity of 'integrated, vulnerable and disaffiliated [by others named excluded]' and he applies the same metaphors of 'in' and 'out' to describe the social structure as did Touraine, adding that the conditions of those left out of mainstream society is determined by the insiders (1995, p.21). In an article from 2000 he expanded this scheme when talking about four 'zones' of social life and added the category of assistance onto the previously mentioned three: 'Now, the zone of integration is breaking up, the zone of vulnerability is expanding and continuously feeds the zone of disaffiliation. Is our only adequate response to strengthen the zone of assistance?' he asks (2000, p.526).

The Underclass Debate

As indicated above the social exclusion discourse has, by and large, been a European phenomenon, although it has been suggested to split it up into three distinctly different paradigms: the solidarity paradigm, which is identical to the one given above; the specialisation paradigm, which is a liberal understanding of exclusion reflecting discrimination against contractoral obligations and rights, dominant in the US; and the monopoly paradigm, which sees exclusion as a consequence of the formation of group monopolies (social closure) somewhat influential in the UK and elsewhere (Silver, 1994). Rather than maintaining this distinction, they have been collapsed into one, or, more precisely the specialisation and monopoly paradigms have been subsumed into the solidarity paradigm in the present discussion. Instead the underclass discourse shall be presented as the most distinctive alternative to the 'French' discourse on social exclusion. The term underclass in its more recent appearances has developed in the US where it has been presented in two variations: a normative one and a scientific one.

The normative discourse – or, as Westergaard (1992) has it, the 'moral turpitude version' as opposed to the 'outcast poverty version' – was strongly promoted with Charles Murray's *Losing Ground* from 1984. Instead of viewing the disadvantaged as victims of structural changes, he perceived them as trapped in a dependency culture produced by too generous welfare benefits. It created 'perverse incentives' which made it profitable for the poor to behave in the short term '... in ways which were destructive in the long term' (Murray, 1984, p.8, quoted from Andersen and Larsen, 1995, p.157). Another influential input to the normative discourse was Lawrence Mead's *Beyond entitlements: the social obligation of citizenship* from 1986. He assumed that everyone wanting a job could get one; so unemployment was self-imposed. He explained the idleness of the urban poor with reference to their ethnic culture: 'Where western culture had sought to overcome material hardship through rationalising economic activity, non-western culture, on the whole, has counselled acceptance.' In other words, blacks and Hispanics are poor because their culture teaches them to accept instead of fight situations of hardship! The solution to the problem of the underclass according to Mead is workfare, a strengthening of the obligations that the disadvantaged should have to society.

This normative discourse emphasises the development of segments of the population culturally detached from mainstream society because of deviant behaviour. They have developed a dependency culture where they expect public support without any aspiration of self-supportiveness. This is a traditional 'blaming the victim' approach to socially excluded people.

Under the heading 'them' or 'us' Michael Katz (1989, pp.236-237) summed up the American perspective on underclass and the poor:

> ... in the language of social science, as well as in ordinary conversation and political rhetoric, poor people usually remain outsiders, strangers to be pitied or despised, helped or punished, ignored or studied, but rarely full citizens, members of a larger community on the same terms as the rest of us ... Poverty in America is profoundly individual, like popular economics, it is supply-side.

The poor are clearly excluded, outside society.

From the 1980s and onwards North American social science and political discourse began to phrase contemporary urban poverty an underclass issue. Richard Nathan (1987) represents the scientific approach. He identifies the use of the term 'underclass' as an indicator of '... a distinctive structural change in social conditions in the United States over the past two decades ...' (Nathan, 1987, p.57). This structural change is the development of an *urban* poverty among ethnic minorities: the underclass is an '... expression for the concentration of economic and behavioural problems among racial minorities (mainly black and Hispanic) in *large, older cities*' (ibid., emphasis added). And later on he expresses that '... the underclass is a distinctively urban condition involving a hardened residual group that are hard to reach and relate to. This condition represents a change in kind, not degree ...' (Nathan, 1987, p.58). The reasons for the difficulty in reaching the urban poor are, according to Nathan, centred around issues like the minority status of the urban poor; their refusal to vote, i.e., participate in regular political activities, including getting support from ordinary interest groups.

The scientific discourse is also promoted by William Julius Wilson (1987), for example. He identifies the economic restructuring which took place from the 1960s and onwards to have a number of severe spatial consequences for the American working class, especially the unskilled workers. The changes within industrial production and the change from industrial production to various service industries has hit the inner cities very hard, since jobs traditionally open to the unskilled either left town or disappeared altogether. When the jobs left, so did a large number of the better off ghetto population (the black middle class, professionals, and other minority groups, such as Jewish segments), while the in migration to the inner city consisted of unskilled blacks, thus changing the class and ethnic composition of inner cities. The consequence has been a dramatic increase in poverty levels in inner city neighbourhoods, since there simply are not nearly enough jobs available, thus forcing people to try and sustain a life without public support, hence creating the so-called welfare dependency. The chronic lack of job opportunities influences the whole community:

> Thus, in such neighbourhoods the chances are overwhelming that children will seldom interact on a sustained basis with people who are employed or with families that have a steady breadwinner. The net effect is that *joblessness, as a way of life*, takes on a different social meaning; the relationship between schooling and post school employment takes on a different meaning (Wilson 1987, p.57; emphasis added, P.A.).

With the term *concentration effects* Wilson sums up the experiences of inner-city low-income families:

> The social transformation of the inner city has resulted in a disproportionate concentration of the most disadvantaged segments of the urban black population, creating a social milieu significantly different from the environment that existed in these communities several decades ago (Wilson, 1987, p.58).

One of the most devastating consequences of the changes within the communities is a disintegration of the social networks. Social interactions between families in the ghetto and families outside are rare or non-existent, and interaction in the ghetto is often related to idleness, welfare 'performance' or some or other kind of criminal activity, which leads Wilson to point to the concept of *isolation* as central in understanding the social dynamics of the urban ghetto (Wilson, 1987, p.61, ff.). The disintegration effects have very often been discussed in relation to the substantial increase in the number of teenage pregnancies, childbirth and subsequent female single-headed households. Among conservative scholars these effects have been related to the expansion of the American Welfare State, especially the rise in the AFDC programme (Aid to Families with Dependent Children), leaving the impression that the possibility of receiving AFDC has been the cause of the increase. In a very careful examination of these matters Wilson and his colleagues make a strong point in rejecting this welfare dependency hypothesis. By constructing a so-called '*male marriageable pool index*' they show that there exists a long-term decline in the proportion of black men, especially young black men, that are in any way at all, in a position to support a family (see Wilson, 1987, p.81, ff.; and Wilson and Neckermann, 1986). In other words, the reason for the 'feminisation' of poverty is most probably related to the lack of jobs than to any 'scrounging' behaviour among black young women. This statistical discussion leads to the sane conclusion '... that the problem of joblessness should be a top-priority item in any public policy discussion focussing on enhancing the status of families' (Wilson, 1987, p.105).

What can be learned from the scientific discourse on the underclass is the stratification consequences of a *qualitative shift* following the change from industrial to postindustrial society and the accompanying employment crisis. This has also come out of European scholarship '... the emergence of the notion of an "underclass" ... does seem to mark a moment in which the social vision of a continuous quantitative variability of civility becomes re-coded as a qualitative distinction' (Rose, 1996, p.345).

The normative discourse is a re-emergence of an age old understanding of the poor as undeserving and it has been influential with regard to the policy side of exclusion. The idea is that the socially excluded should be obliged to do something in return for assistance, which in Europe has been termed activation.

Defining Exclusion *vis-à-vis* Poverty

Table 4.1 juxtaposes poverty and social exclusion with respect to a number of aspects. The critical variable when it comes to poverty is *resources*, while the critical variable when it comes to social exclusion is *discrimination*. A poor person is someone lacking sufficient resources to live a life in accordance with human dignity. His or her needs are not met. Social exclusion characterises a situation where people are denied access to institutions of social integration; they are discriminated against; they do not have, or cannot exercise, social rights. Poverty is often understood and measured as a condition, i.e., in a static fashion, while social exclusion indicates a process, i.e., the dynamic dimension is emphasised. Poverty refers to a vertical societal stratification where the poor are those at the bottom, while social exclusion refers more to a horizontal stratification; the socially excluded are the outsiders; they belong to the periphery not to the centre as the insiders do. Eradication or elevation of poverty points to providing the poor with a sufficient income, e.g., a guaranteed minimum income, while social exclusion is combated via enabling access to service delivering institutions. Measurement of poverty has often been carried out by economists, while social exclusion calls for sociological studies.

Table 4.1   Making distinctions between poverty and social exclusion

Aspect	*Poverty*	*Social exclusion*
Situation	Lack of sufficient *resources*	Denial of exercising *rights*
Cause	*Needs'* frustration	*Discrimination* from institutions of integration
Perspective	Static (a *condition*)	Dynamic (a *process*)
Type of societal stratification	Vertical (upper- vs. lower *classes*)	Horizontal (*insiders* vs. *outsiders*)
Suggested remedy	Social *transfers* (guaranteed minimum income)	Social *services* (activation measures)
Disciplinary approach	*Economics*	*Sociology*

Source: Abrahamson (1998)

Sometimes the poor are also socially excluded and sometimes the socially excluded are also poor. But social exclusion as a concept for contemporary misery is sensitive to processes of keeping segments of the population out of, for example, the housing market because of ethnic discrimination; or consider the case of exclusion from parenthood because of discrimination against same sex couples. Gays and immigrants may be socially excluded without being poor.

Social Exclusion in the Russian Context

In this study the following indicators were developed to capture the process leading citizens into social exclusion (with their working titles in brackets):

- the right to secure, paid work (the Work scale);
- the right to essential medical assistance when needed (the Health scale);
- the right of access to education and culture (the Education and Culture scale);
- the right to significant relations of primary sociability and to inclusion in a community (the Relationships scale);
- the right of access to social networks as one of the main mechanisms – alongside social protection – for the redistribution of resources (we called this the Networks scale, but our respondents called it 'Connections', and that is certainly more appropriate to the Russian situation);
- the right of autonomy – understood as the ability to initiate action, formulate goals and carry through goal-oriented actions; we agree with Ian Gough and Len Doyle (1991) and others who stress the role of autonomy – alongside physical health – as the most important prerequisite for active participation in social life (the Autonomy scale);
- the right to adequate housing (the Housing scale).

Here is emphasised the extent to which citizens are denied rights that otherwise would enable them inclusion or participation in society.

5 Social Exclusion in Russia

Nataliya Tikhonova

Не житьё, а каторга
Not living, but penal servitude

Concepts of Social Exclusion in the Russian Context

Analysing social exclusion as applied to Russian conditions represented one of the most difficult issues in our research. Firstly, although 'social exclusion' is a well-established concept in the Western literature (Abrahamson, 1998; Doyal and Gough, 1991; Gough, 1994; Leonard, 1997; Littlewood, 1999; Paugam, 1996; Touraine, 1991 and others) and has been very productive in helping to analyse social policy issues (European Commission, 1993), research in this area in Russia is in its infancy. Following Tchernina's ground-breaking work in Novosibirsk in 1993-98 (Tchernina, 1998), further research was carried out in that region in the late 1990s and, more recently, there have been some smaller-scale studies in other Russian regions. Secondly, definitions of social exclusion used in Russian research tend to equate with specific forms of deprivation and to identify exclusion primarily with unemployment, so that the real problem of households falling out of the mainstream has remained outside the scope of research.

However, our *most challenging* problem lay in trying to establish whether the concept of social exclusion can actually be applied to contemporary Russian society at all. Surely it is a concept created for and most effectively applied to other types of societies altogether? These are societies in which horizontal stratification has to some extent replaced vertical, where inequality is associated more with discriminations that exclude particular individuals or families from the main integration mechanisms than with belonging to poor classes or groups – and where, therefore, the solution to inequality lies in providing access to integration mechanisms rather than in income redistribution: societies, in other words, which are at a particular stage of modernisation.

This society has been given a variety of names – 'post-industrial society' (Bell, 1973); 'risk society' (Beck, 1992); 'informational society' (Castells, 1998) – but is clearly at a particular stage of development, in which the situation of individuals matters more than their group membership. Although relations of inequality still exist, the individual is called on to act with unprecedented scope and dynamism. This 'social surge of individualization' (Beck, 1992, p.87) means that people are beginning to depend more on themselves – while their individual fates depend more on the labour market, with its risks, chances and contradictions.

Russia has a history of many decades of planning for a 'socially uniform society', where it was a central tenet of the State's ideology that the whole population was to have a similar standard of living. This was to a great extent achieved, bringing with it uniformity of lifestyle. Those who did not work were parasites, and even subject to criminal prosecution: a strict system of social control and mutual assistance operated through the workplace and the place of residence. Although there were poor families in the Soviet period, the concept of social exclusion – at least as any kind of mass phenomenon – did not apply: everyone had to be in the mainstream, willingly or not.

However, more than ten years have now passed. Social differentiation processes have penetrated Russian society, and the old mechanisms of social integration have almost completely broken down: no one talks about 'uniformity' any more. At the same time, there have been no serious large-scale class-based manifestations during the whole reform period, which raises questions as to whether any kind of class analysis can still be applied to Russian society (a discussion that is current among those researching social stratification, e.g., Piirainen, 1997; Tikhonova, 1999). Perhaps it is now more relevant to describe what is happening in Russia through the application of more up-to-date concepts – like social exclusion.

Recent Russian research provides some indirect evidence about people's identities. The project 'Citizens of the new Russia: how do they see themselves and what kind of society do they want to live in?'[1] showed that neither belonging to a particular social or professional group nor living at a certain material standard was the dominant factor in creating identity, whether for Russians in general or for those who were materially less well-off (Tikhonova, 2000).

In the light of all this, we decided to test whether either or both of the concepts of poverty and social exclusion could be applied to the process of increasing social differentiation and the changes taking place in the structure of Russian society today. We were already aware that there is undoubtedly a specific group in Russia who are almost deliberately 'socially excluded'. These are people who do not have a 'permit' (in Russian, *propiska*) or – to use the more up-to-date term – 'residence registration'.[2] Any Russian citizen without permanent registration is automatically excluded from generally accepted mechanisms of integration and social support. This is because social services in Russia are delivered through State bodies at the territorial level, and because the system whereby formal employment depends on having a permit for a given population centre remains unchanged since the Soviet period. So, a permit for a particular address functions as a marker dividing the formally successful section of Russia's population from the section that is deliberately placed in a position of social exclusion.

The latter include vagrants (people of no fixed abode) and the homeless, many seasonal workers, refugees without formal refugee or settler status, professional beggars, illegal immigrants, ex-prisoners who, for some reason, have not been able to get a permit for their old place of residence, and some others. In some major cities, such as Moscow, they also include people who migrate from elsewhere in Russia in search of casual work, but cannot get even temporary residence registration.

Many people and organisations are involved in tackling this scandalous situation as it affects these various groups, though without particular results. But this form of social exclusion lies outside the parameters of our research. We saw our task as being, rather, *to try and assess whether the concept of social exclusion applies to people who have permanent housing, a certain degree of income security and the right to social services, benefits and allowances – in other words, people who are, at first glance, ordinary members of Russian society.* So, in our research, we investigated only those households whose members were registered at a particular address or had official refugee status: in other words, people who are accepted as full members of society and have the right of access to free medical assistance, free education, benefits and allowances, including housing allowances and benefits at the level currently guaranteed by the Russian State. We also tried to determine the validity of applying the concept of social exclusion specifically to such people in the Russian situation and to evaluate how effective it might be as that situation becomes increasingly difficult.

Of course, the limited size of our sample and the nature of our research meant that we were not in a position to give an exhaustive picture of all forms of exclusion in Russia, nor to determine how widespread it is. Similarly, we could not assess social exclusion among any non-poor sections of the population, since our study dealt specifically with urban households in need. Therefore, we set out primarily to discover whether social exclusion exists and to define some of its characteristic features in urban communities in large Russian cities.

The first thing we noticed was that, right from the start of the first survey, respondents themselves introduced the issue of exclusion, providing evidence that the concept is highly applicable to the current state of Russian society. Neither interviewers nor respondents used the term 'social exclusion', which is not a familiar one to most Russians. However, on their own initiative, when talking about lack of prosperity and the restrictions on people in Russia today, respondents listed not only lack of money and particular deprivations, but also lack of access to the main integration mechanisms. Moreover, respondents associated this exclusion very closely with lack of resources (both material and social) for normal integration into society:

> I know people who can't afford to eat or dress properly, and have to go without a lot of things; they are in bad health, but they can't afford treatment – or education for their children; and they can't find work because they are ill. Each of them is in a different situation, but in a lot of cases it's not their fault they can't work – and those are the worst off.

This quotation clearly shows that our respondents associated the various manifestations of social exclusion with a certain standard of living, stressing the psychological state of hopelessness and powerlessness to change anything, with a painful awareness of lack of access to good education and medical assistance. We often heard complaints about work-related problems, feelings of loneliness and an absence of the 'connections' needed for successful integration and access to social support networks.

Thus, when we analysed the 1999 interviews, two things immediately became clear. Firstly, we established *as fact the existence of social exclusion in families who appeared, at first glance, to be completely ordinary (they had a home, residence registration and formal access to all the mechanisms of social integration and social protection, including free education, higher education and health care). Secondly, we found that they associated their social exclusion primarily with their own very difficult material circumstances.*

This gave rise to several problems, which had to be tackled in the course of our research. First and foremost, we needed to find *indicators* that would allow us to divide excluded households from those of the sample who were simply poor. Secondly, having singled out such households using these indicators, we would have to analyse their situations so as to define *the main forms of the social exclusion phenomenon at the micro level*. Then we would have to determine whether this actually was social exclusion, and what had given rise to the situation in each individual case – was it a random occurrence, or are there are some *objective factors that sharply increase the risk of becoming excluded?* Finally, we would have to define the interrelationship between *poverty and social exclusion* in Russia, and try to evaluate whether different groups experience social exclusion in specifically different ways.

Naturally, we had to start by defining indicators of social exclusion. We decided to derive these indicators from seven scales, using classifications based on human rights: this was because manifest instances of discrimination had very often been mentioned in the interviews and because discourses on social exclusion issues often refer to the rights that should be guaranteed by society (Abrahamson, 1998; Da Costa, 1995; Friedmann, 1996; Room, 1995). Given the specifics of the Russian situation, we decided, in developing our social exclusion scales, not to include certain of the human rights characteristically invoked by Western specialists in this field:

- professional assistance at the birth of a child – this is available to all those living in towns and cities, if the mother is a registered resident: we were studying citizens in precisely that position;
- adequate nutrition – specialists have already concluded that, according to a number of nutritional parameters, most of the population of Russia does not have access to this;[3]
- political participation – in principle, this right is guaranteed to every Russian, but demand from the population to exercise it is very low, as RIISNP and other sociological research has shown (Gorshkov, 2000);
- dignity in old age – according to statistical data, only 22.2 per cent of women and 18 per cent of men over pension age in 1999 had incomes below the amount of the subsistence minimum: this was lower than the corresponding figures for the Russian population as

a whole (Goskomstat, 2000, p.183). In addition, over the following two years, the situation in this sphere improved very rapidly, and a series of significant pension increases was planned for 2002;
- a number of other rights were also omitted – security and a healthy environment, non-harmful working conditions, a secure childhood and several others – because we could not measure them in sufficient detail within the parameters of our research.

Here are the indicator scales we established (with their working titles in brackets):

1) the right to secure, paid work (the Work scale);
2) the right to essential medical assistance when needed (the Health scale);
3) the right of access to education and culture (the Education and Culture scale);
4) the right to significant relations of primary sociability and to inclusion in a community (the Relationships scale);
5) the right of access to social networks as one of the main mechanisms – alongside social protection – for the redistribution of resources (we called this the Networks scale, but our respondents called it 'Connections', and that is certainly more appropriate to the Russian situation[4]);
6) the right of autonomy, understood as the ability to initiate action, formulate goals and carry through goal-oriented actions; we agree with Peter Abrahamson (1998) and others who stress the role of autonomy – alongside physical health – as the most important prerequisite for active participation in social life (the Autonomy scale);
7) the right to adequate housing (the Housing scale).

The method of calculating the index for each scale and the combined Social Exclusion Index (ISE) is described in Appendix 1 (Project Methodology). Here, we will merely note that the indicators on the combined Social Exclusion Index, calculated as the sum of the indicators from all these scales, varied in intervals 1-19 across the whole sample for 1999 and in intervals 2-21 for 2000, with the higher numbers representing greater social exclusion.

We should also add that the respondents we identified as representing excluded households answered our question about their most worrying problems in terms that confirmed the relevance of the particular rights covered by our seven scales. Issues of health and autonomy were especially significant, then came problems in gaining access to social networks and to work. Access to education and culture, relationships and adequate housing were relatively less significant for the group as a whole. However, for some types of household, exclusion from mechanisms that would allow them access to these rights was very significant, and lack of them caused a great deal of stress. For example, discrimination in the area of education and culture was, in the main, very significant for families with children under 18; the so-called 'new poor' suffered from their lack of significant relations of primary sociability; and housing problems were perceived as especially serious by migrants and refugees.

In our qualitative analysis, we took into account a range of factors – dynamics of change in the households; their own assessments of their situation in comparison to the situations of others; how satisfied they were with their lives; their specific problems – and found that the indicator threshold for defining a household as excluded was nine points in 1999 and 11 points in 2000. The boundary below which a household was profoundly excluded was defined as 14 points in 1999 and 16 points in 2000. These boundaries are to a large extent notional, of course, but we found them a vital aid to our analysis, and they subsequently demonstrated their fairly high effectiveness and heuristic capacity.

Main Forms of Social Exclusion Manifest at the Micro Level

By applying this Social Exclusion Index (ISE) to our whole sample, we were able to define 47 excluded households in 1999 and 57 in 2000. Some fairly typical life histories will help to give a clearer picture of the realities and complexities of life in these households, what the exclusion consisted of and how it arose.

1. A Chechen family, headed by Abukhasan, a man of 66 with higher education, who had worked in Chechnya as an economist until 1986 and then moved to Moscow. He worked for the first few years after the move as head of an auditing department in the town hall. Despite his fairly senior position, he was given only a one-room flat in Moscow, because his family had remained in Chechnya. However, during the first Chechen war, in 1995, he brought his wife and children to Moscow, so his housing conditions immediately deteriorated sharply. Further events – illness, leaving work, starting in business

on his own account, which took almost all the savings he had, and the collapse of his firm after the 1998 crisis – propelled a person who had previously been completely successful into one of the worst-off sections of the population.

Here are some extracts from his interview: 'The main problem for refugees now is unemployment. They have lost everything, they couldn't bring anything out with them; everything has been looted. If my age allowed me to, I would be earning, but my wife can't find a job either. There's no kind of help from the State, only a housing subsidy; we're barely surviving, and the children aren't getting enough vitamins. We have to start again from scratch; they don't create any jobs for us. If there were no war in Chechnya, I would send the children home: life there isn't so expensive. They don't give us any help. You have to rely solely on yourself. It's the same in Chechnya, except that there, if someone asks for something, others always help him. Here, the people are like wolves – although there are bandits in Chechnya now. It's easier to live anywhere in Russia than in Moscow, even in Moscow Province. But here, they just kick a man when he's down. There's no kind of compensation for your house being destroyed … Children have to be given the chance to study, and they need vitamins, but we can't provide them' (1999, score on ISE – 13 points).

Abukhasan's situation had not improved even a year later. '2000 has been a very unlucky year … Our finances are at the same level as in 1996-7, but with children growing up, you need more money, so things have become harder. Our consumption has gone up by 30-40 per cent, mainly because of the children and my illness. An awful lot of money goes on medicines and treatment. My hopes for future improvement relate solely to the children growing up: my personal prospects are hardly likely to improve. I always planned for my children to study; they've got the brains, so the main thing is that their health should be up to it. You start to do something, the deal is taking shape, but everything falls through if illness strikes. We lost an awful lot in the 1998 crisis. It was hard for everyone, not just me, with the value of savings and possessions falling by almost half. And now the government is stealing everything, prices are increasing and they ask for dollars. Their policy is clear: they're going to ruin us one way or another – it's being done deliberately. It's straightforward deceit … Crooks have stolen everything I managed to earn last year from my business. Now it'll have to go to a settlement. You know what I mean by 'settlement'.[5] That'll have a big effect on my life and on the state of my nerves. So that's why the past year has been unsuccessful.' (Their ISE score had risen to 17 points.)

2. A two-parent family with five children, of whom four were under 18 at the time of the 1999 survey. The head of the family was Viktor, a chief engineer at one of Moscow's scientific research institutes; his wife did not go out to work, but stayed at home with the children. All members of the family over 18,

including the eldest daughter and her husband, either had higher education or were students at the time of the survey. Judging by their IMD (Multivariate Deprivation Index)[6] score, in 1999 the household belonged to the ranks of the poor. In 2000, the situation in the household was worse still and they had crossed the threshold into indigence.

This is how Viktor described the situation in 1999: 'A lot of people I know are almost on the poverty line. Old friends, neighbours, acquaintances – everyone I meet … It's hard to define poverty in two words, you can only define it by comparison. People use or consume just what's necessary, what is directly required for life. Going to visit our relatives outside Moscow is already tough: it means getting into debt. In the past, it wasn't an issue, even though I was earning less. Or medicines: I've been getting subsidies[7] for a little while now, but all the same we can't afford medicines even though the treatment is free. We can't afford to pay doctors' fees, even for essential dentistry.[8] We haven't got any kind of savings or reserves; everything goes on just keeping alive. Every price increase tells on our budget, and a lot of illnesses arise from that. Being on the poverty line means you can't really live – just survive. Poor people can't consume anything extra, only what's necessary. Take us, for example: our youngest child is ill, but I'm forced to buy the kind of foods I can afford, rather than the ones needed. If I buy what he needs, the others will go hungry' (ISE score – 10 points).

In 2000, Viktor assessed his situation as follows: 'It feels pretty much the same – at least, as far as the dynamics of our material circumstances are concerned, it's no better. There have been periods when life has been harder, because of wage delays. And when they do finally pay the money, it's already worth nothing: in real terms, we've been robbed. For the family to get back to our former standard of living now, our income would have to double. In fact, there are no hopes our situation will improve: we'll be moving out of the 'large family' category soon, because our son will be 15.[9] I just pray that the children will be able to provide for themselves when they grow up. I've got no kind of hope' (ISE score – 17 points).

3. A two-parent Ossetian family from Vladikavkaz, living with their two school-age children and the pensioner mother-in-law of our respondent, Yevgeniya. Yevgeniya herself was a housewife of 43; her husband, who was a doctor of economics, worked as a lecturer at Vladikavkaz State University. The family had arrived in Vladikavkaz in 1992 as refugees from the Georgian-Ossetian conflict in Tbilisi; they had lost all their possessions as a result of this conflict. At the times of both the first and second surveys, the family was badly-off rather than poor. In her interview, Yevgeniya said that in recent years 'a lot of people have found themselves in a difficult position, all the more so those who have been refugees. Among them are families who have lost all their possessions. In our family, there have been times that were worse than now –

1992, for example, when we had just settled here from Georgia and we were refugees. I wouldn't say that our situation now is very hard, but it's true that we have no particular hopes for the future' (ISE scores – 13 points in 1999 and 11 points in 2000).

4. Another two-parent family of refugees from Tbilisi, with one child at home; they had moved to Vladikavkaz in 1993, also fleeing the Georgian-Ossetian conflict. Their older son had gone to Ukraine to work in a private business for relatives who ran several kiosks. The respondent's wife was unemployed. 'In Tblisi we had a good three-room flat – our neighbours took it over.' At the time of the survey, they were living in a hostel belonging to the factory where the respondent (49 years old with secondary education) had worked as a gas welder; following long-term non-payment of wages, he had left the factory and applied to the Employment Service. The household lacked any secure source of income at all. The respondent did go to the Employment Service for help and made other efforts to look for work, but was not successful. Finding work was harder because the members of this household found it difficult to express themselves in Russian: at home, they all spoke Georgian or Ossetian. In addition, in recent years, the head of the family had developed a serious alcohol dependency.

By the time of the survey, this household was completely indigent; their neighbours in the hostel had bought the younger son a pair of shoes – otherwise he would have had none. The family had no television or fridge and no money for medicines; essentially, they went hungry. At the first stage, we interviewed the head of the family, but his wife was the second stage respondent: he could not take part because he was on a drinking binge. Their social exclusion indicators remained consistently high (12 points in 1999 and 17 points in 2000). Here is a quotation from the 1999 interview: 'Most Russians probably don't know what situation refugees are in – the ones who have no housing, no work, even sometimes no clothes. I think our family is living below the poverty line: we have no money to eat normally or to buy clothes for the children, so that they aren't ashamed to be seen by their peers.' And a quotation from the 2000 interview: 'At the time of the Ossetian-Georgian conflict, in 1991-2, things were even worse than now. I had a stroke then. Before the war everything was fine for us. That period (the war) was hard – we lost our job and flat in Tbilisi, and after that, things became difficult.'

5. A two-parent family with eight children from Vladikavkaz. The respondent, Al'bert, was disabled (1st category) and in receipt of a pension. He had an alcohol abuse problem. The only working person in the household was his wife, who worked in a grocery run by the mosque. They lived in part of a house, without water or sanitation and with less than three square metres per person. According to the Multivariate Deprivation Index (IMD), they were

profoundly indigent in 1999 and poor in 2000; they steadily scored highly on the Social Exclusion Index (ISE) – 16 points in 1999 and 15 points in 2000. They refused to acknowledge that they were poor and tried to give the impression that 'everything was OK'. 'Most people we know live better than we do ... Pensioners and families with very young children (or a lot of those families) are below the poverty line. There are certainly a lot of people who live worse than we do, who are poorer. Generally, we don't feel ourselves to be poor. [1999] These are difficult times, but a year ago it was especially hard. All the children are studying, and I'm on a disability pension. Over the year, things have become a little bit better. They've added a tiny bit to the pension (about 100 roubles) and my son sometimes earns something.'

These five histories have been included as very brief examples of households where distinct signs of social exclusion were recorded in the course of both surveys (1999 and 2000). As can be seen, socially excluded survey respondents varied greatly – there were families that appeared, at first glance, to be prosperous and families with obvious problems; large and small families; those who saw themselves as poor, and others who were trying to keep up appearances; households whose head was in a fairly high-status job or had a postgraduate degree, and others where the head of the household had a low standard of education. Only one thing united these very different families: their high level of social exclusion. Even from the few histories recounted, it is obvious that things are very bad for these families, although for different reasons; they had no hopes of altering their position in the near future, and none saw any way of improving their situation.

We wanted to look more closely at our excluded households in the context of Russian urban communities: to understand what united them, what were the specific features of their position and the attitudes of household members – and we felt that quantitative analysis of the pre-coded parts of our interviews would help us in this. We divided all the households into three groups: 1) non-excluded (below nine points on the Social Exclusion Index for 1999 – this applied to 57 households; below 11 points in 2000 – 42 households); 2) excluded (9-13 points in 1999 – 40 households; 11-15 points in 2000 – 37 households); 3) profoundly excluded (14 or more points in 1999 – seven households; 16 or more in 2000 – 20 households).

Although it is not possible to dwell here on all the details of the analysis we carried out, we will try to give a picture of some of the patterns that emerged. First and foremost, it was striking how few excluded households saw any improvement in their *material* circumstances over the year of observation, when compared to the control group: seven out of 57 compared to 18 out of 42. In parallel, a downward dynamic in material circumstances over the year was much more common for excluded households (one in three, as against one in 20 non-excluded households); and the higher their indicators of social exclusion, the more this was the case. It was no accident, obviously, that a clear thread of belief in the inescapability of their situation ran through many of the interviews in excluded households (*'I understand myself that I am literally sliding towards nothing. There's already nothing to hope for'; 'Debts and other problems just pile up, to such an extent that you can't find any way out'; '... a feeling that there's no way out'*).

The feeling that it was impossible to escape their situation was closely related to certain significant features of these households – notably to the absence of any feeling that they were capable of somehow managing their own lives, of exercising any significant influence over them. The more profound the social exclusion, the more clearly manifest was this particular feature. Seven out of ten 'non-excluded' families felt that, on the whole, things were going well for them, but fewer than five out of ten 'excluded' and only one in ten 'profoundly excluded' households felt this. Moreover, a constant sense that they themselves couldn't influence what was happening to them was typical only of the 'profoundly excluded' group; the 'excluded' households were no different from the 'non-excluded' in this respect. The same pattern was true for a sense of injustice at all that was happening around them: 80 per cent of profoundly excluded households felt this, as against just under half in the other two groups. Unsurprisingly, therefore, as the year 2000 drew to a close, over half of the profoundly excluded felt predominantly fearful, depressed, in low spirits and embittered, as against a quarter of the excluded and only 5 per cent of ordinary households.

The next most frequent feature of excluded households (both the 'excluded' and the 'profoundly excluded') was that they had found it impossible to use fee-paying educational, medical and health services or to go away on holiday during the year before the survey: this applied to about 70 per cent of each excluded sub-group, as compared to about 30 per cent of non-excluded households. It should also be noted that, in over three-quarters of excluded households, no family member had taken part in any organised sporting, social or leisure activity outside the home (including clubs, evening classes, visiting theatres, museums, exhibitions, concerts, discos, cafés and restaurants) in the previous three months – and not one single household in the 'profoundly excluded' group had done so.

There were other particular features of their way of life which revealed that these households were excluded from important channels of socialisation. Of the 47 excluded households with children under 18, 28 said that they could not afford to pay for extra private lessons or clubs for their children. Another 12 said they did not need them, and five replied that their children rarely took part; in only two households did the children regularly attend such activities. It should also be added that only 14 of the 47 said they could afford to buy essential school supplies for their children.

Excluded households found it practically impossible to subscribe to or regularly buy magazines, newspapers and books, and this was one of the clear markers of the group: 38 out of the 57 never bought them (although they wanted to), another seven did so only rarely, and only five (i.e., less than 10 per cent of all excluded households) could afford to do so regularly.

In Russia, visiting and receiving friends is the most important channel of integration, yet half of our excluded households could not do this. Because no tradition of visiting restaurants, cafes, etc. has grown up, it is social contact during 'visiting' that is the most important way to maintain significant relations of primary sociability and to keep one's informal networks – 'connections' – in working order. Lack of access to this social institution in their everyday practice inevitably condemned a family to a downward spiral of increasing exclusion. It is no exaggeration to say that their motto could be: 'Abandon hope all those who enter here'.

Table 5.1 shows some notable examples of other particular features of their lives. Compared to other people, members of excluded households scored very badly in their responses to our 'short version' General Health Questionnaire ('GHQ') (Manning, Shkaratan and Tikhonova, 2000; Banks, *et al.*, 1980).

Table 5.1   Indicators of respondents' health, in per cent

	Non-excluded poor households (n = 42)	Excluded households (n = 37)	Profoundly excluded households (n = 20)
TOTAL NUMBER OF POINTS out of a possible 84			
Up to and including 24	36	11	20
25-30	27	18	15
31-35	11	29	0
36-40	5	8	5
41-45	10	18	15
Over 45	11	16	45
Points on the physical ill-health scale, out of a possible 21			
Up to and including 6	45	22	30
7-14	45	62	45
15-21	10	16	25
Points on the anxiety/insomnia scale, out of a possible 21			
Up to and including 6	38	30	20
7-14	55	32	35
15-21	7	38	45
Points on the social dysfunction scale, out of a possible 21			
Up to and including 6	33	16	5
7-14	75	78	85
15-21	2	6	10
Points on the severe depression scale, out of a possible 21			
Up to and including 6	71	46	35
7-14	29	51	65
15-21	0	3	0

As can be seen, two-thirds of respondents from excluded households scored 31 or more points on this questionnaire; 60 per cent of those in the profoundly excluded group scored 41 points or higher. The comparable numbers of non-excluded respondents with these scores were 37 per cent and 21 per cent respectively. The most significant deviation was on the 'anxiety and insomnia' scale: about 40 per cent of members of excluded households scored 15 or more points out of a possible 21 on this, while the comparable figure for the non-excluded was 7 per cent.

Respondents from excluded households much more frequently said that their lives had been disrupted by the poor health of a family member, by the absence of social protection from sickness, old age, unemployment or disability (75 per cent of the profoundly excluded complained of this, as against 26 per cent of the non-excluded), by loneliness and lack of attention from others or by lack of social contact with relatives and friends.

It should be added that members of excluded households had more often been the victims of crime (theft, violence, etc.) than others: only half of them had avoided this in the two years preceding the first survey, as against two-thirds of the other households.

Finally, unlike the non-excluded households, where half thought that many people might complain about or even exaggerate their poverty, three-quarters of respondents from excluded households were sure that, as a rule, people are ashamed of their poverty and hide it from others.

To conclude this brief review of some aspects of the lives of excluded households in the cities where we conducted our research, we would like to draw attention to another typical feature of those who fell into our excluded category: by and large, households that used to be in the mainstream have fallen out of it because of recent events, and this is a painful experience for them. It is no coincidence that three-quarters of the 'profoundly excluded' noted that they used to buy newspapers, use various leisure facilities, etc. (in other words, engage in forms of social participation), but now could not do so – only five out of the 57 households said they had always lived as they do now.

Thus, adding quantitative to qualitative analysis showed that the *chief manifestations of social exclusion in Russian cities are lack of access to the main forms of social participation:* regular purchase of newspapers, etc; using cultural and leisure facilities; social visits, including to relatives living at a distance; being able to afford either extra lessons for children or to get the best out of their school studies; good health and access to essential treatment. *All this is accompanied by a feeling that it is impossible to change one's own life, a constant sense of the injustice of events, bitterness, pressure, malaise, disappointment and shame.*

Moreover, social exclusion is gradually taking hold of more and more people who were well-off only a few years ago. From the beginning of the reforms to the mid-1990s, their material circumstances declined sharply, and their chances of solving their problems gradually became slighter. Those in the worst circumstances have become profoundly excluded and have little realistic prospect of returning to a normal life.

'Risk Factors' for the Onset and Growth of Social Exclusion

It will be evident to the reader by now that all the problems of excluded households basically relate to lack of effective social mechanisms for tackling their accumulated problems, which could mean access to social networks, to secure, adequately paid work, to effective State social protection, etc. The reasons for each family's situation are very individual and do not have a single cause: rather, there is a whole complex of reasons, coming together in the widest variety of combinations. Yet they do have certain things in common: we can attempt to define some markers that account for the risk of sharply increased marginalisation, anomie and social exclusion. These are:

- *disability or serious illness* of a household member, especially a man of working age (there were quite a lot of instances in our sample). Quantitative analysis also fully confirmed that family members' state of health was one of the most important factors in falling into the excluded group. It is sufficient to note that 36 per cent of excluded respondents named sickness or disability of a family member as a cause of their present situation;

- *exclusion from mutual assistance networks.* The role of this factor was distinctly visible both in the quantitative data and in the interviews: *'People who have no one to help them are poor, and we have no relatives'; 'Our lives have become so hard: I have absolutely no friends – I live with my mother and Jesus Christ'.* Fourteen per cent of ordinary households received no help from others – but this isolation applied to about 40 per cent of the two excluded groups. Where those in the excluded groups did receive some help, this most commonly took the form of assistance with simple household tasks and everyday matters.[10] The availability of such assistance varied according to the degree of social exclusion. Only one excluded household in five had to ask for help as a special favour, and two-thirds were simply offered it.

Among 'profoundly excluded' households, however, almost half of those who received help had to beg it as a favour; and profoundly excluded respondents received social transfers from the city or district council or from the workplace, charitable help, or money, food, clothing, etc. from relatives and friends much less frequently than other households. Nine of them – half the 'profoundly excluded' households in 2000 – never received any such help, whereas only 27-28 per cent of the other excluded and the non-excluded received nothing;

- *migration* (particularly typical in Vladikavkaz) has become closely associated with lack of social network resources over recent years. *Refugees* are in an especially difficult position, since their exclusion from social networks in their new place of residence is combined with lack of any kind of economic resources (indeed, some migrants arrive with money, only to have it stolen). All the refugees in our research fell into the excluded category, regardless of variations in their material circumstances and standard of education, or even whether they were officially registered as residents (a status which confers colossal advantages but cannot be obtained by the vast majority of refugees in Russia);

- *collapse of small businesses* started by people who are completely ill-equipped to run them. On this level, as applied to the Russian situation, Wacquant's ideas have proved very effective: he attests to the fact that today's marginalised people are forced to resort to 'individual strategies of "self-provisioning", "shadow work", underground commerce and quasi-institutionalised "hustling", which do little to alleviate precariousness' (Wacquant, 1996, p.127). Even in a small sample like ours, we encountered one instance of small business collapse in each of the three cities, and that was without taking into account people self-employed in small-scale trading or services, who had also, in several cases, been forced to abandon this source of earnings. It was also a factor mentioned by other respondents as a frequent cause of extreme poverty, even though they had not experienced it themselves. *'Our friends are living worse and worse. They started a business, but then they were ruined.'*

As a rule, this situation is connected less with the instability of the Russian economy than with the infiltration of criminal elements into the small business sphere, in a climate where there is complete lack of social and legal protection for such businesses. In our sample, small businesses were more common in non-Russian milieux: the ruined businessmen were a Russian, a Chechen and an Ossetian, even though our sample was 70 per cent Russian; while the percentage of self-employed people in the Ossetian Vladikavkaz sub-sample was 30 per cent, as against 7 per cent among Russians in Vladikavkaz. A typical cause of the failure of a small business was some form of theft, ranging from misappropriation of funds by business partners[11] to direct robbery.

> Solpan from Vladikavkaz worked as a taxi driver using his own vehicle: it was stolen, and the thieves then demanded that he buy it back from them. In his 1999 interview, he said: 'now I'm trying to get my car back (I know where it is and who has it), but they are asking too much money. In the meantime I am taking goods from a wholesaler. I stand in the market as a "salesman" – but nothing sells. Another couple of months like this, and I'll be destitute'. He didn't manage to get his car back, and over the year between the surveys, his family's already low standard of living really did deteriorate markedly without it.

- *numerous dependants*: large number of children; multi-generational family; divorced parent with two or more children under 18; death of main breadwinner in a family with children; birth of children outside marriage.[12] So, for example, out of 29 households consisting of a lone parent and one or two children, 17 were excluded, and six of these had very high scores on the ISE (2000); out of 19 families with a large number of children, ten were excluded – four profoundly so. However, just being a two-parent family with one or two children was no guarantee against social exclusion – 19 out of 32 such households in our survey were excluded.

Our analysis paid special attention to the issue of *gender as a prominent factor in social exclusion*, but our quantitative data did not demonstrate any significant links between gender and the situation of poor urban families in Russia. Interviewees themselves did not mention it even once as a cause of their problems. We should also emphasise that, at both stages of the survey, the percentage of excluded households headed by women was similar to that among ordinary households; in fact, the percentage of profoundly excluded households headed by men was actually higher than the average for the sample. Of course, there may well be gender-related forms of social exclusion in Russia, which simply did not come to light in this part of our research – this is an area that merits further investigation, and which is presented in Chapter 6.

It is necessary to emphasise again that none of the above 'risk factors' – with the possible exception of being a refugee from an armed ethnic conflict zone – can be seen in itself as a cause of social exclusion or as an absolute predictor of becoming excluded. Rather, it was the *build-up and interaction of several of these risk factors* that led to social exclusion, as the negative effects of each increased the negative effects of the others, through a distinctive form of synergism. If network or some other kind of resources helped to neutralise the way these factors acted together, then the household did not fall into social exclusion.

So, for example, the only ruined Russian businessman in our sample had a family with three school-age children and a non-working wife. In 1999, before the survey, he had just started to have serious problems with his business, and the situation in the family, according to his wife, was quite difficult. 'I'm having to cut back on literally everything – I sew, knit and cut our hair myself, I buy the cheapest food and medicines. You'd think that we'd be able to sell something and solve some of our financial problems. But it's not like that ... We don't even have enough in our pockets to get on public transport – but if you ask the children, they'll choose the computer (bought during a period when the husband's business was developing well – N.T.) and walk the four stops to school and four stops home.' Over the year between the surveys, the situation with the business did not normalise and, in Yelena's words at the time of the second survey, this was the 'hardest period. This is not because of any specific events, but simply because my husband's income level is low, the family has three children and problems are piling up like a snowdrift. The children are growing and the time has come when a lot of money has to be spent on them. Our situation hasn't changed since the time of the first meeting – it might even have got more difficult.' Nevertheless, this family could not be categorised as excluded at either stage of the research. After the collapse of his business, the head of the family found work, through old connections, as deputy head of a repair and construction directorate in Voronezh, which – although it brought in a smaller income than his own business had – was a fairly good, securely paid job, bringing with it high social status. This was completely different from the situation of the ruined Ossetian businessman in Vladikavkaz, who also had a number of children: there, the absence of corresponding social network resources led the household into social exclusion.

A second aspect of social exclusion, closely linked to the first, is that of duration, and many experts have drawn attention to it (Da Costa, 1995; Delors, 1996; Room, 1990). A socially excluded household does not simply suffer at the time when it is first placed at a disadvantage in terms of education, skills, employment, housing or financial resources, or when it is discriminated against in access to social institutions, but – most importantly – when such restrictions *are prolonged over time.*

Our research showed that it is not simply the duration of restrictions that constitutes a significant marker of social exclusion, but also the effect of an accumulation of risk factors. There is a certain time lag, during which the family is in a borderline situation, before the effects of several risk factors lead to profound social exclusion. This 'grey area' or borderline situation was manifest in our research as the first level of social exclusion. At this stage, a household's exclusion from the main institutions of integration was already leading to social exclusion, and the household was already starting to become objectively different from others. Subjectively, though, they did not yet feel excluded; they still had some possibilities of warding off or slowing down the process of marginalisation and movement towards profound social exclusion – even of remaining in the mainstream, if things worked out well for them: by getting a good job, inheriting money or finding '*a sponsor, who will help us with money*' (we did find a few examples of this in our sample).

The length of time that people spent in the 'grey area' before becoming marginalised to the point of profound social exclusion was, judging from our research, fairly prolonged: for the households in our sample, this period was no less than five to seven years. We had been monitoring 19 of our households since 1996,[13] when our earlier research project began (Manning, Shkaratan and Tikhonova, 2000); in these cases, we saw an accumulation of the negative effects of risk factors over the longer period. However, there were households in this group which, even in 1999, were not displaying the main signs of profound exclusion, yet by 2000 had suddenly fallen into that group. It was as if their exclusion had accumulated to a certain threshold, over years, but they were not aware of it (or were only partially so): then there came a certain moment when the family realised that these were not temporary problems, but marked a transition to a qualitatively different way of life. Details of the 19 households are presented in Appendix 2.

Further evidence of this accumulation of the negative consequences of exclusion from the main integration mechanisms over a period of five to seven years was provided by respondents whose scores on the Social Exclusion Index had been comparatively low in 1999, but were high in 2000. Most people in that position, when asked whether they had ever had more difficult times than the present, all said that an earlier period (generally, 1993-96) had been materially harder for them: '... it's difficult to say that things are harder now than at some other time. Everything started two or three years after the beginning of perestroika, and it's got worse every year'; 'our life has always been hard, but the situation has deteriorated gradually, especially roundabout 1994-96'; 'it's hard to say that now is "worse" – how could it be any worse? Things started to decline when the reforms began in Russia ... and nothing's changed in that respect. We've got no kind of hope'; 'Materially, "difficult" is not the right word for it, but it was even harder in 1993-95 – those were the most intolerably difficult times, just one thing after the other', and so on.

The boundary between the 'grey area' and the 'black hole' of profound social exclusion, with its accompanying feeling of hopelessness, was well expressed by one of our interviewees: 'We had a lot of difficulties before, too, but they were episodes – you could get through them. Now we just have the feeling that there's no way out.' Many respondents also talked (though sometimes using other words) about the division between those who are 'simply poor' and those who have already crossed this boundary and are 'below the poverty line':[14] those below the poverty line are 'those who have got caught up in material need and have no possibilities at all of getting out of it'; 'someone who has the energy to survive will not be below the poverty line'; 'when everything is OK, people are smiling, but now there are no smiles. The fire has gone out in those people's eyes'; those below the poverty line are 'people with sad eyes'.

Feelings of not being able to escape one's situation were particularly typical of profound exclusion, and tended to arise when existing problems – such as housing problems or enforced retirement on grounds of age while there were still dependent children – had worsened. Such situations often affected those who were not by any means the poorest respondents, but (yet again) they served to demonstrate that there was a time lag between the originating factor and the characteristic markers of social exclusion being expressed as pressing problems for the household.[15]

Thus, there were actually many households in our research, which had been really well-off before the reforms, but – judged on their level of material welfare, the particular features of deprivation they were experiencing, their socio-demographic type, their ability to work, their type of work, etc. – should already have had high scores on the Social Exclusion Index in 1999. However, this was not the case, and most 1999 excluded households were those with conventional risk factors: social problems, a large number of children, a disabled or bedridden family member, etc.

By 2000, however – as we have already noted above – the number of excluded households in our sample had markedly increased, even though some had seen an improvement in their material circumstances. In our view, this was primarily due to the 'accumulation effect' and/or to problems that had suddenly arisen in the course of that year. People had become aware of their new situation, not just because of their low material standard of living, but also mainly because of the impossibility of solving their most pressing problems (housing, health, children's education) to the same extent and in the same ways as most people in society can.

Many households that had high indicators on the Social Exclusion Index in 2000 had identified themselves as below the poverty line in 1999, even though their social exclusion indicators at that time were within the bounds of normal. The 'accumulation effect' represented the main difference between them and other households which, at the same level of deprivation in 1999, were still not inclined to identify themselves as below the poverty line (they were more likely to talk in terms such as 'we're still not over the line, but close to it', 'we're not quite there yet', 'we're poor, but for us it's a temporary state' and so on). In other words, in 1999, the first group had started to change their view of themselves, but had not yet completely realised that this was a new state – not just a low income level, but broadly another way of life: they were entering a new world, a 'black hole' that would be practically impossible to get out of.

It seems obvious that, in a few years, as social structures typical of market economies (but new to Russia) become more fully formed, people who enter the borderline 'grey area' will become more quickly aware of what is happening to them. During our research, we met many people who, by the time they had joined the ranks of the excluded, with no hope of returning from the grey area to the mainstream, had realised that this was not a temporary situation connected with the reforms. This will mean that, at least as far as social structure is concerned, Russia will be entering the era of postmodernism, as defined by Alain Touraine, passing from the vertical to the horizontal society, where it is more important to know whether people are at the core or on the periphery, rather than at the top or the bottom (Touraine, 1991).

Social Exclusion and Employment Problems

The interrelationship of social exclusion and lack of access to secure, adequately paid work is the key to understanding the development of social exclusion processes; we have consciously not mentioned it up to now, because it is extremely important and merits a special review.

Of course, we took into account that social exclusion is less strongly associated with unemployment than is poverty. In addition, there is already research data suggesting that social exclusion is less often generated by unemployment than by a particular type of employment: insecure, heterogeneous, differentiated employment, which is more likely to lead to fragmentation and unreliability than to guaranteed security and homogeneity – the type of employment that Wacquant has characterised as 'advanced marginality' (Wacquant, 1996).

Therefore, the first thing we must say is that we did not observe any significant distinguishing features in the nature of employment of members of the excluded households in our sample. This could be because the 'accumulation effect' had not yet done all its work. But it is no less the case that, in the Russian situation, secure employment in itself is far from being a guarantee against social exclusion. As is well-known, even completely secure employment in Russia does not always mean receiving wages regularly or (even less) in full.

Forty-nine per cent of 'grey area' respondents and 35 per cent of profoundly excluded households gave reasons connected with work (job loss, employer in difficulties, non-payment of wages, etc.) as typical causes of their deteriorating situation. A number of respondents also linked their hopes for improvement with the possibility of finding work; therefore, the issue of job-seeking in excluded households became a special focus of our attention.

Analysis showed that a general feature of most excluded households was that they were not satisfied with the job or jobs held by family members. However, fewer than half included a person seeking work. Thus, in 32 excluded households, there was no one looking for work, even though almost half of them included unemployed people of working age – and in only ten of these households was it because the jobs suited them.

Why, then, in 22 excluded households (including nine profoundly excluded ones – practically half this group) was nobody trying to find better work (or any work at all, where they were not employed) or even trying to make more effective use of employment to overcome their social exclusion? This inactivity was in no way related to age: only two of the 22 households consisted entirely of pensioners. After all, employment is a key integration mechanism. So why did this mechanism not prevent the social exclusion of working households?

To help answer these questions, here are examples of some of the 19 households we had observed since 1996, of which ten had become socially excluded by 2000 – three of them profoundly so.

The first case comes from Moscow, where the labour market is vast, and is an example of the degradation of a household where there was a drug addict. Aleksandr lived with his mother, who worked as a nurse. At the time of the first survey in 1996, he had a permanent paid job, but was already under notice of redundancy. Since then, he had not had a steady job, although he had tried to earn extra on a casual basis (he had small temporary jobs restoring a church, building cow sheds, etc.). At the time of the 1999 survey, he was in hospital in a serious condition related to his drug dependency. In 2000, he was not working anywhere and was visibly inadequate.

The second example was that of an underprivileged household from Voronezh. The family of Tat'yana – a woman of 37 years with incomplete secondary education – consisted of her 75-year-old aunt and her three daughters aged 18, 11 and seven years; at the time of the first survey, she was working as a cleaner in a block of flats belonging to an aircraft factory, following a period of registered unemployment. Although Tat'yana had a secure job throughout the whole period of observation, she received a low wage and could hardly expect to find a job with higher pay. She associated her position with alcoholism: 'If everyone who can work didn't drink, it would be easier. Both my former husbands went downhill that way. And I did too, because of them.'

At the time of the first survey, the Employment Service had found Nataliya work as a teaching assistant in a children's nursery, after a period of registered unemployment; she later independently changed her job and became a cutter and seamstress in a private firm. Nataliya's family problems were related not so much to her or her school-aged children as to her husband. 'Our material circumstances have improved a little, and I hope for more improvement because my husband is working now. However, these improvements took place literally a month ago, and before that my husband hadn't been working for two years (they didn't pay his wages, he changed his job several times, he drank, he really went to pieces). And it went on for a very long time.' Although her husband was trained as a gas welder, the only work he had been able to get recently was as a porter, because of his alcoholism.

In contrast, there were excluded households with no problems of substance abuse or social deviance. Vladimir, a man in early middle age with poor health, who had higher education, was already having employment problems in the mid-1990s, and since then he had not had a steady job. By 2000, he was partially self-employed, running a small business in the motor transport protection and repair line, which he had started with a temporary arrangement as a car park attendant. His family's standard of living was not poor, but 'badly-off': their situation had even improved slightly over the previous year, because his son had started work. However, according to Vladimir, 'the factory might let my wife go at any moment, unless there's some improvement there'. In effect, spending many years in insecure employment (despite being willing to work and having – at first – actively sought work) had combined with his poor health to prevent him from finding steady, well-paid work as a way of overcoming exclusion.

Sergei, who lived with his two school-age children and his disabled mother, already had problems with work in 1996, when he was placed under notice of redundancy. In 1997, the Employment Service found him a job as a fitter in a radio electronic equipment factory. However, almost immediately he came up against problems with wage delays and insecure employment (unpaid leave during a period of stoppage at the factory). He was still working there in 2000, but his assessment of the job was 'bad, because they pay very little. The factory's situation is insecure, and there are wage delays. Our hopes are connected with the elections: we need a complete change of both city and provincial leadership. The hardest period was when I was unemployed (1996-99). But having a job hasn't especially changed anything: things have stayed the same, but now people are being fleeced – pay is low, prices are going up.'

From these histories – and those of ten other excluded households, which we had observed since 1996 – we can draw the general conclusion that there was no direct connection between the respondent's employment status (or that of others in the household) and the dynamic of change in their situation, whether this was for the worse, for the better or stayed the same. On the contrary, their problems were almost all connected with alcoholism or with the poor health of members of the household who were of working age. Both these situations meant it was possible to get only insecure, badly paid work – work that could not have any significant effect on the household's position. As one of our respondents remarked, 'everything's bad for us now, because of me, because of my health. I can't work at full strength now. The situation ... has deteriorated. Our problems have increased, piled up.'

These situations can be compared with an example of a household that managed to escape the 'grey area' and get back into the mainstream.

> Valentina was married, with two children living at home, who reached adulthood during the period of observation; at both stages of the research, this Voronezh family was categorised as 'badly-off'. This was the level of welfare where, we found, social exclusion was equally likely to exist or not. Valentina had lost her job as an engineer because the enterprise was in financial difficulties, but she did not want the job to which she had been directed by the Employment Service in 1996 (cashier in a shop): from 1997, she was self-employed. She worked as an interviewer and could always earn more by working on the elections, of which Voronezh had a lot at that time. She had moved into a new social circle, of people involved in servicing the elections, and her phone rang continually with offers of temporary work. The fall in the family's standard of living in the period 1996-97 had resulted not only from her unemployment, but also from wage delays experienced by her husband when his employer was in difficulties. Her husband subsequently became self-employed; however, his small business did not bring in much money. In later years, the family noted an improvement in their circumstances, as a result of the daughter's work, greater security in the husband's situation and the son going to university.
>
> Valentina was completely content with her working routine: she had 'found herself'. She hoped for further improvement: 'Our material situation hasn't changed much. But now we have work, my husband isn't earning too badly, and I've found myself some very convenient extra work, on the pre-election campaigns – Voronezh is building up to the elections for Provincial Governor. I'm sure that my children will manage to build their lives well and find good jobs: they might even be able to help us. Overall, I think that the difficult times are behind us, although who knows what life will bring – things are so complicated nowadays.'

As we can see, although this family did not find a source of full, secure employment, their situation had stabilised: they were actively involved in social networks, they had prospects of improvement, and their children were starting fairly happy, independent lives. Of course, the parents were active in their outlook and had a good standard of education, no serious illnesses, etc. But this interesting example, showing that it is possible to 'leave the grey area', was not by any means the only one in our 1999 sample: out of 40 households in the 'grey area' in 1999, 16 had managed to get out of it a year later.

Thus, our households demonstrated that the reason for their social exclusion was not absence of work as such, but lack of a 'good job' –

i.e., secure, well-paid work. As to why they couldn't get such work, only two out of 57 excluded households thought there was nothing stopping them from getting a good job (although in fact these two both had problems that objectively meant they could not really do so). The rest gave health (46 per cent) and age (41 per cent) as the main reasons for their not getting a good job (half as many again as the number giving these reasons in non-excluded households) and this was confirmed by the results we obtained from qualitative analysis of interviews.

Looking at the interrelationship between social exclusion and access to work for our 1996-2000 households, we concluded that, where family members of working age were fairly effective workers and the dependency ratio was no higher than 2:1, then they had managed, by the end of the period, to overcome their problems sufficiently to avoid social exclusion. However, this certainly did not mean that they had found secure, well-paid work, or that they were no longer in need. The exceptional cases of social exclusion against such a background were all refugees, who were fairly numerous in our sample.

In other words, the relationship between exclusion from effective employment and social exclusion is not a direct one, but is mediated by risk factors which make it difficult for a person to seek work that will protect them from social exclusion – primarily, health problems – or which (like alcoholism in the family or a high number of dependants) negate the beneficial effects of already having such a job. Most members of excluded households who were capable of working were already doing so: moreover, most excluded households had no unemployed members of working age. However, these workers were mostly low-paid, had suffered long wage delays, and/or had numerous dependants: if this situation continued for long enough, then the household was at high risk of becoming excluded.

This leads to the conclusion that the globalisation processes triggered off in Russia since the start of reforms have, in recent years, led the country to changes in social structure that are typical of such processes all over the world. There are some specifically Russian characteristics, including the relatively small role of gender differences in generating social exclusion; the fact that discrimination tends to lie less in breaches of civil rights than in exclusion from effective social networks, which – in the absence of a civil society in Russia – have assumed the burdens carried by civil society in other European countries; long-term non-payment of wages (or, where there is formally secure employment, low wages[16]) as a risk factor for the onset of social exclusion. However, the overall picture of the development of social exclusion is essentially the same as elsewhere. The only misfortune is that Russia has been gripped by these globalisation processes when it was not ready for them: it has little attainable social policy, relevant legislation or – most importantly – real understanding of what is happening.

In this regard, we would like to recall Manuel Castells' characterisation of social exclusion:

> Comparative data show that, by and large, in all urban societies, most people and/or their families work for pay, even in poor neighborhoods and in poor countries. The question is: what kind of work for what kind of pay under what conditions? What is happening is that the mass of generic labor circulates in a variety of jobs, increasingly occasional jobs, with a great deal of discontinuity. So, millions of people are constantly in and out of paid work, often included in informal activities ... Furthermore, the loss of a stable relationship to employment, and the weak bargaining power of many workers, lead to a higher level of incidence of major crises in the life of their families: temporary job loss, personal crises, illnesses, drugs/alcohol addictions, loss of employability, loss of assets, loss of credit. Many of these crises connect with each other, inducing the downward spiral of social exclusion ... (Castells, 1998, pp. 344-345).

Castells describes with amazing precision the 'starting mechanism' of the process of social exclusion that applies to millions of people in Russia today. It is the particular nature of the work available to millions of Russians, which does not prevent either poverty or social exclusion, that predetermines the low level of interest that most of them have in finding a job as a way of tackling their problems or as a means of successful integration into society. Perhaps a more favourable labour market situation would allow many excluded households to return to the mainstream, but for now they just continue to sink further into the 'black hole' of social exclusion and growing poverty.

Social Exclusion, Deprivation and Poverty

One of our most important research objectives was to define the interrelationship between poverty and social exclusion in the Russian situation. Are we just using different words to describe the same thing, or are these two different phenomena?

In fact, this is an issue that has already been tackled by both Western and Russian sociologists. In the course of these discussions, it has been said that, although social exclusion encompasses poverty, it is a much broader concept, which includes lack of rights and limitations on access to the institutions that distribute resources (De Haan, 1998; Delors, 1996). On the other hand, it is far from the case that poverty, always and in all societies, means social exclusion – for the poor may form a majority in a given society (Paugam, 1996).

> Poverty casts a long shadow. It mars every aspect of life – meeting basic needs, joining in social activities, access to services and the chance of good health ... Not all of these [facets to the problem] are experienced by all those in poverty or only by those in poverty; yet there is no doubt that people in poverty are much more likely to suffer each of these forms of deprivation, and often multiple deprivation, than people who are better off (Oppenheim and Harker, 1996, p.88). [The relationship between social exclusion and poverty in Russia has already been demonstrated by Tchernina (1998).]

The key linking element, or 'bridge', between the concepts of social exclusion and poverty was established by Peter Townsend: poverty is defined less through standard of living than via way of life and nature of deprivation. In fact, Townsend was attempting to describe a new social phenomenon – social exclusion – and testified to its beginnings and significance, giving the traditional conception of poverty a new meaning. As a result, he devised a set of deprivations that would act as criteria of poverty – including being deprived of social participation, so that it becomes impossible to maintain the way of life traditional in a given society. Thus, relying on the habitual concept of 'poverty', Townsend tried to record and measure a largely new phenomenon – social exclusion, which also means the onset of a different way of life from that of the mainstream (Townsend, 1987; 1993).

Therefore, in analysing our interviews, we tried to find out whether our respondents could identify the characteristics of poverty, and whether, for them, being poor still did not mean being excluded. Many separated the two, identifying social exclusion as a particular way of life and poverty as simply the low standard of living that is now typical for most Russians.[17] 'We are poor, but so is everyone else' – in the words of one respondent – was a leitmotif of our interviews, repeated by many others in describing their own poverty.

Thus, our respondents did not uniformly associate poverty with social exclusion; rather, they perceived poverty as, in certain conditions, creating the danger of becoming excluded. Therefore, we decided to try and use quantitative methods to define at what level of poverty the threat of social exclusion became practically inescapable. In the light of ongoing debates about ways of measuring poverty, two criteria were used: 1) absolute criteria of poverty, comparing household incomes with subsistence minima, and 2) relative criteria of poverty, using our own Multivariate Deprivation Index (IMD).

The Townsend approach measures the impossibility of maintaining a certain generally accepted way of life and, consequently, records external, more obvious or 'substantive' manifestations of social exclusion – which, in our view, should include the often-ignored socio-psychological strand. The relative concept of poverty turned out to be more strongly linked with profound social exclusion than the absolute concept of poverty. That is, social exclusion was more closely linked to actual deprivation than to income level – not surprisingly, given the 'accumulation effect'.

The general trends established were that profound social exclusion, as a rule, was connected with indigence, and 'simple' social exclusion (the 'grey area') with poverty or being badly-off; to avoid social exclusion, at least 'badly-off' status was required; social exclusion almost never affected the averagely well-off households in our sample. Nevertheless, a fairly large number of households (12), in which no social exclusion had been recorded according to our Social Exclusion Index, still had a high level of deprivation.

What kind of households were these 12, and why was this the case for them? The only household that was indigent but did not have a high score on the Social Exclusion Index was a completely degraded Moscow couple, who both drank: the man was unemployed and the woman, a hospital cleaner. They had rejected the wife's daughter, sending her first to live with her paternal grandmother and then, after the death of the latter, to a boarding school. We interviewed both the man and the woman in this household, and they both said 'we've always lived like this'. Thus, because of the specific features of their way of life and consumption, fixed for years, they were simply unaware that they were excluded, and consequently the depth of the kind of exclusion in which they lived was not measurable on our Social Exclusion Index. However, it was clear that, in most cases, real indigence – measured according to deprivation criteria –

was practically a 100 per cent guarantee that the family would, objectively, be socially excluded.

Here are just a few typical examples of the other 11 households that were poor but did not have high Social Exclusion Index scores.

1. A pensioner couple, who had migrated to Moscow from the country when they were young. In 1999, they said 'we are poor, but so is everyone else', and in 2000, 'things have become a bit better, because they've increased the pension'.
2. A working pensioner in Voronezh (an electric welder), with a disabled wife. He was also pleased at the improved pension payment situation – 'now they pay the pension on time, before it was always late. But our material circumstances haven't changed particularly, because prices are going up. This isn't a difficult period for us, I'm receiving my pension on time: there were difficulties when it was delayed. Our hopes for the future lie … in a pension increase'.
3. The family of a young porter from Voronezh, the son of prosperous parents; he lived with them, but his father had died not long before the survey. Although the respondent himself had been unemployed or partially employed for a fairly long time, the family's standard of living had been quite high until his father's death. In fact, despite the sharp fall in their standard of living in the period before the survey, this household's material difficulties were only just beginning.
4. The household of a lone mother, a student at the Vladikavkaz Medical Institute, who had a permanent job as a hospital nurse, additional nursing work and a lone parent's student grant. Their low standard of living was substantially due to the illness of the respondent's parents – 'Mum is on a Category 2 disability benefit, and Dad is paralysed. His earnings as a lathe operator were the family's main income. We're pinning our hopes on my earning more in future, so I'm relying on my professional training. Now, I'm working for a firm as a cosmetics consultant, just occasionally, but I'm enjoying it – it's a good job. I'm also a distributor for a Swiss firm'.

From these examples, it is clear that poor, non-excluded households were: 1) families who had recently become poor, where the level of need had not yet led to social exclusion (no 'accumulation effect'); 2) households consisting entirely of pensioners with very modest aspirations; or 3) households which have become so degraded that their way of life no longer bears any relation to that of the mainstream, and they do not feel any desire for greater integration into the social formation.

It thus became clear why not all poor families were excluded and/or did not feel excluded. But, at the other end of the spectrum, why did many 'badly-off' families and even a few households who were – by Russian standards – materially prosperous have high scores on the Social Exclusion Index?

We have already said that, in general, excluded households were those which had earlier been in the mainstream, but had left it in recent years as a result of what had happened to them – and that the experience was very painful for them. For example, 75 per cent of the profoundly excluded indicated that, in the past, they had bought newspapers, etc., and had made use of cultural and leisure facilities, but now they could no longer afford to do so. A number of the most significant questionnaire responses from the excluded group were connected with the loss of highly important characteristics of social inclusion, of integration into social life.

This brings us to the issue of 'old' and 'new poor' in Russia. The 'old poor' are people from households that could have belonged to the poor strata of Soviet society (large families, lone mothers, those with serious alcohol problems, people with disabilities) – although they were considerably less poor then. The 'new poor' are completely ordinary households, which used to have the same way of life as most of the rest of society, but have now fallen into poverty as a consequence of Russia's economic reforms in the 1990s. In our sample, profound social exclusion was more typical of the 'old poor', while the 'new poor' tended to be in the 'grey area'.

Sketching a 'socio-demographic portrait' revealed that the chief particular characteristic of the 'new poor' in our sample related to their employment: they were mostly white-collar workers in the budget-funded sector. About half the heads of these households were specialists with higher education or white-collar technical/service sector employees, while most other working family members were not specialists, but still held white-collar jobs. Blue-collar workers – including unskilled workers – were more widely represented among the 'old poor'.

In addition, we encountered twice as many 'old poor' as 'new poor' households where no one was working. Life-story analysis of 'old poor' households showed that they were much more likely to have a history of chronic economic inactivity or have gradually ceased to be economically active. Thus, across the whole sample of 105 households in the three cities, 14 per cent of heads of 'old poor' households had not been working in 1990 (as against 5 per cent of 'new poor'). By 2000, this had risen to a third (as against a tenth of 'new poor' households).

'Old poor' and 'new poor' households also have differing income structures, especially as regards the role of social transfers. Seventy-three per cent of 'old poor' households listed pensions among their three most important sources of income, as against 50 per cent of the 'new poor'. Other benefits (unemployment, lone-parent, low-income, etc.) were in the top three sources of income for 36 per cent of the 'old poor', but only 9 per cent of the 'new poor'. Help from relatives and friends was also comparatively important for the 'old poor', while in the income structure of the 'new poor', a greater role was played by various types of supplementary labour activity – regular secondary employment, occasional additional earnings, working on a plot of land.

Thus, the 'new poor' were largely oriented towards an active model of economic behaviour, and tried to carry it through. Many of them were prepared not only to work but also to study or retrain and were fairly active in doing so, while many members of these households had accepted lower social status rather than be unemployed. So, in 2000, 18 per cent of respondents from 'new poor' households worked as unskilled blue-collar workers, although in 1990 only 8 per cent had done so: in parallel, the number of 'new poor' white-collar technical or service sector employees decreased sharply.

Naturally, this meant not only that they had become excluded from their accustomed secure, well-paid, skilled work and propelled into the 'grey area' of social exclusion: it also entailed the loss of their usual way of life and social circle, intense frustration, and extreme pressure on their highly developed system of consumption – all of which created a much more distinct awareness of their own social exclusion. Therefore, if a 'new poor' family with specialist occupations was at one of the two lowest levels of deprivation ('indigence' and 'poverty'), this was a 100 per cent guarantee that they would have high indicators of social exclusion – a fact that did not apply to unskilled workers, for example. This was especially evident in families where the head of the household had higher education: previously, they had typically had a much more complex and varied way of life than now, and they felt their social exclusion much more keenly when they fell into poverty. It was no accident that, in our 'poor' group on the IMD, half the families whose heads had higher education were in the 'profoundly excluded' group on the ISE. The idea that they felt their present position more sharply, because they had no experience of poverty, cannot be discounted: the income level that the 'new poor' viewed as essential was about double the level cited by the 'old poor', since the latter were used to a life with low aspirations.

The difficulties experienced by the 'new poor' were connected less with the high level of *de facto* unemployment in Russia than with the restructuring of the economy and, in particular, with lengthy non-payment of wages (up to 18 months in some cases) to all kinds of workers, including those in budget-funded organisations and in various types of enterprise. It is no coincidence that more than half the 'new poor' gave problems with work as reasons for their lower standard of living – but only a quarter of the 'old poor'. The latter were generally much less oriented towards active labour participation, and they were more likely to cite illness or alcoholism of a family member as reasons for their own poverty.

When it came to identifying themselves, the 'new poor' had still not accepted their new status. They were more likely to see themselves as 'on the borderline of poverty', even though their position was objectively little better than that of the 'old poor'. Specifically, their position with regard to resources accumulated in the past (both property and social resources) still protected them somewhat from experiencing certain deprivations. However, their average level of *per capita* income was markedly lower than the official subsistence minimum.

Neither their own poverty nor their unpleasant experiences had led to a sharp change in the social circle of the 'new poor' – unlike the 'old poor', the 'new poor' were mostly surrounded by people who also did not consider themselves poor. In addition, the structure of social contact for the 'new poor' was fairly varied, in contrast to that of the 'old poor', who mostly came into contact with neighbours.

In a word, most of the 'new poor' were – according to a number of markers – still in the 'grey area' and their marginalisation had not yet begun. The logical consequence of this was that the 'old' and the 'new poor' had different chances of getting out of social exclusion and poverty. Over the year of observation, almost one in four 'new poor' households improved their position, while for 45 per cent it had deteriorated. The situation of the 'old poor' improved in only 14 per cent of cases, deteriorating in 82 per cent. So, both groups were characterised by a trend towards a worse position – but for the 'old poor', this was a really catastrophic trend.

Thus, where there is a prolonged process of growing deprivation (i.e., over many years), poverty leads to social exclusion. In our research, we found a certain poverty threshold (usually coinciding with the boundary between being 'badly-off' and actually 'poor' on the deprivation scale), at which many markers of social exclusion start to appear and the household will enter the 'grey area'. Moreover, 'indigence' on the deprivation scale will undoubtedly mean that social exclusion objectively exists – although it may not always be recognisable. In cases of a slide into social exclusion over many years, where there is an unsophisticated structure of consumption or self-imposed restrictions, people may be unaware of their actual requirements, which they cannot satisfy because of their income level and their exclusion from all alternative ways of tackling their problems (State support, network resources). These cases are very difficult to record quantitatively in empirical research. However, we demonstrated fairly convincingly that, where a particular level of poverty lasts for seven years or more, it is a definite predictor of the onset of profound social exclusion – leaving the 'grey area' for the 'black hole', adopting a new way of life and a new psychological state.

This time lag of several years – from the point when they fall into poverty to the point when the formation of social exclusion is complete – is a fairly long period, and the family may use it in different ways depending on their potential. Therefore, the individual features of the household situation and the probable nature of the influence of various risks predetermine not just the individual reactions of households to their new situation – but also how long they spend in the 'grey area', their prospects for return to the mainstream, whether they get stuck in the 'grey area' or slide into even more profound social exclusion. However, as we have argued here, some common traits can be traced.

The natural consequence of this must be a rethinking of social policy objectives, in order to try and take into account the 'individualisation of risks' – an approach that has already tentatively begun in the UK (Manning and Shaw, 2000). Unfortunately, in Russia today, neither public awareness nor wider academic circles nor policymakers seem ready to accept or even recognise the need for vital measures to neutralise the negative effects of social exclusion.

In conclusion, we would like to say that we did not in any way set out to throw light on all forms of social exclusion that exist in Russia today – and even less, on social exclusion in general. Our objective was much more modest: to determine whether there are excluded households within the poor sections of the population in large Russian cities, to attempt to define how their social exclusion manifests itself, what are the main risk factors that influence the onset of social exclusion, how the social exclusion process unfolds, and what its interrelationships with poverty may be. We see our results as information to be used in further reflection, rather than as a set of exhaustive answers to these questions. However, we are sure of one thing: we clearly recorded a trend of qualitative change in the social structure of Russian society, with the establishing of a large section of excluded people and all the consequences that flow from this – far wider consequences than those of the large-scale poverty that Russians now simply experience as fairly common.

Notes

[1] Research conducted in 1998 by RIISNP (the Russian Independent Institute for Social and National Problems) for the Moscow representative of the Ebert Fund (Germany), on the basis of a pan-Russian sample of 3,000 people.

[2] The *propiska* system presupposes that every individual must be registered with the local organs of the Ministry for Internal Affairs at his permanent place of residence, with a corresponding notation in his passport. For someone who has come from elsewhere in Russia (let alone from abroad), obtaining this registration is fairly difficult, since quite a number of conditions are imposed.

[3] The statistical data show that, for the majority of food groups, there is steady growth from one decile group to the next, right up to the tenth group, who have the most resources. In 1999, the only exceptions to this pattern were potatoes, sugar and confectionery, as well as vegetable oil and other fats, consumption of which stopped increasing with the sixth decile group (Goskomstat, 2000, p.145). Moreover, expenditure on buying foodstuffs constituted over 50 per cent of all expenditure on household consumer goods in the five lowest decile groups; for the sixth to the ninth groups, it fell to between 49.2 per cent and 46.4 per cent, only reaching 40 per cent in the tenth group (ibid, p.135). See also materials from the conference 'Food security in Russia: economic, social and medical aspects' held by UN FAO and the Russian Academy of Medical Sciences Institute of Nutrition in Moscow on 10th April 2001.

[4] In this regard, it should be noted that 'connections' in Russia today are definitely not the same thing as the 'fixing' (*blat* in Russian) that used to exist as a large-scale phenomenon until about the mid-1990s. From then on, the significance of this kind of corrupt string-pulling lessened, partly because of the increasing severity of competitive processes in the market sector of the economy, and partly as a result of the relative drop in incomes in the majority of institutions in the budget-funded sector. Nowadays, 'connections' are, firstly, access to private networks of support, whose roles and functioning mechanisms are highlighted in the chapter that focuses especially on that theme, and, secondly, a means of obtaining opportune information about job vacancies, along with an equivalent to the system of written references in Western Europe. Written references are only just starting to be used in Russia, and in the meantime oral recommendations may be given by former work colleagues and other people who know the applicant well; however, the effectiveness of these recommendations also presupposes that the referee himself can facilitate access to secure, well-paid jobs.

[5] The respondent is referring to extra-legal methods of resolving economic disputes, which are now widely used in Russia. Although relatively rare by comparison with a few years ago, criminal 'settlements' (in Russian, *razborki* – where the essence of a dispute is

thrashed out not by court arbitration, but by criminal elements representing the interests of the two sides) are nevertheless still fairly widespread, and cost both parties a great deal in terms of nerves and health – not to mention money. Nevertheless, entrepreneurs, especially small businessmen, often have to take recourse to them because of the incomplete nature of Russian economic legislation, the fact that the details of what does exist are not well understood, and the high cost of going to court for arbitration.

[6] For details of the IMD, see Chapter 3 and 'Project Methodology' in Appendix 1.

[7] A system of subsidised payments for medicines exists for certain population categories in Russia (either received completely free or purchased at 50 per cent of the normal price). Local authorities in each region may add their own categories to the federally-determined list of those entitled to the subsidies. In this case, as a family with a large number of children, the household had already had the right to half-price medicines under Moscow legislation for a long time. Unfortunately, the use of this subsidy is fairly complex – only your local doctor is entitled to write a prescription for subsidised medicines, and it can sometimes be difficult to get a consultation with him. In addition, the doctor has a strictly limited list of medicines that can be prescribed with a subsidy: prescribing a medicine not on this list requires a great deal of extra effort, since it is necessary to get permission from the senior doctor of the municipal clinic for the district. Next, pharmacists are very unwilling to accept subsidised prescriptions, since payment for them by the municipal authorities is often delayed. Finally, each pharmacy has a quota for the sale of subsidised medicines: so, it is perfectly possible that, having obtained a subsidised prescription with great difficulty, you will find it impossible to buy the medicine you need urgently at your pharmacy, even though it is available there at full price.

[8] Minor stomatology is free, but all kinds of prosthetic dentistry have to be paid for.

[9] In Moscow, from the point of view of receipt of benefits and subsidies, a family is viewed as having 'a large number' of children where they have no fewer than three children aged 14 or under.

[10] For a more detailed picture of the different forms of help given in the context of informal networks, see Chapter 3.

[11] Contracts between partners in small and medium-sized businesses are often not formally put in writing: everything is done on oral agreements, and two out of our three ruined businessmen had suffered as a result of this practice.

[12] These groups, according to data from the Goskomstat of the Russian Federation, have the greatest probability of falling into the category with the lowest living standards. So, although in 1999 the nationwide average correlation of available mean *per capita* resources to size of subsistence minimum was 128.9 per cent, in the group of households consisting of five or more people, it was 88.2 per cent. For the whole of Russia overall, this indicator was 99.1 per cent for households with two children, 71.1 per cent for those with three children and 47.0 per cent for those with four or more children (Goskomstat, 2000, p.163).

[13] They joined the sample formed for the research project 'Employment and social policy in Russia, 1995-1998' (headed by Nick Manning, INTAS grant 94-3725), as representatives of various groups affected by the labour market crisis.

[14] The concept of 'social exclusion' simply does not exist in Russian at the moment, since the phenomenon is new to the country. Of course, in both Tsarist Russia and Soviet Russia, there were people who were outside the mainstream (tramps, prisoners, etc.). But society itself did not look on them as part of society, perceiving them as 'social rejects', 'the dregs of society'. Nowadays, as our research has shown, the situation is substantially

different: within society itself, rather than outside it, among completely ordinary people who are trying to 'live like everyone else', a fairly large group of people has arisen who really are excluded. However, this is so new for Russia that it is not yet reflected in the language or in the public consciousness.

[15] Naturally, the existence of such a lapse in time between actually entering social exclusion and becoming aware of the fact makes it difficult to attempt to measure the phenomenon empirically or to distinguish a group of affected households. However, we feel certain that these difficulties are not related to lack of development of research instruments with which to analyse social exclusion or to any absence of indicators of social exclusion: they are largely inevitable, since, unlike poverty – which, strictly speaking, can be recorded at any given moment – social exclusion is dynamic in nature.

[16] The minimum wage in Russia at present is about £15 a month.

[17] The monthly average *per capita* cash income of the population in Russia at the time we carried out the first stage of our research was about £40, although two-thirds of the population received incomes of less than this sum and about 23 per cent had monthly average *per capita* incomes of no more than £29 a month (calculated according to Russian Statistical Year Book, 2000, pp.143, 155). However, the catastrophic nature of this situation should not be exaggerated – according to the statistical data, consumption of basic foodstuffs, including in the lowest decile, in the late 1990s was roughly at the level of the 1960s. In other words, there has been experience of this standard of material deprivation within living memory, although the picture of social participation for that group of the population in the 1960s was, of course, qualitatively different from that of the socially excluded in the 1990s.

Part IV

Special Issues in the Study of Poverty and Social Exclusion

6 Special Issues in the Study of Poverty and Social Exclusion

PART I – ETHNIC AND CULTURAL ASPECTS OF POVERTY

Andrei Zdravomyslov and Artur Tsutsiev

Ночью все кошки серы
All cats are grey in the dark

Formulating the Question

In this chapter, we propose to focus on aspects of poverty that are connected less with economic factors than with ethnic and cultural ones. The general premise here is that the phenomenon of poverty can be understood only in relation to the particular cultural features of the society within which it exists. Criteria and perceptions of poverty established in so-called welfare states cannot be transferred to countries with developing economies. The overall level of deprivation viewed as tolerable and the scale of social differentiation are defined not only by the level of economic development and welfare in the country as a whole, but also, in many ways, by specific cultural traditions, by standards of conformity and by living habits at a given level of prosperity. Consequently, the same is true of 'indigence', 'poverty', 'having enough' and 'wealth'.

The average standard of consumption of an inhabitant of Germany, Great Britain, France, the USA, Sweden or any other country on the highest rungs of the welfare ladder represents an almost unrealisable dream of wealth for the overwhelming majority of people in the countries of the developing world. Cultural differences are expressed in the small details of daily life, from the perception of money itself as a symbol of welfare, to consumption of drinking water, use of hygiene products, range of foodstuffs and size and type of equipment in the home, as well as access to modern means of communication and to social activities.

According to the level of welfare of its population, Russia is not among the most highly developed countries in the world, but it is also not one of the poorest. The position of Russia on the wealth-poverty scale is at the same level as countries such as Poland, Romania, Croatia, Estonia, Mexico, Brazil, and India.

There are three very important points that need to be grasped if one is to understand the issue of poverty as it exists today in the former Soviet Union, including Russia.

Firstly, the traditional tendency of Russian culture to condemn wealth, or at least to treat it with suspicion. 'Those who labour righteously do not dwell in stone halls' says a Russian proverb – an ethos very close to that expressed fairly explicitly in the Gospels: 'It is harder for a rich man to enter the kingdom of heaven than for a camel to pass through the eye of a needle'.[1] This thesis was taken up as one of the basic doctrines of Russian Orthodox dogma. The Orthodox Church directed its followers more towards a righteous life than towards wealth and honest toil.

In the Russian cultural tradition, then, the cult of indigence has received strong support. The general opinion was that the voice of the righteous mendicant was certainly heard by God, and, therefore, people who lived in the world, possessing wealth and power, gave alms to the poor with the reminder: 'Pray for me – a sinner'. It should be noted that Russia has never had any laws directed against vagrancy and begging. 'Poverty is no disgrace', says another Russian proverb.

However, the Soviet period was characterised by a break with this cultural tradition and by the assertion of a general obligation to work for the common good. Moreover, Communist labour was seen mainly as altruistic labour. A combination of modest consumption and selfless labour was for a long time the social ideal, and became particularly widespread in practice during wartime and post-war deprivation. In subsequent years, this norm became the official direction of State social policy, aiming for homogenisation of consumption.

Finally, we come to the post-Soviet reform period, contemporary Russia and the ideological turn towards radical liberalism: everyone for himself – especially as far as personal welfare is concerned. This has meant a break with both the pre-Revolutionary cultural tradition and the Soviet State's practical concern about welfare. Personal wealth is now seen as occupying a well-deserved place in the value system, and the most varied means of attaining it have become acceptable. In practice, this has come to entail demonstrations of wealth and disdain for poverty, which is seen as proof of a person's uselessness. At the same time, however, these processes manifest themselves differently in different regions and in different cultural milieux – something we tried to reflect in our research by using a sample made up of three populations of poor families, from Moscow, Voronezh and Vladikavkaz.

The last of these was divided into two roughly equal sub-groups, made up from two ethnic and cultural groups in the Republic of North Ossetia-Alaniya: 26 Ossetian and 24 Russian households. This means that 217 people were covered by our research in Vladikavkaz (out of 396 people across the three cities in the whole sample), including 104 people in Russian households and 113 in Ossetian.

Our hypothesis was that ethnic and cultural differences would be expressed in some way in the economic situation of these households, as well as through the ways they perceived poverty. But what do these ethnic and cultural factors consist of? We have already discussed the general Russian 'ethos of poverty' in relation to Russian cultural traditions and the general Soviet 'ethos of egalitarianism'. But traditional Ossetian culture is not part of Russian culture in the strict sense.

Ossetians are a North Caucasian people; Ossetian belongs to the Iranian group of languages within the Indo-European language family, and its written form came into being at the end of the 18th Century. There are two main dialects of the Ossetian language – Iron and Digor, which have now developed into independent literary languages. Inside Ossetia, Ossetians are divided into three significant groups – Irons, Digors (both groups live in North Ossetia) and Kudarets (they speak a form of Iron and live in South Ossetia).

The religious orientation of Ossetians is also heterogeneous: about 80 per cent to 82 per cent of Ossetians consider themselves Orthodox, and 18 per cent to 20 per cent Muslim. It should be noted that the subjective ethnic boundaries between Ossetian communities do not coincide with their religious denomination. Although Ossetians are the only non-Muslim people in the North Caucasus region and a non-Caucasian peoples in terms of their national language, the cultural values of Ossetians are largely based on traditions common to the whole of the North Caucasus. Wealth and poverty here are not perceived as particular human values; there was no cult of poverty, as was characteristic to a certain extent of Russian culture. Poverty is frequently seen as evidence of the personal lack of worth of the head of the family unit – specifically, his or her worthlessness as a breadwinner. There is a culture of kinship and family, understood more broadly than in Russian culture, with mutual assistance within the framework of belonging to the same 'clan', and this is still partly supported through traditional rituals, despite the undoubted effect of urbanisation and global processes. In developing our research programme, we hypothesised that we would find some strong proof of a higher degree of mutual assistance between Ossetian families, by comparison with Russian families, and that this would compensate to a significant extent for social exclusion.

Another, no less important, circumstance is the increasingly widespread 'ethnicisation' of power and of prestige sectors of the economy in many of Russia's national republics during the later Soviet period and the post-Soviet decade. A particular form of social exclusion has arisen, connected with ethnicity and culture, and has inspired many Russian families to try and emigrate from national republics in the North Caucasus region. This phenomenon has also become widespread in North Ossetia. The ethnicisation of power is connected with the differing extents to which Russians and Caucasians (including Ossetians) have 'capital of primary sociability': social connections – above all, immediate family and other relatives – that can be turned to advantage in finding work, getting into higher education, etc. Making use of this capital as a 'natural resource', Caucasians are coping with social problems through a system of 'positive discrimination' (in comparison with Russians).

This means that Russians (who, according to data from the 1989 census, make up 29 per cent of the population of North Ossetia) – lacking extensive networks of support from immediate family and other relatives – are somehow 'spontaneously' discriminated against within the territory of the national republics. This kind of discrimination, based on selection by ethnicity, is not the result of an organised policy or ordinary nationalism on the part of power-holding groups in the republics. It is, rather, a manifestation of a stable and habitual practice operating in a traditional society, where networks of informal mutual obligation largely coincide with networks of links between immediate family and other relatives (although not entirely incorporated into them). It is not that Russians are excluded from having networks, but – judging from our research data – that their durability and level of performance are frequently not comparable with Caucasian networks.

However, it is vital to bear in mind that the carefully formed sample used for our household research is not representative of the whole Russian or Ossetian populations of the Republic, nor of poor families in the relevant national groups. The groups compared have somewhat the value of 'independent events', enabling a better-founded investigation into the content of problems, without providing any basis for conclusions about the issue of poverty in the region or about regional social policy.

Levels of Poverty

For the first stage of the research, we developed a question to discover the significance of various separate poverty indicators characteristic of the families' standards of living. Among such indicators were employment and level of income, source of earnings, the family's housing conditions, the standard of food they ate, the state of health of individual family members and the ways they organised their leisure time.

At the second stage of the research, we analysed data from the summarised indexes, which allowed us to classify the families into four groups on the basis of all the indicators. These groups were designated as representing four levels of welfare: indigence, poverty, being badly-off, and being averagely well-off. In addition, our questionnaire asked the respondent to give his or her own assessment of the family's standard of living at present, using a seven-point scale from 1, signifying extreme poverty, to 7, meaning very great wealth. Our respondents all placed themselves at the four lowest points on this scale. Thus, we were able to compare two four-point scales, one based on overall criteria of poverty and the other on self-assessment. These data are shown in Table 6.1.

It is worth pointing out that the summarised index seems to provide a stricter criterion for classification than does self-assessment by the respondent. Most Ossetian and Russian families (45 per cent and 61 per cent respectively) situated themselves in the third position, even though the summarised index recorded their situation as 'poor' (27 per cent and 50 per cent). This implies that it seemed to be very difficult for respondents themselves to express their state of poverty. The interviewer felt that people were struggling to preserve their personal dignity. Notably, we most frequently observed this gap between indicators in the summarised index and by self-assessment among Russians: more than two-thirds of them fell into the categories of 'indigence' and 'poverty' (17 per cent and 50 per cent respectively), but they more often assessed their situation at point 3, or 'badly-off' (61 per cent), while 17 per cent even saw themselves as 'averagely well-off'.

Table 6.1   **Level of poverty of Ossetian and Russian families in the Vladikavkaz sample, on the basis of summarised index and of self-assessment (in per cent)**

Level of poverty	Summarised index		Self-assessment		Position on the scale
	Ossetians	Russians	Ossetians	Russians	
Indigence	18	17	14	4	1
Poverty	27	50	14	17	2
Badly-off	41	12	45	61	3
Average	14	21	27	17	4

Table 6.2   **Assessment of various aspects of life by Ossetian and Russian respondents (in per cent of those selecting the extreme points on the scale)**

Aspects of life	Ossetian		Russian	
	Good	Bad	Good	Bad
Family relationships	68	14	79	4
Opportunities for personal contact with friends	57	5	54	0
Work situation	46	0	28	6
Housing	23	36	17	25
Food	9	23	17	8
Clothing	5	14	0	30
Opportunities for leisure	10	35	17	30
Material well-being	0	52	0	46
How life is going overall	9	14	8	4

This tendency was also confirmed by answers to the question: 'How do you think your life is going overall?' Only one respondent in the Russian sample and three in the Ossetian replied that their life was going 'badly'. The overwhelming majority – 87 per cent of Russians and 76 per cent of

Ossetian respondents – indicated that it was going 'satisfactorily'. Two Russian respondents and two Ossetian respondents even replied that it was going 'well'. In other words, there seemed to be far fewer cases of low spirits resulting from poverty than one might expect – and this conclusion applied to both sections of the Vladikavkaz sample.

So, the factors with the most favourable influence on positive perceptions of life overall are relations within the family, opportunities for contact with friends, and the work situation. The other five factors – primarily relating to material standards – seemed to have a negative overall effect on the perception of life. At the same time, a comparison between Ossetian and Russian respondents shows that the Russians assessed their situation at work as 'bad' much more often than the Ossetians. In contrast, Russian respondents more often assessed the standard of their food as 'good'.

In answering a direct question about the reasons for their lives not going well, the positions of both groups of respondents were very close.

Table 6.3 shows that, in explaining the reasons for their lives not going well, assessments were very close for nine out of the 15 proposed indicators, with some even coinciding. It was more understandable that there were discrepancies between factors such as lack of opportunity for personal contact with relations, loneliness and change in status, with respondents from Russian families twice as likely to indicate that these were not going as well as respondents from Ossetian families.

Table 6.3   Reasons for life not going well, as assessed by Ossetian and Russian respondents (in per cent of total number of those surveyed in that group)

Ranking	Factor	Ossetians	Russians	Whole sample across all three regions
1	Poor material circumstances	66	79	66
2	Problems with work	50	45	35
3	Lack of opportunities for leisure	50	42	38
4	Health	45	54	45
5	Lack of protection from violence	27	29	22
6-7	Poor nutrition	27	25	19
6-7	Housing problems	27	25	27
8	Problems with clothing	18	33	21
9	Harmful habits (such as alcoholism)	18	4	10
10	Lack of opportunities to socialise	14	29	13
11	Family problems	14	13	11
12	Lack of time	9	38	21
13	Change in status	5	12	23
14	Loneliness	4	8	7
15	Lack of attention from others	4	4	6
16	Other	0	4	4
	My life is OK	18	8	15

Dynamics of Position on the 'Poverty-Prosperity' Scale

One way of revealing the significance of ethnic and cultural factors in levels of poverty is to compare families who improved their material welfare with those whose welfare deteriorated over the year of study.

Table 6.4   Dynamics of material welfare in households under study, by nationality (based on summarised index, in per cent)

	Russians	*Ossetians*	*Whole sample*
Situation improved	21	27	25
Situation stable (badly-off)	8	27	24
Situation of 'stagnant' poverty	50	32	38
Situation deteriorated	21	14	12

When we look at this table, our attention is drawn first of all to the fact that, taking into account all the overall indicators, there was much greater deterioration in the welfare of the Russian households in Vladikavkaz over the year of observation than in that of the Ossetian households. A fifth of respondents were in a worse position and a fifth were in a better position, while half the families were in a position of 'stagnant poverty'. In Ossetian families these summarised indicators were slightly better: over a quarter of the families were in a better position and only 14 per cent were in a worse position.

How did Ossetian and Russian respondents assess the reasons for a fall in their living standards?

Comparison of the reasons for falling living standards shows that there was greater similarity than difference between the two sub-samples. In both cases, job loss came top of the list of reasons, followed by illness/disability, with loss of breadwinner in third place. People found themselves in particular difficulty when these reasons suddenly combined coincidentally. Tracing the stories of two families shows how this might happen.

1. The story of an Ossetian family, the Gs, was very typical in this regard. The family consisted of five people – a couple and three children. They owned a minibus, and the husband used this to earn money, transporting Vladikavkaz residents to market in the town of Goryachevodsk, which brought in enough for them to live reasonably comfortably. The wife was also earning, doing temporary work. In 1995, during a journey to Chechnya to visit relatives, she died in unknown circumstances. (The trip was connected with an attempt to settle some financial affairs with these relatives.) Almost simultaneously, the head of the family became seriously ill and had to undergo an operation. As a direct result of these circumstances, the members of this family experienced a radical change in their material circumstances. The children recalled the time when the father had been able to work at full strength as a 'golden age'. These

two blows, coming one after another, were psychologically intolerable. The father started drinking. The family fell into poverty.

Five per cent of Ossetian families and 11 per cent of Russian families had fallen into similar circumstances.

2. During the 1980s and early 1990s, the Os, a Russian family, had been very well-off. The head of the family worked in Noril'sk, at Russia's largest nuclear plant. Before moving to Ossetia, he had saved a fairly large sum of money, in order to set up his own business. He went on to become Deputy Chairman of the local council of Karts, a suburb of Vladikavkaz, which in 1992 became one of the epicentres of the Ossetian-Ingush conflict. O leased a piece of land, on which he started producing various things. His business partners were Ingush entrepreneurs, who provided him with credit and a stable situation. The family estimated that their income then had been very high: the wife and two children did not go short of anything, and the head of the family helped his own parent and his wife's parents.

However, the Ossetian-Ingush conflict was the reason for the collapse of his business. According to the way he and members of his family told their story in several interviews, it all began because he failed to come to an understanding with the local policeman. The latter denounced him to the Procurator's Office, accusing him of arms dealing. Our entrepreneur was arrested by the police on suspicion of this crime and imprisoned for three months. His daughter (a minor) was also arrested by the police. The aim of all this was to undermine trust in the family as a whole – and it did just that. After three months he was released on bail, but the matter was far from closed and dragged on for another three years. Over that period, relations of trust and mutual understanding with the business partners were ruined, and our respondent went from being an entrepreneur to being semi-unemployed.

Despite making desperate efforts, he could not restore his fortunes, and the family's situation went downhill. The only property they had left was a jeep, which they sold for the opportunity to acquire real estate in Spain! However, this affair was a failure, since the company involved – acting, according to the respondents, in the name of an English firm, Diamond Travel – turned out to be crooked. The family lost $2,400 in this affair – an enormous sum for North Ossetia. This happened in 1997, and in 1998 the family again suffered from the financial crisis. This was a fairly typical trajectory from prosperity to poverty.

The family's situation now depends to a large extent on the wife's earnings – which are not large, but fairly steady – and on the husband's casual earnings: from time to time he can earn extraordinarily large sums of money, specialising in the manufacture of saunas. This whole story and the change in social status over a short period – with arrest, imprisonment and ruin – has become a source of constant stress, which the respondent tries to blot out by the systematic use of alcohol. His bouts of heavy drinking last several days and, naturally, they have become a new source of crisis in family relations.

Returning to our sub-samples, one difference recorded in our data was that misfortune had more often affected Ossetian families (in our sample there were several Ossetian families who were refugees from Georgia), while family breakdown was more frequent among the Russians.

In addition, at least two sets of reasons were in no way equivalent, and were perceived differently by the two groups. The first related to macroeconomic processes, from outside the family concerned. Here the family was 'a victim of circumstances'. The influence of this factor fell somewhat over the period under study: about 50 per cent of Ossetians and 50 per cent of Russians selected it in 1999, but only about 30 per cent of respondents in 2000.

Loss of a breadwinner, illness or disability and retirement were other factors in poverty. These were primarily causes within the family, connected with the composition of the particular family, with age and with state of health. Around 50 per cent of both the Ossetian and Russian sub-samples indicated such reasons. These are direct negative factors, which are generally irreversible – loss of a breadwinner, for example.

In money terms, a fall in standard of living may be expressed either by a reduction in income or by an increase in essential expenditure that cannot be deferred. (A third variant consists of the coincidence of these circumstances.) In the first stage of the research, our attention was chiefly devoted to the issue of sources of income, while the second survey introduced questions to allow us to assess certain new features connected not with sources of income, but with an increase in essential spending.

Thus, very many families named 'increasing costs of growing children' among the reasons for deterioration in their situation. This circumstance was top of the list for the Vladikavkaz sub-sample, selected by 65 per cent of Ossetian respondents and 37 per cent of Russians. To this should be added another 20 per cent of each group, affected by an increase in family size or by the arrival of relatives. The weight of these factors, taken overall, was greater than 'loss of permanent paid job': however, they were factors that were qualitatively different. In one case, it was a matter of change in the income part of the family budget, and in the other, of changes in outgoings. In addition, the dynamics of family welfare were such that increasing expenditure on children could not be seen as a negative indicator. The prospects of many families, especially those with a lot of children, depended on growing children becoming the main breadwinners.

Some of the younger generation in the families we studied were already bringing additional earnings into the household.

A somewhat different order of the causes of poverty emerged when respondents were asked about the reasons for other people's poverty – the families of their relatives, friends and acquaintances, who were in extreme need or practically indigent. First of all, we found that half the respondents said that there were no such families in their circle. Only 50 per cent of each sub-sample said that they knew such families, giving long-term unemployment, unpaid wages and pension delays as the main reasons for their current difficulties. Fifty-six per cent of Ossetian respondents and 31 per cent of Russians thought that this position would be temporary for their acquaintances, but 6 per cent and 19 per cent respectively thought their position was hopeless. Only 37 per cent and 33 per cent of respondents respectively placed their hopes on the children of such families.

We noted that only 17 per cent of Russian respondents and 9 per cent of Ossetians indicated that their family had not had any unemployment problems throughout the reform period; a third of the Ossetians and a fifth of the Russians said they had been registered as unemployed during that time. Thirty-six per cent of Ossetian respondents and 14 per cent of Russians said that their families were still suffering from unemployment.

Social Exclusion

Respondents themselves consistently interpreted the causes of their poverty in terms that related to many and varied forms of social exclusion, which we outline here.

The most frequent was job loss, which leads not only to the loss of the most important, steady source of income, but also to the loss of habitual forms of everyday occupation, perceived as norms. There is a sense of superfluity and uselessness. An unemployed person loses habitual orientations; self-esteem falls sharply; status in the family and wider circle changes. This course of events can be traced in both the cases we have described above.

The second most widespread form of social exclusion arose from poor health. Disability, long-term sickness and limited ability to work are not only an additional burden on the working members of the family, but dramatically limit the individual's social circle. In a number of cases, the sick family member needs constant care from relatives, and the sharing of this responsibility becomes an important component of the psychological atmosphere in the family and among close friends. In the 1999 survey, about 70 per cent of respondents from Ossetian families and 80 per cent of Russians indicated serious problems with their own health or that of close relatives – spouse, parents or children – while 31 per cent of those from Ossetian families and 20 per cent from Russian families indicated that substantial restrictions prevented a family member from carrying out normal work or everyday activities.

The third form of social exclusion was connected with alcohol abuse, which arises from attempts at psychological escape from life's difficulties. The presence of alcohol dependency in the family was carefully concealed by most respondents: public opinion looks on such dependency as a direct cause of poverty and, consequently, places responsibility for the increasingly difficult situation at the door of the family itself. However, we were able to conclude that alcoholism was a live issue for at least 20 per cent of poor families in both the Vladikavkaz sub-samples.

The fourth form of social exclusion directly concerned children. Of course, all the previous circumstances had some impact on their feelings about the world, their degree of openness in social relations with their peers, and the balance of trustful and embittered feelings that became typical of the child's psychology. However, in a number of cases, children from poor families had fallen behind in their education as compared with their peers, and the family could not provide the child with clothing and shoes to go to school or college because of their material difficulties. There were not many such instances, but they occurred in families with large numbers of children. So, in the large family (eight children) of a disabled person with a drink problem, not all the children were going to school. In a number of other cases, older children (16 and upwards) had had to give up their studies in order to earn enough to support other family members.

The fifth form of social exclusion we observed was the predominance of a depressed psychological state, most often connected with the loss of a loved one and with difficulties in overcoming this new situation. Loss of a breadwinner was indicated as a reason for poverty by a fifth of Ossetian and Russian respondents in 1999. It was often the case that the person who had gone was not only the breadwinner, but also the psychological core of the family.

Other questionnaire responses that threw further light on social exclusion came primarily from the material about fears in the respondent's own life.

Table 6.5   Distribution of responses to the question "What do you fear most of all in your own life?" (Respondents could select no more than three answers)

Ranking	Source of fear	Ossetians		Russians	
		1999	2000	1999	2000
1	Deterioration in my health or that of family members	52	77	55	75
2	Not having enough money to exist	45	55	59	58
3	I fear for my life or the lives of those close to me, because of the growth in crime	45	64	35	25
4	Not being able to get a good education or give my children a good education	41	14	7	29
5	Having no work	31	36	21	29
6	Having no friends	17	0	28	21
7	People becoming embittered and not helping each other any more	17	14	17	17
8	All-powerful authorities and complete lawlessness	14	9	14	17
9	Ethnic intolerance from people around me	9	0	14	8
10	Environmental pollution	7	0	3	4
11	Not being able to get medical help even in case of severe need	3	27	17	8
12	Mass civil disorder	3		14	
	Not being able to create or maintain family life	3	0	7	8
13	Other	-	0	-	8

Answers to the question in the 1999 survey about attitudes to politics also told us something about social exclusion. Not one respondent indicated that a family member actively participated in political activity, and a similar lack of interest in cultural activities was also expressed. However, the overwhelming majority – 82.8 per cent of Russians and 69 per cent of Ossetians – indicated that a family member regularly watched the news or read newspapers, while another 20 per cent watched the news occasionally.

So, there was some interest in politics and in maintaining a certain level of information about the most important events, but it did not extend as far as participation. In addition, a very high proportion (over half) in each sub-sample had taken no steps over the last year to stand up for their own interests through the courts, political lobbying or direct action.

The sixth type of social exclusion was connected with forced moves (and sometimes with refugee status in the literal sense) due to interethnic conflicts. In our Vladikavkaz sample, this form of social exclusion had affected several Ossetian families, who were refugees from Georgia. Although the group of refugees did not constitute any kind of special sub-sample, a whole 'cluster' of the social problems that affect poor families was more clearly expressed in their case: primarily, loss of a proper job with stable wages and loss of housing.

Finally, the seventh form of social exclusion was the lack of any social connections that might be converted into a source of support for the family, into additional life chances or possibilities of improving the family's standard of welfare. Both Russian and Ossetian respondents gave a 'nil' rating to 'help from other relatives or friends' as a source of income on which the welfare of the family depended heavily. In fact, friends and relatives represent a primary social institution and a concentration of social connections resources – and respondents themselves stated this distinctly.

Starting from the – completely feasible – hypothesis that the material circumstances of Russian families in the Republic tends towards poverty (or, at least, being badly-off), it should follow that the level of social exclusion among Russians would be higher than among Ossetians. Data on representation in the institutions of power provide indirect evidence of this. The level of ethnic representation falls within boundaries from 0.9 to 1.1: in the Government of the Republic, Ossetians measure 1.48 and Russians 0.54, while for Parliament the corresponding indicators are 1.53 and 0.35.

Table 6.6   Ethnic representation of Ossetian and Russian students in four higher education institutions in North Ossetia[2]

	Ossetians	Russians	Others
University	1.34	0.60	0.44
Medical Academy	1.40	0.50	0.38
Agricultural University	1.52	0.30	0.26
University of Technology	0.86	1.67	0.42

Data on levels of ethnic representation in leading higher education institutions in North Ossetia also give us a picture of a certain level of social exclusion.

Ethnic Discrimination as a Factor in Poverty

A whole range of responses from the 1999 questionnaire gave us a picture of the nationalist orientations of respondents. In both sub-samples, we fairly often came across families with a nationally heterogeneous composition. In addition, it was not very common to count on help solely from members of one's own nationality. In practice, a mononational social circle was slightly more common among Ossetians (10 per cent as against 3 per cent): this is largely explained by the fact that, for 80 per cent of Ossetian respondents, Ossetian is their mother tongue. In both sub-groups, 14 per cent of respondents said that they would prefer to socialise with people of their own nationality, while about 80 per cent declared that they had social contact with several nationalities.

The data on respondents' reactions to the possible marriage of a relative to someone of another nationality is interesting. Only one respondent in each sub-sample said that this would be intolerable. Forty-four-and-a-half per cent of Ossetian respondents and 55.2 per cent of Russians said that they didn't think there was anything special about it. The largest difference was observed in the following response: 'I wouldn't like it, but I wouldn't object' – 41.4 per cent of Ossetians and 10.3 per cent of Russians. In other words, radical nationalism was very weak, even among poor families, while a 'softer' version of nationalism was slightly more common among Ossetian respondents.

In our 2000 survey, the questionnaire included new questions to try and explain the extent to which our respondents linked their poverty with belonging to a particular nationality. They were asked to agree or disagree with the statement: 'We have become poor because we are ... (Russian/Ossetian)'.

In both ethnic groups, the table shows lack of agreement dramatically predominating over agreement: however, this predominance is significantly higher among Ossetian respondents than among Russians.

Another question was intended to find out how frequently respondents '... felt that people from my ethnic background are living increasingly badly, by comparison with others.' Eighty per cent of Ossetian respondents in Vladikavkaz and 40 per cent of Russians indicated that such a feeling had never occurred to them; while 22 per cent of Russian respondents (but not one Ossetian) said that they often felt this.

Table 6.7   Russian and Ossetian respondents' self-assessment of membership of a national group as a factor in poverty (in per cent)

We have become poor because we are ... (Russian/Ossetian)	*Vladikavkaz sub-sample*	
	Russians	*Ossetians*
Agree	17	9
Don't know	22	9
Disagree	56	82

It may be that Russian families in Vladikavkaz have a somewhat heightened awareness of national issues, and this could be explained by the fact that a family's ethnicity reflects its capital of primary informal connections. Russian ethnicity is associated with low levels of such connections and, therefore, with little potential to make use of them in social strategies, whether adaptational or innovative. In his interview, one of the Vladikavkaz Russian respondents observed heatedly:

> I always feel that I just want to get away from here. I was born here and I grew up here, but I just can't stand it. You know, I can't say Ossetian nationalism has sprung up here, but there is discrimination everywhere – in promotion, at work, absolutely everywhere...

This observation was to some degree supported by answers to the question about obstacles preventing the respondent from getting a good job. A higher proportion of Russian respondents in Vladikavkaz indicated that nationality was an obstacle: 25 per cent, as against 5 per cent of the Ossetian respondents and 9 per cent across the whole sample. For Russians, this cause of difficulties in getting work was in fifth place out of 12, while for Ossetians it was in one of the lowest positions. However, it was also noticeable that in both groups, 'lack of connections' was ranked as the biggest obstacle to getting a good job (71 per cent of Russians and 68 per cent of Ossetians in Vladikavkaz – very different from the mononational sub-samples: 50 per cent in Voronezh and only 37 per cent in Moscow). In other words, in North Ossetia, involvement in a network of personal interrelationships is the chief factor in getting a good job. If we accept that such networks will have an ethnic element, then, in practice, ethnic discrimination is a latent factor in the way such important life issues as finding work are dealt with. It isn't mentioned, it just goes without saying.

It seemed to us that the responses given by Russian and Ossetian respondents to the question about whether they would prefer to live in another region, as a factor for improving their situation, was symptomatic of this. Only 5 per cent of our Vladikavkaz Ossetians agreed that 'other regions offer more opportunities to improve one's circumstances', whereas 42 per cent of Russian respondents in Vladikavkaz thought this.

Conventionally, gender is an important aspect of any analysis of ethnic and cultural differences. In our research, therefore, we asked a retrospective question about which member of the family – the man or the woman – had been the family's main breadwinner in previous years and in 2000. We observed a trend towards a growing proportion of poor Russian families in Vladikavkaz having a woman as the main breadwinner. From 1990 to 2000, the proportion of such families in our sample had grown from a third to almost a half. This trend corresponded to that in the Moscow and Voronezh samples – although there, it was noticeably stronger. In contrast, data from the Ossetian sub-group in Vladikavkaz did not confirm the same trend. However, even among Ossetian families – with their more traditional structure – a quarter had a woman as main breadwinner, and by 2000, the proportion of such families in our sample had grown to 29 per cent. This increase was not so significant as in the other sub-samples. It could be said that neither Russian nor Ossetian households in Vladikavkaz had experienced such a nosedive in the status of men as 'main breadwinner' in the family over the last decade as had taken place in the Moscow and Voronezh sub-samples. In both

Vladikavkaz sub-samples, the role of men has remained predominant, although for Russian families the growth in women's role as 'main breadwinner' has been more obvious. The significance of gender is explored in more detail in the second half of this chapter.

Table 6.8   Proportion of families in the four sub-samples with a woman as 'main breadwinner' (in per cent of families under study, with 1990 and 1995 based on respondents' retrospective assessments)

Sub-sample	1990	1995	2000
Moscow	35	39	46
Voronezh	36	39	54
Vladikavkaz:-Russian	33	35	46
Vladikavkaz:-Ossetian	24	37	29

Perceptions of Poverty and Assessments of One's Own Situation

Let us now look at how the respondents perceived their own situation. Most of them, in one way or another, connected this with the outcome of the 1991-2 reforms. The following table provides evidence of this, comparing as it does the present day with the pre-reform period.

Table 6.9   Self-assessment of the family's material circumstances in comparison with other people's

Families	Before the reforms			Now		
	Better	Same	Worse	Better	Same	Worse
Ossetian	34	59	7	3	31	66
Russian	10	62	28	3	17	79

A deterioration in their position was felt by about 60 per cent of Ossetian families and over 50 per cent of Russians.

The control question on this subject used a 10-point scale of status, and resulted in the distribution shown in Table 6.10.

In this case, we can see negative social mobility for 62 per cent of Ossetian families and for 45 per cent of Russians.

Table 6.10 Comparison of self-assessments of status by Ossetian and Russian families: pre-reform period v. present day

Families	*Before the reforms*			*Now*		
	High (1-3)	*Middle* (4-6)	*Low* (7-10)	*High* (1-3)	*Middle* (4-6)	*Low* (7-10)
Ossetian	17	69	14	3	21	76
Russian	17	45	37	0	17	83

Moreover, in answering the question about reasons for the fall in the family's living standard, a fifth of Ossetians and 17 per cent of Russians stated that their family had always lived like this. Consequently, the proportion of traditional poverty was more widespread in Vladikavkaz than in the other regions under study.

Now we shall look at how poverty was perceived, based on levels of agreement with statements put to the respondents in the 1999 survey. In answering the question about attitudes to families in need, from 40 per cent (among Ossetians) to 50 per cent (among Russians) of respondents suggested that the predominant attitude to such families was one of indifference. A quarter of Ossetians and a third of Russians suggested that attitudes to them mainly depended on why the family was in need. A further quarter of Ossetians and 14 per cent of Russians suggested that people in Vladikavkaz tried to help poor families, and only three respondents thought that attitudes to the poor were disrespectful or scornful.

Perception of one's own poverty was assessed using these pairs of alternative statements, as seen in Table 6.11.

We should note that the first pair of statements, which poses a choice between blame and tolerance in relation to the wealth of others, was assessed in the same way by the Ossetian and the Russian sub-groups. In both cases, roughly two-thirds were inclined to resent the wealth of others and to blame them for their own situation, while one-third responded tolerantly. In the second pair, we were checking our hypothesis that there would be a widespread desire to conceal poverty, as being something shameful. Such feelings were slightly more common among Ossetians: only a third of them, as against half the Russian respondents, suggested that people were not ashamed of their poverty and, on the contrary, tried to use the situation to their advantage. Ossetians evidently tended to be more reserved in demonstrating their poverty. However, any interpretation of this difference from an ethnic or cultural point of view should be approached with a great deal of care: respondents from Ossetian families were more willing to admit that they themselves were poor – two out of five would do so, as against only one in five Russians, even where the latter were objectively in a more difficult situation.

Table 6.11 Choice of alternative statements about perceptions of poverty (in per cent)

	Statements	*Ossetians*	*Russians*
First pair	People experience their situation as very painful, and lay the blame for their misfortunes at the door of those who have become rich on the back of others' impoverishment, as well as of the authorities, who have created favourable conditions for this	62	62
	People look on their own poverty with relative equanimity and are even tolerant of the rich: people who become rich are those who are better at turning the situation to their own advantage	38	38
Second pair	As a rule, people in our circles are ashamed of their poverty; they conceal it, and want to give the impression that everything is going well for them	65	52
	Many people love complaining about their poverty, and even exaggerate it	35	49

Resources

Resources used to combat poverty can be subdivided into at least two groups. The first of these can be defined by such circumstances as whether one has a job or outside help, as well as level of earnings and other income. The second is connected with psychological attitudes, striving to combat poverty, and the degree of faith that there will be a successful outcome to this struggle.

It is worth noting that, although these responses revealed great faith in the future among Ossetian respondents, practical business-like approaches were more clearly expressed by Russian respondents: Table 6.12 provides evidence of this.

The practice of mutual assistance of various kinds is an important social resource for survival in conditions of poverty. This theme was explored in quite a lot of detail in both surveys, in relation to our hypothesis that mutual assistance would have greater significance in Ossetian circles. Here we will merely note some of the more important points. Almost a third of Ossetian families said that they did not receive any kind of help from outside, while 50 per cent of Russian families said the same. The significance of receiving help from relatives and neighbours was acknowledged by 73 per cent of Ossetian and 58 per cent Russian families. But the most interesting thing was that poor families themselves – both Ossetians and Russians – helped others: 86 per cent of Ossetian respondents and 62 per cent of Russians. Ossetian families mainly listed relatives as among those who helped them and whom they helped, while Russians put more emphasis on relations of mutual assistance with friends, acquaintances and neighbours. This signals a characteristic difference in the infrastructure of social connections between Ossetian and Russian families.

Table 6.12 Actions directed at improving the family's material circumstances (in per cent)

	Actions	Ossetians		Russians	
		1999	*2000*	*1999*	*2000*
1	Taking any opportunity to earn extra, including casual, temporary or unregistered work	52	50	76	87
2	Forced to borrow money	45	32	41	42
3	Providing some of one's own foodstuffs	21	18	31	25
4	Getting help from other people or organisations	21	14	7	13
5	Holding several permanent jobs	17	23	21	36
6	Renting out living accommodation, garage, dacha, car, etc.	17	9	7	4
7	Selling some belongings	10	4	10	4
8	Retraining	10	9	10	17
9	Selling excess produce from garden/allotment/small-holding	0	5	3	0
10	Not doing anything, because nothing can be done to improve our situation	17	23	10	8

General Conclusions

Let us draw a few conclusions.

Measured by money income per family member, Ossetian families in Vladikavkaz were more likely to be among the very poorest than were Russians, especially where there were a lot of children. At the same time, they more often received significant – for them – support from relatives. Russian families were more active in their choice of life strategy, especially in seeking additional earnings, while Ossetian respondents were more optimistic in assessing their family's prospects.

However, these differences did not lead us to conclude that there are specific Ossetian or Russian forms of poverty: it would be more accurate to say that the characteristics of poverty and its perception were largely similar in both groups.

However, it is an unavoidable truth that Ossetians do not simply dominate the representative and executive organs of power in the Republic – as well as the most prestigious and profitable occupations – but are over-represented in them. ('New Russians' in North Ossetia are almost all of Ossetian ethnic origin.) Similarities in the characteristics of Russian and Ossetian poverty in Vladikavkaz are not evidence of similarities in the position and feelings of Russians and Ossetians in the Republic as a whole: perhaps the ethnic structure of migration will allow this to be judged indirectly. Thus – according to Passport Office data – of the 16,500 people who left North Ossetia between 1995 and 2000, over 15,000 were Russians, while Russians represented no more than 5 per cent of those entering.

One instance of the ethnic factor exerting a significant influence on a family's material welfare occurs when the family is somehow drawn into an ethnic conflict. Vladikavkaz is a city where some residents have been, in one way or another, affected by two armed conflicts on a regional scale. Chronologically, the first was the South Ossetian conflict of 1989-92, in the course of which about 30,000 to 35,000 Ossetian families were forced to leave Georgia and resettle in North Ossetia. The second was the Ossetian-Ingush conflict, which broke out in the autumn of 1992 in North Ossetia itself. It is clear that those who were direct victims of this conflict suffered the heaviest loss. In our sample, there were several Ossetian families who had become poor as a result of the unfolding of the conflict in South Ossetia, and also one Russian family whose fate had become linked to the circumstances of the Ossetian-Ingush conflict.

A key ethnically-related factor in the social exclusion of some of our Vladikavkaz households was their low level of the social capital of primary informal connections, which have the potential to be converted into life chances and real moves towards greater prosperity. In this regard, poor Ossetian and Russian families in our sample were similar: both experienced – and reacted to – lack of such connections. However, such a lack was much more typical for the Russian than for the Ossetian families.

A significant difference between our poor Russian and Ossetian families in Vladikavkaz was that the Russians displayed more initiative and attempted to change their material situation for the better in a variety of ways. In our sample, Russians were less likely than Ossetians to remain in a state of passive expectation. This also suggested that Russians cherish fewer illusions as to their level of connections: they have to rely on themselves to a greater extent. On the other hand, in our Ossetian sub-sample, there was a disproportionately high number of housewives (for the Moscow, Voronezh, Russian Vladikavkaz and Ossetian Vladikavkaz sub-samples, the figures were respectively: 11 per cent, 12 per cent, 13 per cent and 41 per cent). There were also significantly more unemployed people in the Ossetian sub-sample (7 per cent, 8 per cent, 13 per cent and 18 per cent respectively). In fact, as a result of having more children and more problems connected with health or inter-ethnic conflicts, the Ossetian families in our sample came close to the Russian families in terms of social exclusion. This similarity in levels of social exclusion had come about despite the *a priori* factor that the Ossetians had greater resources of primary social connections: it became apparent that such connections do not provide an intrinsic defence mechanism that automatically comes into play to completely block a family's drift into a state of 'stagnant poverty'. These connections must be drawn on and actively reshaped in the context of adaptational strategies and support networks that are both more active and more efficient than those available to many of the families in our Ossetian sub-sample.

PART II – GENDER, POVERTY AND SOCIAL EXCLUSION IN CONTEMPORARY RUSSIA

Nadia Davidova and Nataliya Tikhonova

Муж да жена – одна сатана
A husband and wife are the same Satan

In the Russian sociological tradition, gender has remained a long-neglected social issue. This was to a significant degree connected with the fact that, from the 1920s onwards, the idea of equality between men and women dominated Russia's official ideology – in practice, to the point of monopoly. And although the years of the Soviet regime saw much done to secure the real emancipation of women and their equality with men, the concrete forms taken by these achievements derived in many cases from a latent but deep-rooted premise that the sexes had distinct identities. The idea of 'sexual identity' was represented by equality before the law plus preservation of gender differences. The resulting situation can be accurately summed up in Margit Eichler's warning that 'gender insensitivity in data interpretation takes two basic forms: ignoring sex as a socially significant variable, and ignoring a relevant sex-differentiated social context' (1998, p.160).

Nevertheless, nowadays most Russian sociologists and social policy researchers agree that no socio-economic problem can be adequately reflected without the gender perspective. Moreover, this set of issues has gained special topicality – not so much because of the specific achievements of the feminist movement as because of the practical task of improving social policy and systems of social support for women and for families.

One of the most complex and interesting aspects of gender research is the hidden world of differences and contradictions within the household, relating mainly to the distribution of roles, incomes and responsibilities within the family. There has been a lot of research on this theme in the UK, where some very interesting data has been obtained over the last few years. It is important to note the pioneering work carried out in this field by Jan Pahl (1980; 1989), as well as research by Jackie Goode (1998; 1999),

Lydia Morris (1990), Catherine Vogler (1994), Gail Wilson (1987) and a number of others.

Their research paradigm looks at the issue of who is in charge of the household (on a day-to-day level, this means both supporting the family and running the home) from the standpoint not only of the everyday executive management of financial means, but also from that of power as strategic control over the household (Vogler and Pahl, 1994). Similarly, a distinction has to be made between the strategic and the tactical, everyday levels of decision-making within the household. A lot depends on the specific ways that functions are distributed in the family, and the family's standard of living frequently leaves its stamp on these. Therefore, as applied to poor families or those in need – where inequality in the distribution of power over incomes within the household may lead to varying levels of deprivation for different members of the family – the issue of gender differences in the area of financial control and responsibility within the household stands in its own special light.

Of course, socio-cultural differences and traditions, which vary depending on the type of community (whether this is state, ethnic group or region), have left their mark on the distribution of roles and financial power in the family. Nevertheless, there are also some general trends, and we looked at these within the framework of our longitudinal Russia-UK joint project. Our in-depth gender research focused first and foremost on poor Russian families, looking at specific features of the ways that family roles work and families are managed, and at the distribution of financial power and responsibility. In addition, the research group set itself the special objective of clarifying the issue of inequality in dependency and deprivation within the family, as experienced by husband and wife, and the differences that exist between the ways that men and women experience poverty and survival (depending on their differing everyday situation and type of family). In the UK, the Joseph Rowntree Foundation has successfully engaged in the study of gender differences from this viewpoint over a number of years (Goode, *et al.*, 1998).

Our analysis is based on data from both the longitudinal panel survey of 105 poor households and on methodologically related in-depth gender-based interviews. For these, we selected families of various types from the 105 households taking part in the main survey (in this instance, 'families of various types' refers to the socio-demographic structure of the household – size, generational profile, marital status of family members, whether the family has children, etc.). The essential condition was the presence of a couple in the family – a husband and wife who could be interviewed separately. Participation in in-depth interviews was voluntary and was additional to the main survey interviews. In total, we interviewed 20 couples (three couples without children, four with grown-up children and 13 with between one and six children under 18) and two women from families with children under 18, whose husbands it proved impossible to interview for various reasons. Thus, 42 interviews were obtained from 22 households, tape-recorded and conducted in an open, non-pre-coded form; respondents were interviewed in their own homes. The length of an open, tape-recorded interview was between 40 minutes and one hour.

It is essential to add that one vital aspect of selecting families for gender-based interviews involved examining the issues from an ethnic perspective. We tried to take into account the critical comments that are often made of gender research with a monoethnic sample (Graham, 1992), and so we broadened the ethnic base of our in-depth interviews by including five Ossetian households and one Jewish household among the 22 surveyed.

We wanted to compare our data with the Russian picture as a whole, so we also analysed the results of a pan-Russian research project 'Women in the new Russia: who are they? How do they live? What are they looking for?', which was carried out in January 2002 by the Institute for Multidisciplinary Social Studies of the Russian Academy of Sciences. This research (headed by N.E. Tikhonova) took a sample of 1,400 women aged 17-50, representative for Russia in that it used proportional representation of women from different regions of the country and types of community (from villages to megalopolises).

Some Results from the Longitudinal Panel Survey of 105 Poor Households in Moscow, Voronezh and Vladikavkaz and from the Pan-Russian Representative Survey

The results of a great deal of recent research (and ours was no exception here) provide evidence that the burden of the consequences of Russia's reforms of the 1990s has fallen most heavily on the shoulders of women.

This is shown by – among other things – the predominance of female unemployment, women's limited access to the main institutions of integration (a good job, good-quality education, control, power) and the increasing dependency of families on the woman, when, in the face of a declining standard of living, responsibility for raising the next generation falls completely to her (Coudouel, *et al.*, 1999; Gorshkov and Tikhonova, 2002). Moreover, Russian women's ability to choose between employment in the economy and working in the home is significantly restricted by their standard of living and the income needs of their families. In the absence of any real system of social support for the family, the majority of Russian households with children simply cannot survive without women's wages. In recent years, many Russian households have seen shifts in the traditional models of distribution of responsibility and authority in the family, connected, in particular, with the function of main breadwinner being fulfilled by women. This has been a trend since the early 1990s, and it relates to the structural crisis in the economy, which has led to a growth in both open and hidden unemployment and to the exacerbation of employment problems for a significant proportion of the Russian population. In these conditions, intensification of women's economic activity can partially compensate for difficulties with a husband's job, usually connected with the impact of economic crisis on industrial production.

So, according to the longitudinal panel survey data, in 1990 the function of breadwinner had been – in one way or another – fulfilled by a woman in only a third of the 105 households under study (that is, her wages were higher than the man's at the time, or else she was the only person in the family who was working). However, by the year 2000, this function had shifted to practically half the women in the same households. What is more, this trend was evident among the Russian population in all the regions of our survey, and it was only among the ethnic Ossetians who took part that it was appreciably weaker.

It is obvious that, in the conditions created by an unstable economic situation, the possibilities for females to take on the role of breadwinner come closer to those open to male breadwinners: the traditional model has been replaced by an egalitarian one, presupposing women's more active participation in the material security of the family. It is difficult to say how far such a choice by Russian women has been either voluntary or effective: given the fact that our investigation looked at poor families, it could be hypothesised that, in a number of them, this kind of substitution serves as an indicator not of improved position but of the reverse – a fall in standard of living has required the woman to make active efforts to maintain it.

Indeed, this hypothesis is favoured by the fact that, in the pan-Russian survey, the main breadwinners in 24 per cent of poor couples (those families with an income of less than half the median income for their region) were women. In better-off groups, only in 17 per cent of cases was the woman's contribution to the family budget larger than that of all other family members. However, in one family in four, the woman's contribution was the same as that of her spouse, and this proportion applied in practically all income groups.

Our data on the topic of women's contribution to the family budget provide evidence that up to half of Russian women of working age consider their contribution to the family budget to be – at least – no less than their husband's contribution. Yet this result is somewhat paradoxical since, in fact, the view is usually taken that a family's level of welfare depends as a rule on the husband's wages. It may be that the Russian women's responses indicate that, in many families (and this was clearly the case, for example, even in the very poor families on our panel of 105 poor households), men spend a disproportionately large part of their money on themselves personally (cigarettes, beer, etc.) and that what they put into the family budget is comparable to – or even less than – the woman's contribution. Although this problem requires further research and clarification, it is certainly reasonable to assert that the traditional gender distribution of functions in the family is undergoing serious change in Russian society today.

At the same time, these changes do not always entail re-examination of existing stereotyped views of what being 'the head of the family' actually means. Over 90 per cent of the respondents whom we interviewed in the course of our household panel study were able to name one family member as head of their household. However, in defining the head of the family, they were guided by not one, but at least three, approaches: the traditional (patriarchal) approach, where the oldest member of the family (as a rule, a man) was designated as its head; the economic approach, where the head of the family was its main breadwinner and/or the person who controlled the family budget (in this case, the family might be headed by either a man or a woman); or the egalitarian (equal) approach, where the family did not clearly identify a head (Davidova, 2000). According to data from the pan-Russian survey, 49 per cent of women selected the egalitarian approach as the ideal model for distribution of power in the family. Support for the other models was: patriarchal – 15 per cent, economic – 34 per cent.

The picture obtained from the results of the longitudinal panel survey was as follows. Of the 105 households in need, some were 'male' (headed and/or managed by a man), others were 'female' (headed and/or managed by a woman), with 55 household respondents of both sexes naming men as heads of household, 41 respondents of both sexes naming women and the other nine unable to single out one member as head of household (we referred to these as 'equal' households). However, the ratio of 'male' to 'female' households varied markedly between our different research regions. Moscow households were equally likely to be headed by a man or a woman. A particular feature of the Voronezh sub-sample was the preponderance of 'female' households, while in Vladikavkaz, in contrast, 'male' households predominated. Moreover, we encountered cases where the family member singled out as head was neither the breadwinner nor the person managing the family budget. That is, even when all the functions of head of the family were really being fulfilled by the woman, this role was not acknowledged, either by her husband or by the wife herself. The approximate ratio of 'male' to 'female' households was: Moscow 1:1; Voronezh 1:2; Vladikavkaz (Russian) 2:1; Vladikavkaz (Ossetian) 3:1.

In larger than average families (more than four people), the man was more often head of the family. At the same time, younger and smaller families were significantly more frequently headed and managed by women. Types of families where the head was a woman were fairly varied – they included lone-parent families, separated and single women, young couples, pensioner couples and families with and without children. However, the greatest likelihood that a two-parent family would be headed by a woman was where there were no children under 18. In contrast, where there was a husband/father living in a family with children, he was overwhelmingly more often designated by respondents of both sexes as head of household: only six two-parent households with children, out of 43 taking part in the survey, singled out the woman as head.

However, it should be noted that the main earner/breadwinner was designated by respondents as head of the family in only 60 per cent of cases: for example, in one out of five households with children under 18 where a man was head of the household, he was not the main breadwinner, having ceded that function to the woman. As far as making decisions about everyday budgeting was concerned, in the overwhelming majority of cases, this right (and often the additional duties that went with it) fell on the shoulders of the woman, even if she was not the acknowledged head of the family. In practice, only a third of men recognised as heads of families took part in the practical, everyday running of the home and the day-to-day planning of smaller family expenditure. Thus, the subjectively defined head of a Russian household was not automatically the person who made the main contribution to the family budget or carried responsibility for management within the family.

So, following in the footsteps of specialists in the area of gender research, we set out to investigate more carefully, to 'open the black box' and look at the distribution of duties and responsibilities within the family – an issue still insufficiently studied in Russia. We undertook supplementary in-depth interviews with couples, in order to look at everyday life within the family not just from the position of one family member, but from male and female perspectives separately.

In-depth Gender Investigation of 22 Poor Households in Moscow, Voronezh and Vladikavkaz

Our in-depth interviews with couples confirmed the thesis mentioned above – that each individual family has its own complex gender distribution of functions (and its own fixed view of it), and that it is this as a whole which also defines the model of relations between spouses, as far as distribution of power and responsibility within the household is concerned. However, there are some principal kinds of interrelations between the definition of who is the main breadwinner and the model of distribution/managing financial resources in the family.

Our summarised classification of patterns of domination in the household was broadly based on Goode *et al.*'s proposed classification of distribution patterns of the primary functions within the household (1998), as well as the one first constructed by Pahl (1989) when she classified patterns of management/control over strategic decision-making. According to this, the 22 families we investigated can be divided into three groups.

1. The egalitarian group consisted of eight couples who took joint financial responsibility for their families: this was reflected in the models of strategic control and everyday management used in these households. In such families, 'everything's done by agreement, there's no kind of strict husband/wife division ...' (Aleksandr, Moscow). This is how the situation was described by respondents from families that fitted the egalitarian pattern of ensuring and distributing financial control in the household:

> I think that, as far as earning money nowadays goes, in my opinion, you can't say that the man or the woman is the person who should be earning. In these circumstances, the person who does it is the person who can best do it, the one

with the best opportunity to do it (Larisa, from an Ossetian family with a lot of children, Vladikavkaz).

We often take financial decisions together. Well, the money's all in one pot. Even if it's physically in my pocket and I've earned it – that still means it's in the one pot (Georgii, from a Russian family with a lot of children, Vladikavkaz).

Nevertheless, it was in this group that we noted a distinct feature of the women's economic activity. In half the cases, they were not the associate but the main breadwinner: husbands in these families either were not working or were experiencing difficulties with their permanent jobs. Furthermore, in all the egalitarian households, the woman's contribution to the family budget was no less than that of the man. By comparison with the other family patterns, it was more often the wife who exercised sole strategic control over the financial resources and/or main prospects of the household. However, we also found some cases of independent financial management, where the husband and wife kept their financial resources separate, each taking responsibility for their own portion of the family's total expenditure. Overall, according to our research data, the woman was the breadwinner, controller and overall manager of the family budget in four out of the eight egalitarian households, while in the other half, her authority to carry out all or some of these functions was shared with the man ('equality').

This is how women heading two-parent families typically described their situation:

I'm the main breadwinner in the family, because at the moment I'm working and getting industrial injury benefit.[3] That means I contribute more money to the budget than my husband, who has a disability pension – so I'm the person who has to solve all the financial problems, too. I'd say that, in the experience of people I know, where the husband earns more than the wife, the main decisions are taken by the man (Rimma, from a Russian family with no children, Voronezh).

2. The traditional group consisted of 10 couples where the woman took primary responsibility for running the home, for everyday management and – in rare cases – for strategic management, but did not carry out the function of main breadwinner. Valentina from Moscow expressed the essence of this pattern as follows: 'in the family, the husband should provide for the material side of things, and the wife should take care of the

housekeeping'. The women in over half of these traditional families were not working: to be precise, in seven families out of the 10 (if we accept as justified the position taken by the two Ossetian families who did not view the wives' regular unregistered work, which they were forced to undertake as a result of the impoverished material situation of their families, as regular employment).

So-called 'pooling' – joint strategic and everyday decision-making in running the home and in managing the household funds and major spending – was a fairly widespread practice in this group of families. In regard to this, one of our Voronezh respondents said: 'I think the man should give the woman material freedom, provide for her materially. As for everything else – there's no kind of forced division, we do everything together'. Our interviews showed that in only three families out of the 10 was strategic control in the household exercised mainly by one of the spouses – in two cases this was the man and in one, the woman.

Here are some quotations from interviews with men who headed traditional families:

> Who's the head of our family? Well, of course, the head of the family is always the husband – so, it's me. I earn the money, I'm providing for the family, I'm the financial support. But the dominant role in the housekeeping belongs to the wife, she deals with more of that. In the sense of regulating things, of power in the home – of course, I don't especially display my power, although I might be the stronger one at certain times (Pyotr, from a Russian family with no children, Moscow).

> Ideally, the role of the husband is to earn money, and the role of the wife is to 'keep house' and carry out all the other family duties. My wife and I have never had any kind of disagreement about that distribution of labour. That's how we've always done things (Lev, from a Jewish family with children, Moscow).

> Of course, the wife shouldn't have to earn money, that's the husband's job, and hers is to organise everything around him, arrange things, decide where to make savings, plan ahead. I've always thought that the husband should be the earner and I've tried to keep to that rule all my life. But as far as budgeting for the family is concerned, I think that's the wife's duty (Vladimir, from a Russian pensioner family, Voronezh).

3. Finally, we identified a group of four distinctly male-dominated households, as far as decision-making, control over finances and

management within the family were concerned. This was less typical,[4] but was undoubtedly traditional in its basic pattern of distributing power and duties in the family. The husbands in this group frequently exercised not only strategic but also everyday control over the household's main expenditure, while the wives were alienated from material resources and carried out only housekeeping functions. Usually this situation of male dominance was manifest in families with young children where the woman had no work outside the home and was completely dependent. Vladimir from Voronezh stated this explicitly: 'I am generally in charge at home, but that means I'm in charge of myself, and you – the wife and children – are in my charge'. Two of the instances of male dominance involved fairly prosperous families, whose members had consciously organised this disposition of labour and responsibility:

> That's how we've arranged things. Because I've been at home, not going out to work, I haven't had any earnings of my own – that is, I couldn't bring anything into the house – so, naturally all the money has been my husband's. I've been getting some money for the kid – you know, to buy fruit and small things like that. I've never thought of it as any kind of infringement of my rights, because I've never had any problems with buying food, he has brought everything home. And generally I think that the money in a family should belong to the man. For a man to have no money is just nonsense (Tat'yana, from a Russian family with children, Moscow).

However, in the two other cases, male dominance of the family meant humiliation and increasing deprivation for the woman, as her interests were ignored:

> When the man is the main breadwinner (like my husband), he runs everything himself, no one else is allowed to. And he still goes on at the woman because she isn't earning. He calls her strictly to account if she spends anything at all. Of course, that's the way some are. Not often. In fact, among the people I know, there's only one other family like that now. Everything depends to a large extent on the husband's nature, and mine, for example, has to have the woman feeling dependent (Vera, from a Russian family with children, Moscow).

Thus, our interviews with couples revealed that the most widespread situation was where the head of the family, who fulfilled the primary functions of breadwinner, was the man, but everyday budgeting decisions were taken by the woman. On that level, our sample reflected the pan-

Russian picture, described above, fairly accurately. At the same time, as a rule, the man took at least an equal part in deciding strategic issues. Other obligations were more often distributed according to the principle that the man's business was to provide for the family materially and the woman's to deal with the housekeeping and the children (caring for children and for the home fell entirely to the woman in 17 out of our 22 couples). Svetlana, from Voronezh, said her husband put it as follows: 'this is your duty: when you earn as much as I do, then the household duties and the housekeeping can be shared out differently'. As a rule, the men – and, indeed, the women – had no particular doubts that these functions in the family were primarily 'female':

> The woman can cope with all this better, simply because she deals with it more. I am more removed from it all. Before, when she was working, I did some of it, too – I could go out to the shops, pay the rent on the flat. But, since she's been at home with the children, she simply has more time for it (Lev, from a Jewish family with children, Moscow).

> My wife answers to me for all that. I've never even bought myself so much as a handkerchief. I get what I need without any discussion – what I say, goes (Vladimir, from a Russian family without children, Vladikavkaz).

However, where the family budget was insufficient, the wives' active everyday management of the family (running the home and housekeeping, bringing up the children, providing the family with the most necessary items, etc.) frequently meant not additional power, but an additional burden being shifted onto the women's shoulders: the men obviously tried to avoid carrying out these 'tasks that are not for them' (Vladimir, Voronezh):

> I'm almost certainly the one who has a better idea of where and what to buy, because my husband doesn't go around the shops: he really doesn't like doing it. If he does venture out to buy something, then it's the first thing he sees, and then only so that he can get shot of a duty that has to be done. So, it's mainly me who takes that kind of decision. Nevertheless, you know, given that he is the one earning more, I have to say that without him we wouldn't be buying anything (Marina, from a Russian family with children, Vladikavkaz).

> I always tell him, of course: I've been to such-and-such, I've spent so-and-so. But he's more or less indifferent, he doesn't go into it carefully, and he doesn't remember anything. He knows these functions fall to me, and that suits him completely (Valentina, from a Russian family with children, Moscow).

You mean our everyday affairs? I think the woman copes better with those, because she has more experience. It's her fate to think from morning till night about how and where to economise, how, where, on what ... It's just easier for the husband if the wife takes on more cares and responsibilities – fewer headaches for him (Svetlana, from a Russian family with children, Voronezh).

Of course, I'm more capable of visualising all the problems the family might be faced with. Somehow my husband goes into it less. If you tell him he has to do something – he does it, but he hardly ever takes a decision or notices anything on his own. It's only recently, when I've been ill, that he's found out how much things cost or how much rent we pay. Life forced him to. When I was in hospital, he had to decide and do a lot of things for himself. He was even scared at first. Since then, he hasn't asked me nearly so often where all the money goes ... before that, he couldn't really conceive of it much at all (Mariya, from a Russian pensioner family, Voronezh).

Gender Conflicts

We noted that the views of men and women as to how roles and functions, power and responsibility should be distributed in the family did not always coincide. In most cases, men and women had the same preferences for the ideal roles for a man and a woman in earning money, running the home, tackling family problems, and ideas about which family member has the clearest picture of the whole range of these problems, who – husband or wife – makes fewer mistakes or is better at putting particular ones right, and so on. But there were some cases where they differed fairly significantly.

Table 6.13 Views of the ideal model for distributing management functions within the family, 22 households surveyed (number of persons)

Ideal model for distributing roles and functions within the family	*Women*	*Men*
Egalitarian	8	4
Traditional	11	13
Male dominance	3	3
TOTAL	22	20

As we can see, the predominant ideal for men was a traditional distribution of roles in the family (and this was even more frequently the case in Vladikavkaz, both among Ossetians and among Russians living in Ossetia).

Women, while not rejecting the traditional disposition of labour, were inclined towards the egalitarian model more often than men. In the opinion of Irina, from Moscow: 'the egalitarian model is, generally speaking, the ideal, since everything seems to be tending towards both spouses having to earn money for the family'. Sixteen out of the 22 women surveyed thought that the woman should work, with nine of those interviewed declaring that she should provide for the family's basic needs equally with the man and seven saying that she should work hours that would allow her to do the housework and look after the children. Male opinion on this was more conservative: half the men surveyed would prefer their wives not to work, taking the view that the woman should not work at all:

> In principle, if the economy made the progress that it should, or even started to pick up a bit, with factories and industry back on their feet, then it should be enough for the husband to work and the wife to take care of the house and the children. That would suit me best (Sergei, from a Russian family with children, Moscow).

> It's better when the wife doesn't work. The home is better kept. The children's education goes better. She looks after them – sees them off and meets them. It's not that it's more in keeping with our traditions. It's just that I know it means the children and I are being looked after, their lessons are being done on time and they're being fed at the right times. They're under control constantly. Stay at home and bring up the children – I don't need any more than that (Khazbi, from an Ossetian family with a lot of children, Vladikavkaz).

Others admitted the possibility of the woman being employed outside the home, but would prefer her to work part-time, leaving enough time for the home and children:

> Yes, it's better when the wife doesn't work. Or, if she works, then it should be the kind of work that gives her some moral independence. Even though she might not have material independence, then she should gain some moral independence from the fact that she is doing something useful and interesting. The ideal model is when the woman works a bit. What's more, she shouldn't be working because the family needs the money, but for moral reasons, to fulfil herself (Vladimir, O., from a Russian family with grown-up children, Vladikavkaz).

The best thing for the woman is to do some part-time work, just mornings, say, so that she feels needed and gets out into society, but it leaves her with enough time for the home. It's not her responsibility to bring money into the house (Vladimir, M., from a Russian family with children, Vladikavkaz).

Comparison of our respondents' ideal views with their real family situation showed that they more often coincided for men than for women. Thus, the ideal and real pictures of how power, authority and responsibility in the family should be distributed coincided for 15 out of 20 men in the survey and for only nine out of 22 women. What, then, in the women's opinion, was the nature of this lack of coincidence between ideal expectations and real life? As the quotations below show, it was very varied; also, it rarely meant that the woman was discontented with a difficult situation solely because her rights to take decisions about the administration of all the family's money were being infringed.[5] Often, it was the reverse – she would have liked less responsibility and a lighter burden in terms of her need to earn money, and it was that which made her discontented with the real situation. Sometimes the fact that it was impossible for the husband to fulfil the function of breadwinner also led to more serious family problems, even making it impossible for them to be legally married:

If you take into account that for a woman the home and children always come first, she should have to work less. I wouldn't say that I would like to sit at home all the time – of course not, I would like to work, earn a wage and feel financially stable. But ideally, of course, it would be better for my husband to earn more than at present. At the moment, I'm earning more than him (Svetlana, from a Russian family with children, Voronezh).

That's why I'm not getting married at the moment, in the sense that we're not officially registering our marriage. Igor thinks he should be bringing money into the home, and that I shouldn't work. Well, that's him ... a real man. So I know that if I marry him, I won't be working at the school any more, because he's against it. He thinks the man should earn the money and the woman should stay at home, that it's her duty, otherwise it's not a real family. He said to me straightaway – 'while I'm not earning any money, we won't be able to set up a real family'. And I'm already not far off forty ... (Tat'yana, from a Russian household without children, Vladikavkaz).

In contrast to having to earn outside the home, the woman's management duties inside the home – even though they also meant an additional burden for her – raised practically no protest from female respondents. This might have been connected with the fact that the majority of women were sure that it was they who were better than other family members at picturing the whole range of family problems, that they coped much better with forward planning of the family budget and made far fewer mistakes in taking decisions on one issue or another. Fifteen out of 22 of the wives surveyed were inclined towards this opinion, but only eight out of 20 of the husbands.

> My husband more often makes mistakes. I always say to him: 'You weren't listening to me – look, you've done the wrong thing again'. And he laughs. He's a typical man – Ossetian men think it's a good thing to be the head, that's what he wants. And I say to him: 'It's not a matter of you being the man or the one in charge. It's a case of me getting things done somehow, and you – never' (Larisa, from an Ossetian family with a lot of children, Vladikavkaz).

> In every case, the woman will think about what she needs to feed her children and her husband, so she's less prompted by the thought 'perhaps we'll get by'. It's just that she makes fewer risky purchases – so she makes fewer mistakes than a man (Marina, from a Russian family with children, Vladikavkaz).

> Among the families I know, anyway, it's more often the men who make mistakes, because they put the family at more financial risk. The women are more pragmatic, they have to deal with the more down-to-earth things, organising everyday life. And so you try to make fewer mistakes, because your mistake will affect literally all members of the family (Ol'ga, from a Russian family without children, Vladikavkaz).

Lack of coincidence between views about real and ideal models of management and control within the family, including the problem of the family's material security, could in the end lead to conflicts along gender lines. According to our survey data, such conflicts existed in one form or another in fully half the families we surveyed; moreover, as a rule, they were initiated by women, who were less content with this aspect of life. Conflicts within the family – reflecting the distinctive internal struggle between spouses for the right to more access to control over the budget and over the family's chief prospects – were found in households in all the regions and all the ethnic subgroups investigated.[6]

Gender and Deprivation

Yet another contradiction, which leaves its stamp on the psychological microclimate in the family and provides objective evidence of a tendency towards inequality of rights within the family, was divergence in the degree of deprivation experienced by the husband and by the wife in poor households. (Jan Pahl (1989), was one of the first people to draw attention to this.) The main point here was the fact that neither material resources (including money) nor lack of material resources was distributed in the same way to all members of the family. Although both spouses said that the children's needs were the unquestionable priority for collective expenditure, it was women who were more often inclined to limit their own consumption in order to meet the needs of other family members.

Like others, we found that that even when the woman took everyday decisions independently – about what to buy with the money she has, and for whom – this did not in any way protect her from personal deprivation (Snape and Molloy, 2000). Her duty to make sure 'we've got everything in the house' often led to the woman going without the most essential items.

> I'd like to buy something for myself there and then – shoes or something to wear, but the first thing you think is: 'I can manage without it, but I must buy this for my daughter', 'I can make do, but my husband needs that', because I'm at home more, and they have to go out to different places. But for the sake of the children, I very often go without something myself – that's the way things have gone. I do get upset about it, but not very. I would be more upset if I couldn't buy something for my daughter or for my husband than for myself. I can wait (Valentina, from a Russian family with grown-up children, Moscow).

> Yes, I go without things myself. I buy almost nothing for myself, for my children's sake. I think it's better to buy things for my husband; after all, he goes out to work (Larisa, from an Ossetian family with a lot of children, Vladikavkaz).

Nevertheless, although this phenomenon of unequal distribution of deprivation within the family is undoubtedly widespread, it was not predominant. The results of our in-depth interviews with 22 poor households in Moscow, Voronezh and Vladikavkaz revealed only eight instances of families where the wife experienced greater deprivation than the husband and other family members. At the same time, however there were only two families in difficult material circumstances where the husband was voluntarily undergoing greater deprivation than the wife, which provided evidence that women are much more ready to go to such lengths than men.

This greater deprivation of wives by comparison with husbands and other family members, their greater burden within the family and the enforced neglect of some of their significant needs all left a noticeable stamp on the psychological state of the women we interviewed, which was remarked on both by the women themselves and by their husbands:

> Seeing the problems, well – my husband *sees* them, of course, but I've got more experience of them, like all women. Of course, he can't see all the problems by any means, he doesn't see some of the small things – he doesn't know or doesn't notice (Zoya, from a Russian family with children, Voronezh).

> Well, on the financial level – I'm usually the one who decides. But my wife takes the greater weight of emotional problems on herself: she worries (Vladimir, from a Russian family with children, Vladikavkaz).

In this regard, it should be noted that the psychological state of the women we surveyed was generally fairly poor – as a rule, significantly poorer than that of the men. Moreover, women from those families that had high scores on the Social Exclusion Index were in an especially bad psychological state: during the interview, they were likely to complain about things that were not mentioned by women who were living at the same level of material welfare but had better scores on the Social Exclusion Index. So, for example, references began to appear to the fact that prolonged absence of money for even the most essential items was having an effect on their psychological state, that restricting themselves meant not just going without a particular activity or purchase, but *never* meeting certain specific needs. They even said that the necessity of sacrificing their interests to the interests of their family made them feel they were no longer women:

> When you're in such a long-drawn-out crisis, of course, your nerves just go (Vera, from a Russian family with children, Moscow: 17 points on the Social Exclusion Index).

> I've never had anything, no nice clothes, no make-up. If there's any money at all in the family, I can't ever use it to buy anything for myself, I don't have the right. I just wear whatever people give me ... Of course, I get terribly upset that I can't afford anything for myself. You know, you just stop feeling like a woman, and so you're constantly upset inside ... It's not that I'm going without something specific, but all kinds of things I need. I have to, because there isn't

enough money for the children (Anna, from a Russian family with a lot of children, Moscow: 19 points on the Social Exclusion Index).

From the responses of the couples with children to our question about whether they personally have to go without anything in the interests of the family, and why, and for whose sake they do so, we were left with the impression that, when the family is experiencing material difficulties, the woman mostly prefers 'taking the knocks' herself, while the man would rather spread the deprivation equally across the family. (Although it should be said that in our sample there were practically no cases where the man was trying to further his own interests to the detriment of the family.) Women's readiness to be the ones who mostly went without, added to their already larger burden of everyday management and running the home (far from a simple thing in itself nowadays in Russia, especially where the family is in need), markedly exacerbated their deprivation, leading to gendered inequality in the burden of poverty (Goode *et al.*, 1998). Moreover – and this must be particularly emphasised – in the overwhelming majority of cases, this inequality in the burden of poverty was taken on voluntarily by women. This was not just an individual sacrifice, arising out of love for her nearest and dearest, but also the manifestation of an internalised social norm, whereby, in all circumstances, a woman must forgo her own interests for the sake of those of her family and children:

> I'm sure I'm not the only one who has to go without things; any woman in a family with as little money as we have – where the same thing has happened after all these reforms – goes without a lot, in order to provide for her husband and children (Anna, from a Russian family with a lot of children, Moscow).

> It's somehow naturally simpler for me to hide my own needs or restrict myself in some way, but allow myself to buy something for the child. I have restricted myself like this, no-one has put any pressure on me (Tat'yana, from a Russian family with a child, Moscow).

> Yes, I go without literally everything, because I've just got one goal – to make my child really literate, to educate her, and, of course, it's mainly me who makes the most sacrifices for the sake of that. You know, if I go without something, then in principle I just look at my goal in doing so and that makes me happy. I compensate for this self-denial in some other way: if I've bought my child some good sheet music, I don't feel too unhappy that I have gone

without something (clothes, for example), because I'm buying my daughter a non-material life (Vera, from a Russian family with children, Moscow).

Thus, although the serious psychological state of women from poor families could, in many cases, certainly be explained by gender inequality in the distribution of the burden of poverty, this inequality in itself did not lead women to protest, since they had assimilated certain socio-cultural models of gender behaviour: Russian women from poor families perceived the woman's greater deprivation as a self-evident and natural fact.

It should also be said that, as a rule, women ascribed their lack of access to a 'good' job to the fact that, in conditions of an insufficient and weakly effective system of social support for the family,[7] they put their children's interests first. This could have a decisive effect on the family's material circumstances: for some families, it led to a slide into the 'black hole' of profound social exclusion, which in its turn had a very serious psychological effect on them, especially when they found it impossible to provide the children with all the essentials. Thus, a kind of 'closed circle' has come into being: children – impossibility of getting a steady job with an adequate wage that is actually paid regularly – poverty – impossibility of giving the children everything they need – constant serious psychological stress and health problems – further reduction in the chances of getting a good job. Despite its distinctly gendered nature, women themselves did not connect this cycle with labour market discrimination against them. Indeed, the 'children element' of lack of access to a good job took on very different guises for different women. Some were not prepared to give up looking after their child for the sake of a low-paid job, others, with young children, found it impossible to find a good job because they might have to take a lot of sick leave, while others again had a disabled or sick child who needed constant care:

> It's hard to say whether it's because of our sex that I and other women I know are not working – recently, in many ways, it's become more comfortable not to work, to spend more time looking after the children and the home. And then, what would you be working for? You might say a worthwhile job, for example, but of course there aren't any. It's a matter of waiting – so it's better to devote the time to the children; there's such a lot of crime now, you really have to take them to school ... It's hard to find a highly paid, good job now, regardless of whether you're a man or a woman. I know there are some very active women ... but it's rare nowadays for an employer to give a woman sick leave (Irina, from a Jewish family with children, Moscow).

I've always worked, all my life, apart from the last two years, but that is mainly because my son has been ill ... My business is the children and their school – making sure they get there, meeting them, getting their lessons done. But now I'm busy with my youngest son; he doesn't go to school because he's ill (Anna, from a Russian family with a lot of children, Moscow).

In a number of cases, going out to work in the kind of job available to them actually led to growing deprivation for the women concerned – since new forms of discrimination had arisen – and possibly even to increased social exclusion, but not to improvement in the position of the woman and the family as a whole:

For a woman with children on her hands to find a job nowadays is very difficult. I've already been taking work anywhere, just to get money to keep my child: so, even though I've got higher education, I was doing a manual job ... Of course, if you are talking about what I came up against in the workplace – of course, arbitrariness, crudity, mayhem, because it's a milieu where you find mainly the lowest strata of the working class. And since our enterprise was fairly profitable – a bread-making plant – then, of course, something shocking happened literally every day and literally to everyone. That applied to the wages and to the working hours – it was completely and absolutely arbitrary. For a woman with a child and that kind of job as well, where you simply stop respecting yourself as a person, naturally, it even affects your personal life ... Your personal life as such is reduced to a minimum – just your circle of friends, keeping in touch either on the phone or perhaps seeing them once a month. The only thing I've never gone without is reading real literature. Generally, I think that's become the special leisure pursuit of the poor (laughs), because nowadays the theatre is closed to people who can't afford it; the cinema – well, I've never been especially fascinated by it; and going on holiday, or going away somewhere for a break – in the past, I could afford to go to the south with my child for a holiday, but now the most I can afford is to go to our friends' dacha (laughs). That's the way it is (Tat'yana, from a Russian family with a child, Moscow; a typical member of the 'new poor').

It was not surprising, in such circumstances, that the majority of families preferred the model where the man provided for the family – however badly – while the woman looked after the children and the home, working 'whenever possible'. However, there were also situations where a lone woman found it easier to cope with the family's difficulties than when there was a man in the family, even though these cases meant that gender inequality was replaced by the burden of poverty being transferred totally onto the shoulders of the woman. These quotations from interviews with our respondents throw some light on the specific features of such situations:

> There are families where the fathers drink. In a family like that, all the problems naturally fall on the mother's shoulders. I know families where the men are adults, even aged about 50, and they are using drugs, injecting. What kind of family decisions can someone like that take? He's got kids, but he's selling something on the sly and living that way. He needs a good kick. What good is he to his wife? He's already nothing to his family, he's doing them nothing but harm, he's not bringing anything in. The children and the mother are really forced to go extremes. I know two families like that, where they've simply thrown their own fathers out (Kazbek, from an Ossetian family with children, Vladikavkaz).

> Women cope better with all today's problems. True, it still depends on the kind of man. It can be the case that the woman not only does everything, but also earns more than the man. Men nowadays often don't want to earn, or to work at all – they just drink. I know some cases where men – husbands of my friends – have been dismissed for drunkenness. Women now have more responsibility for the family (Mariya, from a Russian pensioner family, Voronezh).

Conclusion

In summing up, it is fair to state that the reforms of the 1990s have had an ambiguous effect on the situation in Russian families, riddled with internal contradictions. On the one hand, they have led to the mass impoverishment of the population, increasing the burden on women and raising levels of real social discrimination against them, yet on the other hand, they have acted as a kind of 'starter mechanism' for new, very complex processes at the micro level, whereby roles and power within the family have been redistributed in favour of women. In addition, recent research – including our own – has recorded a feminisation of poverty in Russia: that is, a growth in the number of poor households headed by women. (Although this is to some extent the outcome of a general growth in the proportion of families in Russia headed by women.) Of course, this conclusion requires further verification, and so it is as yet impossible to say whether this is a situational response to the structural crisis in the economy, which has primarily affected the 'male' professions, or whether it is a lasting trend.

Nevertheless, it is indisputable that the reforms which started in Russia during the 1990s have markedly altered the country's previous situation: in particular, economic restructuring has led to the emergence of a large body of unemployed men. This is largely new for Russian society (at least, as a mass phenomenon), since under the Soviet regime it was – at least in principle – impossible for men not to work. In addition, the growth in the number of families headed by women is an expression of the fact that men's health is deteriorating more quickly: there is a corresponding increase in disability, as well as a marked growth in alcoholism and drug addiction, among men. Another, though smaller, factor contributing to change in the distribution of power and duties within the family and to increasing social differentiation in the population, is the dependent attitude that these conditions seem to engender in some men, who attempt to improve their position through an 'advantageous marriage', so that the woman is much more likely to occupy a dominant position in the family hierarchy than in the past.

In conclusion, given both the importance and the ambiguity of the process of change in the distribution of duties and power within the family taking place in Russia today, we will simply quote three extracts from our interviews, illustrating our respondents' perceptions of these complex processes:

Now the situation is more often different – reversed, in fact. The man isn't working, the woman is working, and so there are conflicts: 'you go to work', 'when you bring something in, I'll feed you', 'we've got nothing', and so on. Then people start fighting, they even get as far as separating. I know a family where that situation has led to separation (Pyotr, from a Russian family without children, Moscow).

Nowadays men look for a woman in order to find the best way to net her and set sail again ... It's no good expecting men nowadays to take their problems on themselves (or even some of them) ... Disorder around them no longer has any effect on men. So they have to be looked after, and in any awkward situations they become flabby; they can even go so far as to commit suicide because of a personal inferiority complex – you know, suicides happen more often among men (Tat'yana, from a Russian family with a child, Moscow).

It's important for me that the man should keep the family (and it's what I'd like for my daughter). It's been like that since time immemorial, with the man as breadwinner, since prehistoric times, probably that's the ideal of how it should be, although nowadays, in Russia, it's more the women who manage things, who are earning. I think patriarchy is being replaced by matriarchy (Vera, from a Russian family with children, Moscow).

Notes

1   Gospel according to St Matthew, 19: 24.

2   The method for calculating this index was proposed by A.B. Dzadziev. The index is calculated as the relationship of the proportion of an ethnic group in the population to the proportion of students from that group. If there were 'fair representation', the index would be equal to 1. We should also note that, the greater the competition among school-leavers to enter a particular higher education establishment or even a particular faculty, the lower the proportion of Russian entrants.

3   Payments for working in conditions detrimental to one's health.

4   The pan-Russian survey showed that the man handles all types of spending in only 4.5 per cent of Russian couples, while in 5.3 per cent of families there is no common family money and each spouse deals separately with what s/he earns. In 27.3 per cent of families, the woman handles all types of spending; in 28.2 per cent of families, the woman is responsible only for day-to-day expenditure, while big purchases are planned jointly; and in 33.0 per cent of families, the money is in general use and all expenses are planned jointly. Other patterns of responsibility (for example, the man responsible only for day-to-day expenditure, with big purchases planned jointly) figured in only 1.7 per cent of responses.

5   Further evidence of this is provided by the pan-Russian survey, where 87.1 per cent of the respondents who were legally married and 75.9 per cent of those in *de facto* marriages indicated that they were satisfied with the distribution of duties involved in administering all the money within their family. At the same time, 56.1 per cent and 46.4 per cent respectively viewed relationships in their family as 'good'.

6   In this connection, it is interesting to note that the pan-Russian survey recorded even more conflicts than we did in our sample of poor households – practically three-quarters of the married women in that survey noted that they had disagreements with their husbands. However, these were connected with financial problems in only 43.3 per cent of legal marriages and 33.9 per cent of *de facto* marriages; but in poor families (those with an income of less than half the median income for their region), the figure was 49.1 per cent – in other words, practically the same as the picture, outlined above, of the poor households in Moscow, Voronezh and Vladikavkaz where we carried out in-depth interviews.

7   There is insufficient State pre-school provision in Russia nowadays (although a fee-based, fairly expensive infrastructure has become established in this sphere), while social services to assist with housekeeping, which would allow a woman to escape some of the functions involved in caring for children and the home, are also underdeveloped. In addition, there is a covert practice among employers of refusing to grant a man childcare or sick dependant's leave: as a rule, a man going to his employer with a request for this may be sanctioned, even dismissed.

Appendix 1
Project Methodology

Nadia Davidova

Попытка не пытна, спрос не беда
Trying isn't torture, asking isn't misfortune

Subjects Studied

This project involved analysis of poverty and social exclusion in Russia on the basis of data from three methodologically linked pieces of research. Two were qualitative and in depth, while the third formed part of a long-term programme to monitor public opinion and the situation of Russians, conducted by the Russian Independent Institute for Social and National Problems using a pan-Russian representative sample.[1]

- The core of the project data was provided by the results of a panel study of 105 poor households from three Russian cities – Moscow, Voronezh and Vladikavkaz. The first stage of the *longitudinal panel survey* was conducted in November/December 1999, and the second, in November/December 2000. The survey was carried out in respondents' homes (and, in some cases, at the North Ossetian Research Institute for the Humanities and Social Sciences in Vladikavkaz), on the basis of a qualitative, partly pre-coded interview, lasting no less than two hours. At each stage of the research, the interviewers, who were the academic staff of the project research group, used a questionnaire with about 100 responses, of which no less than 20 per cent were open rather than pre-coded. However, even the closed questions were complex and flexible in structure, and always contained an open alternative. The sample and our approach to the panel survey are described in more detail below.
- In the light of the project's objectives, the research team decided to carry out *supplementary open interviews* with some of those taking part in the panel survey: members of 32 households from Moscow,

Voronezh and Vladikavkaz (10+10+12 respectively). Interviews were conducted with couples (husband and wife interviewed separately), with female heads of one-parent households and with young people aged 16-21 in the households concerned. In total, 58 supplementary interviews were tape-recorded in people's own homes, in a free form rather than pre-coded (17+15+26 interviews respectively by city, with 13 interviews in Russian households in Vladikavkaz and 13 in Ossetian). In total, we interviewed 20 couples (five in Moscow, five in Voronezh and ten in Vladikavkaz, of whom five were in Russian households and five in Ossetian), two women who were heads of one-parent households with children (one interview each in Moscow and Voronezh) and 18 young people (six in each city, with three Russian and three Ossetian in Vladikavkaz). Each open, tape-recorded interview took 30 to 40 minutes.

- *The pan-Russian representative survey* took place in October 2000, and included questions suggested by the academic staff of the 'Poverty and social exclusion in Russia' project. One of its aims was to clarify and add to ideas about trends in the socio-economic positions of poor households and how they adapt, as revealed in the course of our longitudinal qualitative study. It was further hoped that combining qualitative research with quantitative population measures might make it easier to draw generalised conclusions from the whole study.[2] In order to do this, the representative survey contained questions identical to some of those in our panel survey of poor households in Moscow, Voronezh and Vladikavkaz. The pan-Russian representative survey collected information about the composition, size, socio-demographic structure and incomes of respondents' families. Some idea of socio-economic differentiation within the population was obtained by applying two criteria – self-assessment of material situation and correlation of *per capita* income with the regional subsistence minimum. At the same time, attention was directed towards how the poorest section of Russia's population felt, and towards their perception of the reasons for the fall in their living standards and their degree of satisfaction with particular aspects of life. Representative data were also obtained on means of survival adopted by the Russian population and on specific aspects of how inter-family mutual aid networks function. The sample for the pan-Russian research consisted of 1,751 people, and true representativeness was guaranteed by forming the sample in accordance with the gender, age, socio-occupational, territorial/local and ethnic proportions of the general population, based on data from the Russian Federation's State Committee for Statistics.

Poor Households Panel Survey

Sample

Within the two stages of the longitudinal research, representatives of 105 poor households from three Russian cities – Moscow, Voronezh and Vladikavkaz – were interviewed (116 adult respondents, representing the households at various stages + 19 young people aged 16-21 from the same households). Twenty-eight households took part in the research in Moscow, 27 in Voronezh and 50 in Vladikavkaz (24 Russian households and 26 Ossetian). The regional, national and age boundaries of the sample were observed and corresponded with the project's stated objectives: to obtain a more accurate view of the essential nature of poverty in different regional, ethnic and socio-cultural communities, and also to analyse the issue of the reproduction of poverty in these communities.

A random sample was formed for the panel survey, using several methods:

- on the basis of information provided by the regional social protection services (the Centre for Housing Subsidies in Moscow, the District Social Security Services in Voronezh and the Centre for Social Assistance in North Ossetia). In total, 29 households (eight households in Moscow, six households in Voronezh and 15 households in Vladikavkaz) were included in the sample *on the basis of a formal assessment of need*. The research interviewers were able to familiarise themselves with lists of people registered with – or who had applied to – the organisations mentioned, to observe the client reception procedures used, and to select those respondents who most closely matched the survey profile;

- additional, *partly formalised ways of assessing need* were used: three households in Vladikavkaz were selected from among the families of university students who received supplements to their grants because they were badly off; four households in Voronezh were found on the database of the 'Sotsis' Sociological Centre, which provided the addresses of potential respondents, whose households – according to the results of a number of previous investigations into living standards – had an average *per capita* income at or below the regional subsistence minimum. Thus, a further seven households were included in the sample on the basis of these methods;

- *'snowball' sampling by informal expert assessment* of household level of need was also used. In this case, the 'experts' were the respondents themselves: at the interviewers' request, they provided information about neighbouring families who were in extreme material need. In total, 38 households (ten households in Moscow, eight households in Voronezh and 20 households in Vladikavkaz) were selected by this method;

- we also included in this research some households from Moscow and Voronezh, which had taken part in the investigation of groups affected by the labour market crisis, as part of the INTAS project 'Employment and social policy in Russia, 1995-1998' (headed by Nick Manning, and conducted by the same research group). Ten households from Moscow and nine households from Voronezh, which had taken part in the 1996 and 1997 surveys and been identified, according to its results, as poor, were brought into the 1999-2001 study. Thus, in total, 19 households were included through the longitudinal *repeat panel method*;

- since the repeat panel of households with members affected by the employment crisis did not extend to Vladikavkaz (which had not been involved in the 1995-1998 research on unemployment), it was decided to try and draw into the sample some households affected by employment problems. In the aim of *ensuring specific comparability* of the Vladikavkaz data, we wanted to include households that had applied to the relevant services for unemployment benefit and/or for supplementary material assistance because the family was badly off during a period of unemployment. The North Ossetian Republic's Employment Centre helped the research group to obtain data about unemployed people who had applied to or were registered with the Employment Service, regardless of whether they received unemployment benefit or needs additions or neither. Using the Employment Centre database, our research group in Vladikavkaz selected a further 12 households as most closely matching the conditions for the 1999-2000 survey.

Thus, 38 households were included in the sample on the basis of informal expert assessment of their level of need; information about another 48 households was provided by various services for the social support of people in need, by the Employment Centre and by other State and public organisations; in addition, 19 respondents (and some other members of their families) took part in the survey because they were, according to the results of the previous INTAS project in 1995-1998, in a high-risk group for falling into poverty. The use of several methods to form the panel was necessary in order to draw in various types of poor families, including those who – for various reasons – were not receiving any specialised social support on the basis of need.

The sample was randomised and did not represent the overall regional situation – but that was not one of the objectives of this qualitative, in-depth study of a specific social group. Nevertheless, in forming the sample, the research group consciously tried to observe particular socio-demographic proportions and to include different types of families in the survey, in terms of household structure both as it represents a particular risk of falling into poverty (the presence in the family of pensioners, disabled people, unemployed people; whether there are a lot of children, whether the children are being brought up by a lone parent, and so on) and as it corresponds to the typology of households applied by statistical bodies.

Bringing the most varied range of poor households into our longitudinal investigation offered us the opportunity to focus on the study of a situation in development, perhaps bringing us closer to an 'understanding of *why* events happen as they do, rather than simply accepting them at their face value' (Giddens 1993, p.676).[3] One of the project's main research hypotheses was that the real picture of poverty and social exclusion in the various regional, socio-cultural, national and ethnic communities in Russia might turn out to be broader than previously accepted conceptions (Neuman, 1991).[4] Therefore, the principles on which we constructed the sample and the qualitative methods used in our research were selected with a view to developing and modifying the initial hypotheses and to pinpointing new research issues as the research progressed.

Panel Preservation/Substitution

One of the chief methodological objectives during the longitudinal investigation was to maintain constant the composition of the household sample established at the first stage of the survey. Overall, despite the fact that six research units dropped out, the panel at the second stage was preserved (the lost households were not replaced). Reasons for households dropping out were: refusal to take part in the repeat survey (one household in Moscow), moving house (one Ossetian household in Vladikavkaz moved to the country and another one emigrated to Greece), and failure to contact the respondents for various reasons (one household in Voronezh and two Ossetian households in Vladikavkaz).

In addition, during the course of the longitudinal survey, we made 11 substitutions of respondents from the households under study. Most often, the spouses of first-stage respondents took part in the second stage of the survey – either because they themselves wanted to and were better informed about the current situation in the household (three cases in Moscow and one in Voronezh) or because it was impossible to interview the same family member (through illness or alcoholism – one case in Voronezh and two in Vladikavkaz). There was also one case of substitution of a respondent because of death (Moscow), two because of family breakdown (Moscow and Voronezh), and one because the family member who acted as respondent at the first stage had moved to the country (Voronezh). In total, five respondents in the Moscow sample were replaced during the year, four in the Voronezh sample and two in Vladikavkaz, although in all cases the same household was represented as at the first stage of the survey.

Some Demographic Characteristics of the Households Studied

Size of Households　The most common family size was four people: there were 31 such families in the study – practically a third. However, the size of households differed noticeably by region and, especially, by ethnicity. In Moscow and Voronezh, about a third of the households studied were small households of one or two people; in Vladikavkaz, however, there were dramatically fewer such households (only four Russian families). By contrast, the presence of large extended families of five or more people was more typical of Vladikavkaz (North Ossetia), and there was a significant proportion of large families in the Vladikavkaz sub-sample – 50 per cent of Ossetian and almost 40 per cent of Russian families (see Table A.1).

Ethnic Type of Households　Taking the stated objectives of the research as a starting-point, the sample was planned around the particular ethnic features of Vladikavkaz, where equal proportions of Ossetian and Russian families live side by side. However, in the other regions, too, both non-Russian and ethnically mixed households took part in the survey. Five Moscow households were not purely Russian in ethnic composition: three families were mixed, while two were of other nationalities (one Chechen and one Jewish). In Voronezh, there was one ethnically mixed family. In multinational North Ossetia, 12 out of 50 families were ethnically mixed. So, across the three research regions, the sample consisted of approximately 62 per cent Russian households, 20 per cent Ossetian households and 18 per cent ethnically mixed households/households of other nationalities.

Table A.1   Number   of   family   members   in   households   studied (persons)

Number of members of household	*Number of households*				
	Moscow	Voronezh	Vladikavkaz (Russians)	Vladikavkaz (Ossetians)	TOTAL *across whole research*
1	2	2	0	0	4
2	6	7	4	0	17
3	5	7	5	3	20
4	9	6	6	10	31
5	2	5	3	6	16
6	1	0	2	3	6
7	1	0	3	0	4
8	1	0	0	1	2
9	1	0	1	1	3
10	0	0	0	1	1
12	0	0	0	1	1
Total	28	27	24	26	105

Demographic Type of Households   Only one in four of the households studied did not include children under 18. Regional divergences were not very marked, since everywhere the proportion of families with children noticeably exceeded the proportion of families without children. Nevertheless, out of 50 Vladikavkaz households, 42 included children (something under 80 per cent of Russians and 90 per cent of Ossetians), while one in three Moscow and Voronezh households did not include any children under 18. In addition, Vladikavkaz households were more often multigenerational (a couple, their children under 18 and their older relations, all living together). Across the whole sample, a third of families with children were one-parent families (children were more often being brought up by women, but the sample also included a few lone fathers), and practically a fifth had a large number of children (we encountered a few cases of one-parent families with a lot of children). In the Voronezh sample and the Vladikavkaz Russian sub-sample, there were more one-parent families, while among Ossetians there were more likely to be large numbers of children. The demographic types of poor families taking part in the panel study were distributed as follows (see Table A.2).

Table A.2   Demographic types of households studied (number of households/per cent)

Family Types	Moscow	Voronezh	Vladikavkaz (Russian)	Vladikavkaz (Ossetian)	Total
Single pensioners	3 (11%)	2 (7%)	0	0	5 (5%)
Couples without children	1 (4%)	4 (15%)	1 (4%)	0	6 (6%)
Couples with children	10 (35%)	7 (27%)	3 (12%)	13 (50%)	33 (31%)
Multigenerational two-parent families *(couples with children and older relations)*	3 (11%)	2 (7%)	4 (17%)	4 (15%)	13 (12%)
One-parent families *(one parent bringing up children alone)*	3 (11%)	4 (15%)	4 (17%)	3 (12%)	14 (13%)
Multigenerational one-parent families *(one parent bringing up children and living with older relations)*	4 (14%)	5 (18%)	7 (29%)	4 (15%)	20 (20%)

Other family types	4	3	5	2	14
(single people, couples with adult children, etc.)	(14%)	(11%)	(21%)	(8%)	(13%)
TOTAL	28 100%	27 100%	24 100%	26 100%	105 100%

Heads of Household The overwhelming majority of households taking part in the research designated a head of household (members of only five households asserted that they were equal, and another four didn't know). The average age of heads of household was just under 50, but the age range varied from 90 (in Vladikavkaz) to 25 (in Voronezh). Overall, heads of household in Moscow and Vladikavkaz tended to be older (with an especially large number of households headed by pensioners in the Vladikavkaz Russian sub-sample), while in Voronezh, by contrast, the heads of respondent families were more likely to be in the economically active age groups.

It was equally probable that a Moscow household would be headed by either a man or a woman. However, a particular feature of the Voronezh sub-sample was the preponderance of female-headed households, while in Vladikavkaz, in contrast, male-headed households predominated. The approximate ratio of households headed by men and women was: Moscow 1:1; Voronezh 1:2; Vladikavkaz (Russian) 2:1; Vladikavkaz (Ossetian) 3:1.

The heads of Moscow households had the highest standard of education – half the heads of families had higher education, and another third had specialised secondary vocational education. The Vladikavkaz sample was also fairly well-educated – 70 per cent of households were headed by people with either higher or specialised secondary education; however, only a third of Vladikavkaz heads of household had higher education. The Voronezh sample was the least well-educated: barely half the heads of households had higher or secondary education, while the proportion of households headed by family members with higher education was even lower than in Vladikavkaz – just a fifth of all families. Nevertheless, cases where a poor family was headed by a person who did not have general secondary education were fairly rare (none in Moscow, two in Voronezh and three in Vladikavkaz), and the research revealed no illiterate heads of households.

The employment status of the heads of our respondent households is presented in Table A.3.

Table A.3   Employment status of the heads of households studied (number of households/per cent)

	Moscow	Voronezh	Vladikavkaz (Russian)	Vladikavkaz (Ossetian)	Total
Employed	12 (50%)	14 (58%)	5 (22%)	6 (24%)	37 (39%)
Self-employed	2 (8%)	2 (8%)	2 (9%)	4 (16%)	10 (11%)
Unemployed	0	2 (8%)	2 9%	4 (16%)	8 (8%)
Working pensioner	2 (8%)	0	4 (17%)	0	6 (6%)
Pensioner	7 (30%)	5 (22%)	9 (39%)	8 (32%)	29 (30%)
Disabled	1 (4%)	0	0	3 (12%)	4 (4%)
Housewife/ husband	0	1 (4%)	1 (4%)	0	2 (2%)
TOTAL	24 100%	24 100%	23 100%	25 100%	96 100%

Data Analysis: Research Indexes

Deprivation Index (IMD)

The project[5] used an approach based on combining the potential of objective (expert) and subjective (survey) methods to define the most significant indicators of deprivation. This approach was first established in Russia in 1997 within the framework of Macauley, Mozhina and Ovcharova's research:[6] Russian and Western experts developed a list of 36 restrictions on a generally accepted way of life, on structure of consumption and on social participation. In the course of their research, and on the basis of this preliminary list, they selected 17 of the most significant deprivations characteristic of a state of poverty in Russia: the presence of at least two of these led to a household being counted as poor. This was the first time that a set of indicators of deprivation, separating poor Russians from the non-poor, had been defined empirically.

In our own research, we wanted to focus especially on how the poor themselves understand poverty, with reference to their different regional, ethnic, national and socio-cultural communities. We therefore decided on further monitoring of the markers that define poverty in Russia today, this time from the point of view of the poor themselves. In 1999, at the first stage of the survey, 105 poor households in Moscow, Voronezh and Vladikavkaz were asked '*In your opinion, what are the markers of poverty in Russia at present?*' To make this assessment, households were presented with a list of items, goods and services, which, according to Macauley, Mozhina and Ovcharova's results, were habitually present and generally accepted in the everyday lives of most of the population: these were items whose absence, according to the same data, was felt most acutely by the overwhelming majority of those surveyed. Our list included 26 indicators in total: that is, it was an amended and somewhat broader version of the most significant restrictions on a generally accepted way of life, structure of consumption and social participation, which might be said to characterise poverty in Russia today (see Tables A.4 and A.5).

Table A.4   Q. – In your opinion, what are the specific markers of poverty in Russia at present? (percentage of households surveyed)

Suggested Indicators	Marker of Poverty	
	MMO[6]	PSE[5]
1. buying necessary medicines and medical appliances (prostheses, glasses, hearing aids, etc.) poses serious financial problems	97	90
2. cannot afford to visit a private doctor if there are no free specialists available	91	79
3. not having enough money to go away on holiday, if only once every two years	63	64
4. cannot afford to use paid forms of entertainment (theatres, concerts, cinema, sporting facilities), even just once a month	57	44

5. not being able to organise a ceremony, such as a funeral or wake, without getting into excessively heavy debt	95	90
6. not being able to afford to take part in a ceremony organised by others	-	66
7. not being able to afford to visit relations (children, parents, etc.) who live a long way away	81	74
8. not being able to afford a subscription to (or purchase of) even one newspaper or magazine	76	66
9. the family budget does not extend to inviting people round to family celebrations or on public holidays	82	83
10. having no money to buy presents for friends and relations for birthdays or other celebrations	82	76
11. not being able to afford meat or fish, even if only twice a week	94	93
12. not being able to buy the family's favourite delicacies, even for a celebration	72	77
13. not being able to afford hygiene products (toothpaste, soap) or washing products in the quantities needed	94	90
14. having no money to replace or repair clothing and shoes	97	92
15. not having a fridge, and not being able to afford to buy one or get one repaired	91	88
16. not having the most basic furniture needed for everyday life, and not being able to afford to buy any or get it repaired	94	89
17. not having even a black-and-white television, and not being able to afford to buy one or get one repaired	93	92
18. not having a washing machine, and not being able to afford to buy one or get one repaired	82	72

19. not having an up-to-date colour television or a video recorder, and not being able to afford to buy one or get one repaired	40	51
20. having less than five square metres of living space per family member; lack of amenities (going without water, heating, electricity)	65	64
21. the family has no possibility, even in case of extreme need, of doing any repairs to their flat or house (mending the roof, replacing faulty plumbing, glazing windows, etc.)	89	91

Table A.5 Q. – In addition, in your opinion, what are the markers of poverty for a family with children?

Suggested Indicators	Marker of Poverty	
	MMO^6	PSE^5
22. not being able to buy fruit or sweets regularly, even for the children	95	92
23. not being able to give schoolchildren or students money to buy food while out at school	96	88
24. not being able to buy the children new clothes and shoes to fit them	98	94
25. not being able to pay to send the children on holiday to camps, health resorts or guest houses	84	73
26. not being able to pay for extra lessons for schoolchildren, whether in clubs, groups or privately	78	70

The Index of Multivariate Deprivation (IMD) is based on an evaluation of the degree of need expressed in our research, and represents the aggregated total of the most significant deprivations present in 105 households in Moscow, Voronezh and Vladikavkaz at the time of our investigation. Because evaluations were initially based on a relative approach to the understanding and measurement of poverty, the presence of particular indicators of deprivation in the household was measured by relating the family's current potential to make certain types of expenditure, to use certain items, goods and services or to afford certain types of activity, to their previous situation (i.e., to the habitual standard of living in that household) – a retrospective comparative analysis, based on the response '*I used to spend money on this, but now I can't afford it*'. Depending on the index values obtained, depth of impoverishment was then distributed along the scale 'indigent' – 'poor' – 'badly-off' – 'averagely well-off'; this was based not only on quantitative indicators (totals of responses selected), but also on their qualitative characteristics (order of preference) at the various levels of deprivation, given also the particular regional and ethnic perceptions of poverty that prevailed in the communities under study. The IMD was calculated separately at each stage of our longitudinal project, and this allowed us not only to obtain a picture of a particular household's current living standards, but also to investigate the dynamics of their situation over time (see Tables A.6 and A.7).

Table A.6   Q. – Please mark each of the following items with the number that most closely describes your present situation: (Please mark the NUMBER that most closely corresponds to your present situation, against EVERY item listed below)

Indicators of Deprivation	*Response 1 Marked: 'I used to spend money on this, but now I can't afford it' 1999 / 2000 percentage of households surveyed in each band*			
	Indigent	*Poor*	*Badly-off*	*Averagely well-off*
Not being able to afford hygiene products (toothpaste, soap) or washing products in the quantities needed	5 / 13	0 / 3	0 / 0	0 / 0

Table A.6 Continued

Indicators of Deprivation	Response 1 Marked: 'I used to spend money on this, but now I can't afford it' 1999 / 2000 percentage of households surveyed in each band			
	Indigent	*Poor*	*Badly-off*	*Averagely well-off*
Not being able to buy the children new clothes and shoes to fit them	-* / 33	- / 6	- / 0	- / 0
Having no money to replace or repair clothing and shoes for the adults	95 / 80	44 / 38	29/ 29	0 / 6
Not having a fridge, and not being able to afford to buy one or get one repaired	25 / -**	0 / -	0 / -	0 / -
Not having even a black-and-white television, and not being able to afford to buy one or get one repaired	35 / 53	19 / 12	2 / 0	0 / 0
Not being able to afford meat or fish, even if only twice a week	80 / 93	75 / 68	43 / 27	10 / 0
Not being able to buy fruit or sweets regularly, even for the children	45 / 60	25 / 21	3 / 6	0 / 0
The family has no possibility, even in case of extreme need, of doing any repairs to their flat or house (mending the roof, replacing faulty plumbing, glazing windows, etc.)	85 / 73	47 / 59	24 / 41	0 / 6

Table A.6 Continued

Indicators of Deprivation	Response 1 Marked: 'I used to spend money on this, but now I can't afford it' 1999 / 2000 percentage of households surveyed in each band			
	Indigent	Poor	Badly-off	Averagely well-off
Buying necessary medicines and medical appliances (prostheses, glasses, hearing aids, etc.) poses serious financial problems	40 / 27	16 / 15	5 / 3	0 / 0
Not having the most basic furniture needed for everyday life, and not being able to afford to buy any or get it repaired	85 / 87	53 / 53	26 / 6	30 / 19
Not being able to give schoolchildren or students money to buy food while out at school	80 / 40	47 / 21	10 / 9	0 / 6
The family budget does not extend to inviting people round to family celebrations or on public holidays	80 / 87	59 / 56	29 / 32	10 / 12
Not being able to organise a ceremony, such as a funeral or wake, without getting into excessively heavy debt	45 / 33	25 / 18	5 / 18	0 / 0
Cannot afford to visit a private doctor if there are no free specialists available	75 / 87	56 / 65	24 / 44	0 / 6

Table A.6 Continued

Indicators of Deprivation	*Response 1 Marked:* 'I used to spend money on this, but now I can't afford it' 1999 / 2000 percentage of households surveyed in each band			
	Indigent	*Poor*	*Badly-off*	*Averagely well-off*
Having no money to buy presents for friends and relations for birthdays or other celebrations	65 / 60	41 / 41	33 / 21	0 / 0
Not being able to buy the family's favourite delicacies, even for a celebration	-*** / 80	- / 68	- / 62	- / 19
Not being able to afford to visit relations (children, parents, etc.) who live a long way away	75 / 80	66 / 65	50 / 44	20 / 6
Not having a washing machine, and not being able to afford to buy one or get one repaired	30 / 53****	38 / 68	24 / 50	0 / 12
Not being able to pay to send the children on holiday to camps, health resorts or guest houses	80 / 53	75 / 56	48 / 44	20 / 6
Not being able to pay for extra lessons for schoolchildren, whether in clubs, groups or privately	75 / 67	66 / 44	33 / 35	40 / 6
Not being able to afford to take part in a ceremony organised by others	65 / 60	50 / 29	12 / 12	0 / 0

Table A.6 Continued

Indicators of Deprivation	Response 1 Marked: 'I used to spend money on this, but now I can't afford it' 1999 / 2000 percentage of households surveyed in each band			
	Indigent	*Poor*	*Badly-off*	*Averagely well-off*
Not being able to afford a subscription to (or purchase of) even one newspaper or magazine	65 / 80	69 / 62	62 / 59	20 / 6
Not having enough money to go away on holiday, even only once every two years	90 / 67	87 / 65	93 / 85	70 / 56
Having less than five square metres of living space per family member; lack of amenities (going without water, heating, electricity)	75 / 53	59 / 44	26 / 24	30 / 31
Not having an up-to-date colour television or video recorder, or other up-to date electronic and domestic equipment, and not being able to afford to buy any	75 / 93	88 / 85	74 / 94	70 / 69
Cannot afford to use paid forms of entertainment (theatres, concerts, cinema, sporting facilities), even just once a month	90 / 67	75 / 65	50 / 56	40 / 38

Table A.6 Continued

Indicators of Deprivation	Response 1 Marked: 'I used to spend money on this, but now I can't afford it' 1999 / 2000 percentage of households surveyed in each band			
	Indigent	Poor	Badly-off	Averagely well-off

TOTAL
per cent/number of
  households in each
  band
	100/100
	20/15
		100/100
		32/34
			100/100
			43/34
				100/100
				10/16

* At the first stage of the survey in 1999, there was no separate response for 'children's clothing and shoes', so the calculation was based on the single response 'clothing and shoes for family members'. The next row of the table shows the overall result.

** At the second stage of the survey, in 2000, this indicator was calculated on the basis of the responses 'I do not have/cannot afford to repair basic household items, such as TV set/fridge' – i.e., the two indicators were conflated. The next row of the table shows the overall result.

*** There were no 1999 data based on this response, because the question was not asked at the first stage of the survey.

**** At the second stage of the survey, in 2000, the response 'washing machine' was replaced by a variable relating to 'limiting consumption'. This indicator takes into account those households which, over the course of the year, had been unable to acquire any of the household appliances/equipment or consumer durables that the household lacked, or use any kind of fee-paying services, *regardless of how vital.*

Table A.7 Change in living standards in the households studied in Moscow, Voronezh and Vladikavkaz between 1999 and 2000

2000 (per cent / number of households surveyed)

As grouped in 1999	Moscow				Voronezh				Vladikavkaz				TOTAL			
	I	P	B	W	I	P	B	W	I	P	B	W	I	P	B	W
Indigent (I)	100 /1	0 /0	0 /0	0 /0	100 /3	0 /0	0 /0	0 /0	50 /6	50 /6	0 /0	0 /0	63 /10	37 /6	0 /0	0 /0
Poor (P)	9 /1	55 /6	27 /3	9 /1	20 /2	60 /6	20 /2	0 /0	0 /0	70 /7	30 /3	0 /0	10 /3	61 /19	26 /8	3 /1
Badly-off (B)	0 /0	15 /2	62 /8	23 /3	0 /0	18 /2	82 /9	0 /0	11 /2	26 /5	42 /8	21 /4	5 /2	21 /9	58 /25	16 /7
Averagely well-off (W)	0 /0	0 /0	0 /0	100 /2	0 /0	0 /0	0 /0	100 /2	0 /0	0 /0	20 /1	80 /4	0 /0	0 /0	11 /1	89 /8

Social Exclusion Index (ISE)

The Social Exclusion Index (ISE) was calculated separately for each stage of the 'Poverty and social exclusion' project. Points on the ISE were totalled from indicators on multi-variate scales, as listed below.

FIRST STAGE OF THE POOR HOUSEHOLDS PANEL SURVEY

Scales (1999)

1. The right to secure, paid work (the WORK scale).
2. The right to essential medical assistance when needed (the HEALTH scale).
3. The right of access to education and culture (the EDUCATION AND CULTURE scale).
4. The right to significant relations of primary sociability and to inclusion in a community (the RELATIONSHIPS scale).
5. The right of access to social networks as one of the main mechanisms – alongside social protection – for the redistribution of resources (the NETWORKS scale).
6. The right of autonomy: the ability to initiate action, formulate goals and carry through goal-oriented actions (the AUTONOMY scale).
7. The right to adequate housing (the HOUSING scale).

Indicators within scales (1999)

1. The WORK scale *takes into account the following responses marked on the Stage One questionnaire (each of these response variants corresponds to 1 point on the cumulative ISE):*
   HOW SECURE HAS YOUR WORK SITUATION – OR THAT OF ONE OF YOUR FAMILY MEMBERS – BEEN RECENTLY?
   - one of us has experienced wage delays
   - one of us has been compelled to take unpaid leave
   HOW WORRIED ARE YOU THAT YOU OR A MEMBER OF YOUR FAMILY MIGHT LOSE THEIR JOB?
   - I am very worried
   - I am rather worried

IF YOU THINK THAT YOUR LIFE IS NOT GOING WELL, THEN WHAT ARE THE MAIN REASONS THAT LEAD YOU TO THIS ASSESSMENT?
- problems with work

2. The HEALTH scale *takes into account the following responses marked on the Stage One questionnaire (each of these response variants corresponds to 1 point on the cumulative ISE):*
WHAT DO YOU THINK RESTRICTS YOUR CHANCES OF GETTING A SUITABLE JOB?
- health
IN EVERYDAY LIFE, ARE YOUR ACTIVITIES – OR THE ACTIVITIES OF ANY MEMBER OF YOUR FAMILY – LIMITED BY SOMETHING TO DO WITH HEALTH?
- limited: I, or a member of my family, have to make a great deal of effort to carry out my duties at work and at home
- significantly limited: I, or a member of my family, cannot hold down a normal job or carry on normal everyday life (Category 1 or 2 disability)
- a member of our family is bed-ridden
PLEASE MARK EACH OF THE FOLLOWING ITEMS WITH THE NUMBER THAT MOST CLOSELY DESCRIBES YOUR SITUATION:
- necessary medicines or appliances (prostheses, glasses, hearing-aids, etc.) (*response 1 marked – 'I used to spend money on this, but now I can't afford it')*
- visiting a private doctor if there are no free specialists available (*response 1 marked – 'I used to spend money on this, but now I can't afford it')*
WHAT DO YOU FEAR MOST OF ALL IN YOUR OWN LIFE?
- not being able to get medical help, even in case of severe need

3. The EDUCATION AND CULTURE scale *takes into account the following responses marked on the Stage One questionnaire (each of these response variants corresponds to 1 point on the cumulative ISE):*
WHAT IS THE FIRST THING THAT YOU GO WITHOUT WHEN MONEY IS TIGHT?
- visiting theatre, cinema or other entertainments
- magazines, books, newspapers

PLEASE MARK EACH OF THE FOLLOWING ITEMS WITH THE NUMBER THAT MOST CLOSELY DESCRIBES YOUR SITUATION:
- newspapers and/or magazines (*response 1 marked – 'I used to spend money on this, but now I can't afford it'*)
- visits to the cinema, theatre, museums or other cultural pursuits (*response 1 marked – 'I used to spend money on this, but now I can't afford it'*)

WHAT DO YOU FEAR MOST OF ALL IN YOUR OWN LIFE?
- not being able to get a good education or give my children a good education

PRESENT LEVEL OF EDUCATION OF ADULT MEMBERS OF HOUSEHOLD
- incomplete secondary education
- basic education
- illiterate/no basic education

4. The RELATIONSHIPS scale *takes into account the following responses marked on the Stage One questionnaire (each of these response variants corresponds to 1 point on the cumulative ISE):*

PLEASE MARK EACH OF THE FOLLOWING ITEMS WITH THE NUMBER THAT MOST CLOSELY DESCRIBES YOUR SITUATION:
- visiting/inviting friends/family at birthdays or on public holidays (*response 1 marked – 'I used to spend money on this, but now I can't afford it'*)

WHAT ARE YOUR USUAL PERSONAL SOCIAL CONTACTS, APART FROM FAMILY MEMBERS LIVING IN YOUR HOUSEHOLD?
- nobody except members of my family
- nobody at all

5. The NETWORKS scale *takes into account the following responses marked on the Stage One questionnaire (each of these response variants corresponds to 1 point on the cumulative ISE):*

IF YOU THINK THAT YOUR LIFE IS NOT GOING WELL, THEN WHAT ARE THE MAIN REASONS THAT LEAD YOU TO THIS ASSESSMENT?
- loneliness

DO YOU SOMETIMES RECEIVE HELP FROM YOUR
NEIGHBOURS OR RELATIVES WHO DO NOT LIVE IN YOUR
HOUSEHOLD?
- don't receive help
DO YOU SOMETIMES RECEIVE HELP FROM YOUR
FRIENDS, WORKMATES OR ACQUAINTANCES?
- don't receive help
DOES YOUR FAMILY GIVE HELP TO ANYONE WHO DOES
NOT LIVE IN YOUR HOUSEHOLD?
- don't give any help
IN A CASE OF EXTREME MATERIAL DIFFICULTY, WHO
WOULD YOU TURN TO FIRST FOR THE HELP YOU
NEEDED?
- no-one

6. The AUTONOMY scale *takes into account the following responses marked on the Stage One questionnaire (each of these response variants corresponds to 1 point on the cumulative ISE):*
HOW OFTEN THIS YEAR HAVE YOU EXPERIENCED THE
FOLLOWING FEELINGS?
- everything happening around me is unjust *(response marked: 'often')*
- I feel that I cannot go on living like this *(response marked: 'often')*
- it is impossible for me to have any influence on what is happening around me *(response marked: 'often')*
- I am satisfied that things are going according to plan for me *(response marked: 'never')*
- I have felt that I only need to put up with things a bit longer, and then life will improve *(response marked: 'never')*

7. The HOUSING scale *takes into account the following responses marked on the Stage One questionnaire (each of these response variants corresponds to 1 point on the cumulative ISE):*
WHAT IS YOUR HOUSING SITUATION?
- I rent part of a room, a room or a flat
- I live in a hostel
- part of a house
- room/s in a communal flat or part of a house
- homeless

WHAT IS THE AREA OF YOUR TOTAL LIVING SPACE, CALCULATED IN SQUARE METRES PER MEMBER OF YOUR FAMILY?
    - less than 10 square metres per household member
IF YOUR HOUSING CONDITIONS DO NOT SUIT YOU, PLEASE GIVE THE TWO MAIN REASONS FOR THIS.
    - we live in the same flat as neighbours or relations
    - overcrowding
    - lack of amenities (bathroom, toilet, heating, electricity)
    - the building needs capital repairs

SECOND STAGE OF THE POOR HOUSEHOLDS PANEL SURVEY

Scales (2000)

1. The right to secure, paid work (the WORK scale).
2. The right to essential medical assistance when needed (the HEALTH scale).
3. The right of access to education and culture (the EDUCATION AND CULTURE scale).
4. The right to significant relations of primary sociability and to inclusion in a community (the RELATIONSHIPS scale).
5. The right of access to social networks as one of the main mechanisms – alongside social protection – for the redistribution of resources (the NETWORKS scale).
6. The right of autonomy: the ability to initiate action, formulate goals and carry through goal-oriented actions (the AUTONOMY scale).

Indicators within scales (2000)

1. The WORK scale *takes into account the following responses marked on the Stage Two questionnaire (each of these response variants corresponds to 1 point on the cumulative ISE):*
    HAVE YOU OR ANY MEMBER OF YOUR FAMILY BEEN DIRECTLY AFFECTED BY UNEMPLOYMENT (REGISTERED OR DE FACTO) DURING THE REFORM PERIOD?
        - member(s) of our family were unemployed for a long time
        - member(s) of our family are still unemployed
    HOW SECURE HAS YOUR – OR YOUR FAMILY MEMBER'S – WORKING SITUATION BEEN OVER THE LAST YEAR?

- one of us has experienced wage delays
- one of us has been compelled to take unpaid leave
- one of us has been put on part-paid leave or short-time working

2. The HEALTH scale *takes into account the following responses marked on the Stage Two questionnaire (each of these response variants corresponds to 1 point on the cumulative ISE):*

WHAT DO YOU THINK NOW RESTRICTS THE CHANCES OF GETTING A SUITABLE JOB FOR THOSE WHO NEED IT (FOR EXAMPLE, UNEMPLOYED FAMILY MEMBERS, YOUR ADULT CHILDREN LOOKING FOR A JOB FOR THE FIRST TIME, ETC.)?

- health

IF YOU SEE YOUR FAMILY'S LIVING STANDARDS AS WORSE THAN THEY WERE 12 MONTHS AGO, WHAT HAVE BEEN THE MAIN REASONS?

- illness or disability of a family member

MANY PEOPLE NOW FIND THEMSELVES FORCED TO CUT DOWN ON, OR SOMETIMES EVEN TO COMPLETELY GIVE UP, SOMETHING THEY HAVE BEEN USED TO HAVING. WHAT HAS YOUR FAMILY BEEN PRACTICALLY FORCED TO GIVE UP RECENTLY BECAUSE OF MONEY DIFFICULTIES?

- medical treatment and drugs that we really need, but which are expensive

TRY TO ASSESS YOUR APPROACH TO THE FOLLOWING ITEMS OF EXPENDITURE IN YOUR PRESENT SITUATION:

- necessary medicines or appliances (prostheses, glasses, hearing-aids, etc.) *(response 1 marked – 'I used to spend money on this, but now I can't afford it')*
- visiting a private doctor if there are no free specialists available *(response 1 marked – 'I used to spend money on this, but now I can't afford it')*

HAVE YOU EXPERIENCED THE FOLLOWING FEELINGS THIS YEAR:

- I have been feeling in excellent health, with a sense of well-being *(response marked: 2 – 'not really' or 1 – 'no')*

WHAT DO YOU FEAR MOST OF ALL IN YOUR OWN LIFE?

- not being able to get medical help even in case of severe need

3. The EDUCATION AND CULTURE scale *takes into account the following responses marked on the Stage Two questionnaire (each of these response variants corresponds to 1 point on the cumulative ISE):*
   MANY PEOPLE NOW FIND THEMSELVES FORCED TO CUT DOWN ON SOMETHING, SOMETIMES EVEN TO COMPLETELY GIVE UP SOMETHING THEY HAVE BEEN USED TO HAVING. WHAT HAS YOUR FAMILY BEEN PRACTICALLY FORCED TO GIVE UP RECENTLY BECAUSE OF MONEY DIFFICULTIES?
   - buying newspapers, magazines and books
   IN ADDITION, WHAT HAVE YOUR CHILDREN BEEN FORCED TO GIVE UP ALMOST COMPLETELY (WHERE THERE ARE CHILDREN UNDER 18 IN THE FAMILY)?
   - extra sports, music or language lessons
   - taking part in events for children and activities involving extra expense (e.g., visits to the theatre, cinema or circus)
   TRY TO ASSESS YOUR APPROACH TO THE FOLLOWING ITEMS OF EXPENDITURE IN YOUR PRESENT SITUATION:
   - subscription to (or regular purchase of) newspapers, magazines, books *(response 1 marked – 'I used to spend money on this, but now I can't afford it')*
   - visits to the cinema, theatre, museums or other cultural pursuits/entertainments *(response 1 marked – 'I used to spend money on this, but now I can't afford it')*
   IF YOUR FAMILY HAS CHILDREN, PLEASE ASSESS YOUR APPROACH TO THE FOLLOWING ADDITIONAL ITEMS OF EXPENDITURE:
   - paying for extra lessons for schoolchildren, whether in clubs, groups or privately *(response 1 marked – 'I used to spend money on this, but now I can't afford it')*
   WHAT DO YOU FEAR MOST OF ALL IN YOUR OWN LIFE?
   - not being able to get a good education or give my children a good education

4. The RELATIONSHIPS scale *takes into account the following responses marked on the Stage Two questionnaire (each of these response variants corresponds to 1 point on the cumulative ISE):*
   HOW WOULD YOU ASSESS THESE DIFFERENT ASPECTS OF YOUR FAMILY LIFE?
   - personal contacts *(response marked: 'bad')*

MANY PEOPLE NOW FIND THEMSELVES FORCED TO CUT DOWN ON, SOMETIMES EVEN TO COMPLETELY GIVE UP, SOMETHING THEY HAVE BEEN USED TO HAVING. WHAT HAS YOUR FAMILY BEEN PRACTICALLY FORCED TO GIVE UP RECENTLY BECAUSE OF MONEY DIFFICULTIES?

- visiting or inviting friends round
- keeping in touch with relations who live a long way away (even by telephone)

TRY TO ASSESS YOUR APPROACH TO THE FOLLOWING ITEMS OF EXPENDITURE IN YOUR PRESENT SITUATION:

- organising or taking part in ceremonies (weddings, christenings, funerals or wakes) when necessary *(response 1 marked – 'I used to spend money on this, but now I can't afford it')*
- visiting friends, relatives, acquaintances *(response 1 marked –'I used to spend money on this, but now I can't afford it')*
- inviting people round to family celebrations or on public holidays *(response 1 marked – 'I used to spend money on this, but now I can't afford it')*
- visiting relations (children, parents, etc.) who live a long way away *(response 1 marked – 'I used to spend money on this, but now I can't afford it')*

5. The NETWORKS scale *takes into account the following responses marked on the Stage Two questionnaire (each of these response variants corresponds to 1 point on the cumulative ISE):*

IF YOU THINK THAT YOUR LIFE IS NOT GOING WELL, THEN WHAT ARE THE MAIN REASONS THAT LEAD YOU TO THIS ASSESSMENT?

- loneliness

DOES YOUR FAMILY SOMETIMES RECEIVE HELP FROM ANYONE WHO DOES NOT LIVE IN YOUR HOUSEHOLD?

- the family doesn't get any help

WHO EXACTLY GAVE YOU THIS HELP?

- nobody has helped us

DOES YOUR FAMILY GIVE HELP TO ANYONE WHO DOES NOT LIVE IN YOUR HOUSEHOLD?

- don't give any help

DOES YOUR FAMILY MORE OFTEN RECEIVE OR GIVE
HELP?
  - we are not in a position to help anybody, and nobody helps us
HAVE YOU OR ANY FAMILY MEMBER RECEIVED ANY OF
THE FOLLOWING *(DIFFERENT TYPES OF SOCIAL SUPPORT
LISTED)* IN THE LAST YEAR?
  - none of the above
DO YOU KNOW ANY FAMILIES AROUND YOU –
RELATIVES, FRIENDS OR ACQUAINTANCES – WHO ARE
LIVING IN EXTREME NEED, EVEN IN THE DEPTHS OF
POVERTY?
    - yes, three or more families

6. The AUTONOMY scale *takes into account the following responses
   marked on the Stage Two questionnaire (each of these response
   variants corresponds to 1 point on the cumulative ISE):*
   HOW OFTEN THIS YEAR HAVE YOU EXPERIENCED THE
   FOLLOWING FEELINGS?
       - everything happening around me is unjust *(response marked:
         'often')*
       - I feel that I cannot go on living like this *(response marked:
         'often')*
       - It is impossible for me to have any influence on what is
         happening around me *(response marked: 'often')*
       - I am satisfied that things are going according to plan for me
         (response marked: 'never')
       - I have felt that I only need to put up with things a bit longer,
         and then life will improve *(response marked: 3 –'never')*
   HAVE YOU EXPERIENCED THE FOLLOWING FEELINGS
   THIS YEAR:
       - I have felt that on the whole things are going well for me
         (response marked: 1 – 'no')
       - I have felt that I am playing an important part in things
         (response marked: 1 – 'no')

7. The HOUSING scale *takes into account the following responses marked on the Stage Two questionnaire (each of these response variants corresponds to 1 point on the cumulative ISE):*
   WHAT IS YOUR HOUSING SITUATION?
   - I rent part of a room, a room or a flat
   - I live in a hostel
   - part of a house
   - room/s in a communal flat or part of a house
   - homeless
   WHAT IS THE AREA OF YOUR TOTAL LIVING SPACE, CALCULATED IN SQUARE METRES PER MEMBER OF YOUR FAMILY?
   - less than 10 square metres per household member
   IF YOUR HOUSING CONDITIONS DO NOT SUIT YOU, PLEASE GIVE THE TWO MAIN REASONS FOR THIS.
   - we live in the same flat as neighbours or relations
   - overcrowding
   - lack of amenities (bathroom, toilet, heating, electricity)
   - the building needs capital repairs

Notes

[1] The RIISNP Monitoring Survey has been conducted quarterly since 1992 by the RIISNP (Director – Prof. Mikhail Gorshkov) in collaboration with the Centre for Social Forecasting and Marketing (Director – Dr Franz Sheregi).
[2] Silverman, D. (2000), *Doing Qualitative Research*, Sage Publications, London.
[3] Giddens, A. (1993), *Sociology*, 2nd ed., Polity Press, London.
[4] Neuman, L.W. (1991), 'Social research methods: qualitative and quantitative approaches', 2nd ed., Allyn and Bacon, Boston.
[5] INTAS project 'Poverty and social exclusion in Russia: regional, ethnic and socio-cultural aspects', 1999-2000, looking at 105 households in Moscow, Voronezh and Vladikavkaz, headed by N. Manning and N. Tikhonova.
[6] The research project 'Poverty in Russia: deprivation and social exclusion', 1997, looking at 900 households in St. Petersburg and 250 households in Vyaznikov, headed by A. Macauley, M. Mozhina and L. Ovcharova. For results, see: (1998) *Poverty: alternative approaches to definition and measurement.* Joint monograph, Moscow Carnegie Centre, Moscow.

Appendix 2
Histories of 19 Households (A Longitudinal Study, 1996-2001)

Nataliya Tikhonova

Вся семья вместе, так и душа на месте
When the whole family is together, the soul is in its place

MOSCOW

Household 1

Over the whole period of observation, this *typical 'new poor' Moscow household* consisted of three people – an elderly married couple (with whom we conducted 'gender interviews' in 2000) and their daughter (who was the main respondent in 1996, 1997, 1999 and 2000). Until the 1990 reforms, the head of the family, a specialist with higher education, had worked as a test engineer at a vast light vehicle factory. By the time of the first survey he had already retired but, as a pensioner, continued to work as a fitter in the repair shop of the same factory throughout the whole period of observation. In 1996, as in all the later years, his wife was a non-working pensioner.

Their daughter, Anna (d.o.b. 1976), had completed a vocational secondary education and began her working life as an inspector of measuring equipment in the quality control department of the factory where her father worked. From 1994 to 1996, she was on unpaid leave as a result of problems at the factory, and joined our 1996 survey as an insecurely employed person. From her father's account of what had happened, it was roughly at that time (1993-94) that the family's financial difficulties began, and these continued throughout the subsequent period of observation. Until then, the family could be seen as averagely well-off.

Their financial problems related not only to the fact that Anna had no kind of income at all, but also to her father's reaching pension age and transferring to a different post, at exactly the same time as the enterprise began a systematic programme of non-payment or prolonged delay of wages, as a result of problems with the competitiveness of its production output. So, for example, in January 2001, the enterprise was paying wages due for September 2000. In addition, the head of the family had been involved in an accident and crashed his car, so he bought a new Moskvich car (an inexpensive model intended for the domestic market) on a preferential credit loan from the factory, and for 18 months he did not receive any wages at all because he was repaying this.

Anna's situation changed in 1997, when the enterprise released her because of staff cuts. She was then on the unemployment register for over a year. In 1998, she completed computer courses to which the Employment Service had directed her, but even on the vast Moscow labour market she did not find a job afterwards. She was removed from the unemployment register because she refused the Employment Service's suggestions on the grounds that the jobs were 'too far to travel', 'badly paid', etc.

Judging by this respondent's replies in various years, she did not really want to go out to work, and her parents did not condemn her for this, taking the view that:

> It's not so simple to find work, because they don't offer you anything in your usual occupation. That's my daughter's situation ... we worked together for a while, then she worked on her own for a while, and she got a job through the Employment Service for a while, but it was all temporary work. And then that same Employment Service laid her off, dismissed her, took her off the register, as if they didn't need her ... That's affected her situation since then, and her psychological state. Although the financial side of things isn't so important to me, the main thing is for her to work, so that I could know she was mixing with people – but it isn't turning out like that (Anna's father).

However, Anna herself was not unduly worried by her enforced social isolation. As she said, seven years after she had, in fact, stopped working:

> I would have preferred not to go out to work, but it didn't seem entirely right ... Somehow I've never been able to start work again: I have to help Mum around the house and at the dacha. But I'm getting organized to fix something up. Dad has promised to ask at the factory ... We're not rich, but we have everything we need. Our situation is still the same, we have enough to live

modestly. I don't think anything will change, even if I get a job: I still won't earn very much.

Nevertheless, despite Anna's belief the family had easily enough money for a modest way of life and the fact that her family did remain in the 'badly-off' section of the Material Deprivation Index over the whole period of observation, the real situation in the family gradually deteriorated. It was true that, during the period, the family acquired a new car with the help of the enterprise where the head of the family worked; however, all the members of the family consciously went without such components of consumption behaviour as paying for holidays, types of leisure activity that required additional expenditure, visiting, receiving guests and using fee-paying medical services. The thing the family perceived as most difficult was that they were compelled to restrict their spending on clothes. As the head of the family said in 2001:

> I also have to go without buying clothes. It seems impossible that I could have been wearing the same suit for 25 years, but here it is, I'm still in it ... I've torn my sock somewhere – I can mend that myself and wear it, but somewhere else I tore something a bit more serious – the lining of my jacket. I couldn't sew it up straightaway, so I just don't unbutton it, and that's that. The main thing is that everything should be relatively clean ... You know, my wife needs to buy new boots – she already put it off the first season she needed them, but look at her clothes – she hasn't got anything.

So, this family's growing deprivation was evident primarily through the deterioration of what they owned, the exhaustion of the resources they had accumulated in the pre-reform period and the gradual building-up of material problems ('our problems are still growing'). In addition, at the time of the final survey in 2001, Anna's father was already 65 and had serious problems with his health: it was becoming increasingly difficult for him to work. Given that the main sources of income were his wages and irregular material assistance from Anna's brother, who lived separately, this created a real threat of further deterioration in the household's situation.

However, the family's immediate circle and their wider social contacts had not changed as a result of the changes in their material circumstances, while there was nobody among Anna's 'immediate acquaintances' whom she herself regarded as poor. In fact, she did not consider herself poor either, remarking that 'we live relatively normally ... My family does not live below the poverty line, although we are close to it'.

Anna herself described poverty as 'lack of money' and, to solve this particular household's problems, it would indeed have been enough just to increase the pensions received by the parents, since the family was generally in the mainstream. There was no question of their being socially excluded: their total scores on the Social Exclusion Index were 7 points in 1999 and 4 points in 2000.

Household 2

Throughout the whole period of observation, this Moscow household consisted of one young woman (d.o.b. 1965), who came from a family of doctors and she, herself, had higher education in medicine. Like the previous household, she was a typical example of the 'new poor'. But while Anna, from Household 1, was in a passive – even, in a certain sense, dependent – position, Nataliya (the Household 2 respondent) was typically representative of an active, energetic disposition towards life.

Before the reforms, Nataliya had lived in Voronezh (our provincial survey city), but in the early 1990s she moved to Moscow and began her own small business there, selling souvenirs to foreign tourists. After her unregistered trade was forcibly brought to an end in 1993-94, she gradually began to slide into deep poverty. She could not register as unemployed, since she had no official residence permit for Moscow; thus, she was an example of a *de facto* unemployed person who had no possibility of obtaining official unemployed status – a situation typical of Moscow.

After the failure of her small business, Nataliya lived on her savings for some time, but these rapidly ran out, since she had to rent a flat at market price – a problem which the previous household did not have, since they were native Muscovites and their rent was notional. Although the flat she rented was the cheapest available, without furniture or a telephone, it was still fairly expensive. Over almost five years, Nataliya slowly reduced her needs, working only from time to time (if her former friends and colleagues trading on Arbat Street[1] asked her to) and stretching her remaining money just to pay for the flat. Once a month, she received a parcel from her mother in Voronezh, containing food – generally potatoes, cabbage and beetroot and, sometimes, cooked rissoles – which she lived on for a long time. In 1996, when she joined our first survey as a *de facto* unemployed person, and in 1997, she was very highly deprived. In fact, throughout that period, Nataliya lived practically at the level of indigence.

Her situation was aggravated by serious depression resulting from lack of success in her personal life, and it was this that actually prevented her from going back to regular work. Some time in 1998, Nataliya attended meetings of a pseudo-religious cult, which, she claimed, helped her a lot in regaining her psychological stability. After this, she asked an old friend, who also came from Voronezh and had her own tourist business in Moscow, to lend her money, to train first as a masseuse and then as a homeopath. Having received this money, she was putting these plans into effect. As a result, both initial direct help with food from her relations and, more importantly, later substantial financial assistance from friends (to train in a field for which there is demand on the Moscow labour market) allowed her to overcome a difficult period in her life successfully. Thus, Nataliya's case was a *clear example of the significance not only of particular personality traits, but also of social network resources, in helping people to get out of poverty.*

As a result, at the time of the 1999-2000 surveys, Nataliya was self-employed as a masseuse in private practice, charging $10 per session, which was a fairly high rate for Moscow. Because of her increasingly difficult material circumstances and the need to pay off her debts, Nataliya was working practically every day of the week. As a result, in 1999, she had already risen to 'badly-off' on to the Material Deprivation Index, and by 2000 she was 'averagely well-off'. She continued to rent the same cheap flat (although she was doing repairs there and had obtained a cell phone, since having no telephone in the flat had made her work impossible) and to economise on literally everything, even going without new clothes – but she was doing this with the aim of having a flat of her own after some time.

Of the reasons behind the change in her material circumstances and the fact that she had survived her earlier difficulties, Nataliya herself said:

The improvement in my material circumstances is a result of my greater professionalism: it means I have got more clients and my income has increased. I hope I will have the strength, the time and the intelligence to master homeopathy – then my prospects will be limitless. I'm doing something I love – if it's going to be well-paid, all well and good. Plus it's a good way of feeling you are in control of yourself, your feelings, your situation. That difficult period in my life was basically connected with the fact that my personal life wasn't going well, I felt that I couldn't do anything, I couldn't work. It used up all my strength, and I ended up in a very sorry plight.

As far as social exclusion – as opposed to deprivation – was concerned, Nataliya spent a fairly long period in the 'grey area' as a result of all her difficulties. However, she managed to escape it and came to represent a successful example of reintegration into the mainstream. Her Social Exclusion Index scores were 7 points in 1999 and 4 points in 2000.

Household 3

This Moscow household, *also an example of the 'new poor'*, consisted of four people – a married couple with a student son and a daughter at school. Both spouses had worked as engineers at a scientific defence research institute until 1995, when they were released because of staff cuts. On this level, their problems can be seen as relating to the restructuring of the Russian economy that took place following the reforms of the 1990s. As a result, Irina had been officially registered as unemployed from June 1995, and this was why she was recruited as a respondent for our 1996 survey. Since then she has not managed to get a job, a fact which both she and her husband attribute primarily to her stammer. She has not tried to retrain, since she thought that her usual occupation was a good one. She refused any work offered by the Employment Service that was not in her usual occupation, on grounds of low pay. In 1998, Irina applied for and received a disability pension,[2] in addition to which she sometimes had extra income from unregistered typing work. In 2001 she said:

> I've already practically stopped looking for work now, although I regularly look at the adverts. I haven't given up hope, but up to now I haven't found anything. It's strange because my specialized training is IT-related … there should be some work on that basis, with worthwhile earnings, and it's just a matter of waiting a while – so it's better to devote that time to the children.

Irina felt she could not aspire to a highly-paid job: when she took part in the interview, she expressed interest in whether there might be any interviewing work for her.

Her husband, Lev, said that, following his redundancy, he had not changed his 'usual occupation, but the kind of thing I do' and started to work repairing electric hotplates. Possibly it was easier for him to take up a manual job than for many of his other colleagues who also lost their jobs, since he had real experience of working in a manual occupation: before he went into higher education and moved – literally just a few years before being made redundant – to the post of engineer, he had worked as a foreman, adjusting visual measuring equipment. This move back to manual work solved the family's more acute problems and halted their rapidly growing deprivation for some time. But after the crisis of August 1998, which involved the devaluation of the rouble and the collapse of many firms, Lev's wages fell sharply. Although he had some additional earnings from repairing electrical equipment privately, these did not have any serious impact on the family's material circumstances. Just two weeks before the 2001 survey, he was left entirely without a job, since the firm where he worked 'went bust'. Lev attributed the impossibility of getting suitable work primarily to his age:

> I'm getting older and older all the time, there are already fewer chances for me, it's hard to find anything ... Because of my age, I'm already going nowhere fast ...

Their son, who reached the age of 18 and became a student during the period of observation, sometimes had unregistered earnings, working as a programmer in a private firm and taking orders home (computer design, modelling, programming, computer repairs). But he became ill and lost this source of unregistered earnings, even though he only had a common cold, for which the employer should simply have granted him up to two weeks leave on grounds of temporary incapacity for work. He had spent his earnings mainly on his own needs, but nevertheless, the loss of this job created additional problems for the family.

The family viewed the period 1995-6 as their most difficult. At the time of the final survey, they were categorised as 'badly-off', but in fact they were increasingly going without a number of things they needed. Lev noted in 2001:

> Basically, we haven't got enough money to clothe ourselves. I mention that first because, for example, we need to change our furniture, but even talking about doing that is absolutely impossible – I've set it aside as unreal, an impossibility. We haven't got enough money for repairs, and we won't even mention holidays – that would be impossible for us, and for the children ... Material problems are piling up, we can't solve them ... You see – the plaster's

falling off, it urgently needs to be repaired, and we can't do it yet, the same as everything else.

The family pinned their hopes for the future mainly on their son graduating from the institute, but they understood that such hopes were somewhat shaky because he might get married.

Like the two preceding 'new poor' households, this family perceived poverty simply as lack of money. Moreover, because they had enough food, they did not consider themselves to be poor, although they did complain about not having enough money to meet their other needs. There were poor people in their circle, but these were not the majority. This family never fell into the group of socially excluded households, although they were teetering on the brink of sliding into the 'grey zone'.

Household 4

From 1996-9, this family of native Muscovites consisted of a woman something over 30 years old, disabled from infancy (Ol'ga, who suffered restricted growth, was intelligent, literate and a valuable, active worker) and her pensioner father. Both had higher education. In 2000, the respondent's sister and niece, who had previously rented a separate flat, moved in with them.

In 1996, Ol'ga joined our sample as someone under notice of redundancy. However, when applied to her, this description was merely notional, because the enterprise where she had worked until then (having been hired under a disability programme) was semi-fictitious and suddenly disappeared with all documentation, including the employees' personal work records. Ol'ga went to court to establish her rights to unemployment benefit, sought out the former director of the enterprise on her own initiative and phoned him personally. She finally achieved the status of registered unemployed person with all associated rights, including that of having her benefit calculated on the basis of her last real wage rather than the minimum wage (which would have been the case if she had not managed to present her work record with a signature confirming that she was made redundant due to staff cuts).

In later years, Ol'ga had not found any permanent work, although from time to time she took part in American programmes for training and job placement for disabled people (she trained as a financial trader or share dealer, which meant she could work in a bank and had computer skills).

These enabled her to get some work from an American fund to support disabled people, although her earnings from this were sporadic. Ol'ga always made use of any opportunity to get extra income from any source. However, she could not find a steady paid job, since even on the relatively favourable Moscow labour market *our research revealed that there is distinct discrimination against disabled people.* As a result, no-one in the household had had secure employment for several years. Over the period of observation, the family's deprivation grew noticeably, and they fell from being badly-off into real poverty.

Two quotations from our interviews with Ol'ga allow us to imagine life in this household more fully.

> You can see that people are getting poorer, just by looking at my neighbours and friends. The costs of services and food are going up a lot. I think our lives are hard, we're poor now ... (1999).

And a year later:

> The situation's still the same. It's true that things were harder when Mum passed away in 1996. I don't know myself how we coped then, the Americans supported me a lot, I went on their courses. It's humiliating when you have to depend on your father and your sister. I'm pinning all my hopes on finding a job. I don't know anyone, and it's everyone for himself. It's been easier to make some arrangement with the Americans than to deal with Russians. Now I'm getting organized to earn on my own account: I don't want to take a penny from anyone. My difficulties aren't only material, they're more a question of morale: I don't want to be dependent ...

Ol'ga's experience of discrimination, her lack of social and cultural integration and the general social discomfort with disability were also reflected in her high total scores on the Social Exclusion Index, and on the Networks scale and the Relationships scale in particular.

Household 5

This household began as an example of a comparatively secure lone-parent family. From 1996-99, it comprised a divorced woman, born in 1964, who had come to Moscow from a small town when she was young, under a workers' quota scheme for Moscow enterprises,[3] and her two children under 18. Valentina joined our panel in 1996 as a person in insecure employment, as a result of the difficulties being experienced by the factory where she worked. Since she was a very active woman, taking the attitude that she should achieve everything for herself, and had worked extremely hard all her life, she left the factory and took a manual job with the Moscow Metro. At the time of the first survey, Valentina, despite all the difficulties she had experienced, retained fairly optimistic views on life. Her children were well-behaved and well-cared-for. The single small room where the three of them lived was tidy. Despite a modest average *per capita* income, the family had managed to acquire a new television and a music centre. From the point of view of level of welfare, Valentina managed to maintain her standard of living steadily at the level of 'badly-off' over the whole period of observation.

Valentina always had a realistic, appropriate view of her own situation. So, in 1999, she remarked:

> A lot of people now have got into a difficult situation, regardless of their education. It's hard for people, and this results from the way life is structured – prices, inflation, wage delays. Both from people I know and from what I see on the television – everyone's talking about the impoverishment of the population ... Poverty means having no tomorrow. In the past we weren't afraid of becoming poor, we could rely on stability (we'll get our wages, we'll buy this now, and wait to buy that). Our family doesn't live poorly, but we're badly-off.

Nevertheless, problems with the two children, hard work, life in a communal flat in a room with only 14 square metres for three people and the impossibility – despite all her efforts – of improving her life in any way meant that, in 1999, the household had a fairly high score on the Social Exclusion Index, because of high indicators on the Autonomy and Housing scales.

In April 2000, between our two final surveys, Valentina got married. This event, happy in itself, transformed the family's life into an absolute nightmare, because of certain particular features of Russian legislation. The family was already living in overcrowded conditions, and after Valentina got married, they had to manage with just 3.2 square metres of living space per person. Moreover, because Valentina's husband had been registered as resident in Moscow for less than ten years, the family lost all rights to municipal housing: according to Moscow by-laws, a family that intentionally makes their housing conditions worse (which had been the effective impact of Valentina's marriage) forfeits all rights to help with housing from the municipal authorities for five years. This is how Valentina herself described her difficult circumstances.

This is a very hard time in my life. I'm in dispute with my neighbour over a room that's become free in the communal flat. There are four of us living in a room 14 metres square, while they've got 17 square metres for three people. But she says I got married for convenience sake, just in order to get the room. I've collected so much paperwork, I've been everywhere, but in the end she got the order, because she's a widow.[4] Her husband died of drink, but she's been getting a pension for him, and all that time I was bringing up my children alone. Now I've just reached the point where I want to blow the lot up. There's no way out. I've been offered a grant of 200,000 roubles, but I have to put in 300,000 myself – and where am I going to get that kind of money? I haven't even got 10,000[5] to pay a lawyer, but you can't get one to do the work for less. If a lawyer was prepared to defer the payments, I could pay him back over a year, but no-one will do that either, and the court case is in two weeks' time. I'm on tablets, the pressure is terrible, I'm completely devastated. At every stage, people just say – you've brought this situation on yourself, why did you get married?

Household 6

When we started our observations in 1996, this two-parent Moscow family consisted of a married couple and two children under 18. In 1996, 1997 and 1999, our respondent, Vera, viewed herself as the head of the family. She had been recruited into our sample because she was officially registered as unemployed. Before that, she had worked as a labour planner in a construction enterprise and had been made redundant in 1994, due to staff cuts.

In 1996, her husband, who also worked in the construction industry, was seriously ill in hospital after an accident and was not receiving any wages: the family was in a great deal of difficulty – Vera herself said 'we haven't had enough money for even the most essential things'. She indicated that her only source of income at that time was help from relations, since she had already stopped receiving unemployment benefit by then. From the point of view of deprivation, the household was really in poverty at that time.

However, the family's other conditions could be described as modest rather than poor. They lived in a small two-room flat, where each person had about 9 square metres; they owned a fridge, a washing machine, a colour television and a carpet, all bought before the reforms, as well as a piano acquired in the early 1990s for their daughter's music practice. The family had no suite of furniture, no car, no video recorder, nor any other – even old – expensive belongings at that time. This was a fairly standard picture of a badly-off family, which – together with their housing conditions – led us to suppose that the family had not been poor before the reforms either, but poised somewhere on the boundary between being badly-off and averagely well-off.

Just before the 1997 survey, Vera received a small legacy following the death of her sister. This noticeably altered the family's situation: they began to live significantly better from a material point of view. In addition, her husband found a job as a works superintendent in a construction firm, while Vera managed to get a job as a social worker. (However, this did not suit her because of the low pay, and for the whole period of observation she continued to talk about her desire to find another, more highly paid job, but with flexible hours.)

In 1999, the household's circumstances were favourable, if insecure. As before the reforms, the family was again poised on the boundary between being badly-off and averagely well-off. However, by this time, three things had severely shaken Vera out of her previous optimism, leaving a noticeable stamp on her assessment of the situation in the household and on her generally fairly high score on the Social Exclusion Index, where she was in the 'grey area'. Firstly, the legacy she had received had practically run out. Secondly, her husband's affairs were very patchy – he was working in a private construction firm and experienced temporary interruptions of income, which generated a constant fear in the respondent of getting into the same terrible position that they had been in during the mid-1990s. Finally, the fact that their son had left school and they had to get him into an institute (which costs a great deal in Moscow) made her painfully aware of how restricted her own means and potential were.

In 2000, at first glance, it seemed that the family's situation had stabilised. The elder child had entered a good higher education institution to train as a production manager and had moved out of his parents' home. They had recovered the car they bought when they received the legacy (it had been stolen in 1999). However, the time had come for the younger child to leave school, creating the problem that they had to spend money on coaching to get her into a higher education institution. In addition, the husband's insecure situation at work continued – he had not received any wages for three months before the survey. Their Material Deprivation Index score had increased again, since they had finally exhausted the 'insurance' potential of the legacy.

This contradictory picture was also revealed in the interview: 'I think our situation has deteriorated', said Vera at the time of the 2000 survey.

> Our problems have increased, they've piled up ... Our daughter is leaving school, the dollar is falling, there's inflation ... But the hardest period was in 1994-5, when there were difficulties with employment, with changing values; there are other values now, in the recent past there was none of that, everything's come to a halt again now. I don't think of the present as difficult for us, the children have grown up, they're off our hands, but it's bad for people whose children are small. If my husband can move from this job to a better one, it will be better still – I can't pin my hopes on myself. My husband wants to leave this job, everything's going to rack and ruin there, there's no stability ... You know, I'm afraid for the future. Every day you think about seems dark, and you just don't want it to be dark, dark, dark ... And then there are already health problems, ageing: we had our second child late, and so it has been pretty difficult bringing her up at our age.

This insecure situation, lasting many years, was reflected in an increase in the family's score on the Social Exclusion Index: in 2000, this corresponded to profound exclusion. Of course, another cause of this increase was that, for the sake of her children's future, Vera had been going without almost everything herself for years, trying to ensure that her children were not deprived of anything. This, of course, became increasingly difficult as the children grew and their needs increased, and it was hard for her to accept that it was impossible to give the children everything they needed. Her husband also suffered because he couldn't provide his children with the way of life that their peers had:

> My daughter asks me, 'Daddy, how are things for you at work?' So I say, 'Everything's all right at work', and she comes back with: 'All right' would mean there were no problems, that we could easily afford to go to McDonald's.

This household offers an example of the effect on the overall circumstances, behaviour and psychology of the 'new poor' of insecure incomes, the experience of temporary poverty and fluctuations in standard of living, depending on the situation (both Vera and her husband losing their jobs, his prolonged illness, the unexpected receipt of a legacy, the husband's insecure situation at work, their son's independence, the need to find funds for their daughter's education, etc.). It demonstrates that, when personal income is insecure, even the unexpected receipt of a legacy – although it might keep the household from complete degradation – cannot entirely stabilise the situation. On the other hand, this household is also a fairly clear example of how the socialisation of children in a 'new poor' family can be successful, even with very limited resources, where there is the slightest possibility of spending on their education by cutting back on entertainment and social contact with their peers.

Household 7

A two-parent family consisting of three people – a couple and their daughter, who was born in 1987. In her heart of hearts, Ol'ga (our respondent in this household) would have preferred to be a housewife, but worked throughout practically the whole period of observation 'because I have to'. This necessity derived from the fact that both spouses had worked in the private sector of the economy practically all the time since the early 1990s, and, as Ol'ga said, there were 'times when either my husband or I was left without work'.

In 1997, she joined our sample as someone who had returned to work after a period of registered unemployment. She lost this job after the August 1998 crisis, and in 1999 she was again registered as unemployed with the Employment Service. By 2000, she had found another job, through the influence of friends, as a bookkeeper in a private firm.

At first glance, this was a completely secure, averagely well-off family, where both spouses had higher education. However, Ol'ga assessed her family's situation very critically. So, comparing the family's material circumstances with those of others, Ol'ga noted that in 1990 they had been the same as everybody else's, but by the end of the 1990s they were much worse. According to her:

> The poor today are those who can't provide a normal life for their children and give them a worthwhile education. There are a lot of people like that now, especially because you have to pay to study practically everywhere. Among my acquaintances, there are still two or three who can just about provide their

children with a normal situation. Even if our family isn't poor, then it's on the edge of being poor – that's exactly right.

In 2000, Ol'ga said:

Our material circumstances are largely unchanged. Things are a bit worse, mainly because life in general is getting more expensive. As our daughter grows, spending on her goes up, but our income is the same as before.

These assessments seemed strange, given their comparatively well-off standard of living. However, closer analysis showed that they resulted from a feeling of insecurity about this standard of living, from an understanding that it could all collapse in an instant. Ol'ga felt this all the more intensely because she came originally from a family that was materially very successful, and the situation in her own family was worse than when she had lived with her parents.

Ol'ga was aware that she and her husband had achieved as much as they were going to and that, even if one or other of them succeeded in finding a new job, this would not have a significant influence on their situation. At the same time, the forthcoming end of her daughter's schooling, with all the additional expenses this entailed, required mobilisation of all the family's resources: thus, although the household remained in the averagely well-off category, its circumstances were gradually deteriorating. In addition, the family lived in a communal flat, and as her daughter grew up, this depressed Ol'ga more every year. All their household possessions dated from no later than the early 1990s and needed renewal, just as their home needed repair. Although the family managed to buy a car in 1998, this required enormous economies. By 2000, the family had mounting debts, which in the past it had always avoided.

It seems that this feeling of insecurity was also influenced by the fact that, in Ol'ga's opinion (which she expressed more than once in the course of our surveys), her husband, although not an alcoholic, had an alcohol abuse problem, and this could not fail to affect the family's standard of living and prospects. In any case, this apparently completely secure household had very low reserves, and any deterioration of the situation – serious illness of one member of the family (Ol'ga's constant fear), the simultaneous unemployment of both her and her husband, her husband's increasing propensity for alcohol, etc. – threatened the household with significantly poorer circumstances. Ol'ga herself understood this: 'There's hardly likely to be any significant change for the better. It'll be good if things don't get any worse' (2000). And, given how things had developed in other households where there were alcoholics or drug addicts, her fears seemed entirely well-founded.

Household 8

A Moscow household consisting of two people – a divorced, unemployed man born in 1977 and his mother, who worked as a nurse. A fairly typical example of the degradation of a household where there was an alcoholic or (as in this case) a drug addict.

In earlier years, Aleksandr, who joined our sample in 1996 as someone under formal notice of redundancy, had a family, a child and secure paid work: he was a theatre sound operator and had additional earnings from restoration work. From the point of view of material welfare, the family was a fairly typical 'averagely well-off' family. In other words, when we carried out our first survey, this household was still completely successful.

During the period of observation, Aleksandr's wife left him and refused him any contact with their daughter. Aleksandr regularly complained about his loneliness, lack of friends and lack of support. Both his drug dependency and his feeling of being abandoned and superfluous had a marked effect on his psychological state.

After being made redundant, he mainly did seasonal work just outside Moscow – he had small temporary jobs restoring a church (Aleksandr was religious), building cowsheds, etc. At the time of the 1999 survey, he was in hospital with a serious drug-related condition, and he then underwent a course of therapy for drug addiction, but without success. At the time of the 2000 survey, he was not working at all and was obviously inadequate. His mother was in a very bad psychological state as a result of all she had been through; she was ashamed of her son and avoided any contact with our interviewer.

The household was basically badly-off in a material sense, although its deprivation increased between 1996 and 2000. Substantial help from Aleksandr's brother, who lived separately, helped to slow the household's material degradation: he gave the family a colour television and a music centre, and helped their mother financially.

The family's material difficulties had resulted in the first instance from Aleksandr's unemployment, but the root of both his unemployment and his gradual degradation was his poor health, caused by drug dependency. He himself understood this, and in 1999 he said: 'I'm poor because I'm unemployed, now I'll just have to piece myself back together, recover a bit ...', and a year later:

> Everything's bad for us now, because of me, because of my health. I can't work at full strength now. I understand that I'm sliding towards nothing. There's already nothing to hope for. However, I think that I will be able to survive this period, it's impossible that it should never end. If only I could manage to get my family back, my daughter, I would have some meaning in my life again. Recently nothing has been going right with work, or with life.

In contrast to their scores on the Material Deprivation Index, which, although they became worse over the period of observation, did so slowly, this household's scores on the Social Exclusion Index rose quickly, reaching 13 points in 2000. In other words, Aleksandr was close to the boundary between 'the grey area' and 'the black hole' of profound social exclusion. His worst scores in that respect were on the Health scale and the Autonomy scale. It was also impossible not to notice the marked deterioration in his indicators on the Networks scale and the growth of his social isolation. This corresponded to what we recorded in the interviews – that although in the initial period he had a circle of permanent social contacts, consisting of old friends and acquaintances (of whom most were not poor themselves), by 2000 Aleksandr was unable to name anyone with whom he was in permanent social contact.

Household 9

A three-generation family of Muscovites, which was in a state of stagnant poverty and social dysfunction throughout the whole period of observation. None of the three couples in the household (which was made up of parents and two sons with their partners and children) was legally married. All of them constantly fought amongst themselves, and prior to the 1999 survey, one of the sons had beaten his mother. The parents had a metal door on their room, since, they said, their sons were stealing their money.

The respondent in the 1996-1999 surveys was Ol'ga (d.o.b. 1945), the partner of the head of the family, a woman with higher education, who joined our panel as a registered unemployed person. In 1998 she survived a stroke, but she died in 1999, shortly after the survey. The household member who took part in the surveys in 2000 and 2001 (the latter being the 'gender interviews') was one of her daughters-in-law, Oksana (d.o.b. 1979), whose second child was born and died in the period between the 1999 and 2000 surveys.

The household had both a joint budget (based on general expenditure on housekeeping and food and on the father helping the daughters-in-law with day-to-day expenses for the grandchildren – according to Oksana, 'he's always been like the breadwinner; when Ol'ga Petrovna was alive, he supported her, and he helps me ... He sees to everything himself, he knows where to help, it's his house') and an independent budget for each of the three families. However, out of nine people, including six adults, only three were working. The family's main breadwinner was the father, who had secure employment throughout the whole period of observation, working as a driver for a construction directorate. Ol'ga had decided not to look for work, but to stay at home with her young grandchildren; she was first in receipt of unemployment benefit and then of disability benefit. The sons' employment was insecure, involving small-scale trading. One of the daughters-in-law, Oksana, did not work, saying: 'my child is totally dependent on me' and 'I don't have the strength to do everything', while the other had some occasional unregistered earnings.

Both their 74-square-metre three-room flat and their furniture were in very bad condition throughout the period of observation. In addition, one of the sons had an alcohol abuse problem, and an oppressive atmosphere hung over the whole household.

Here is a quotation from Ol'ga's 1999 interview, not long before her death.

> I've been ill, mostly in hospital. Everyone is poor because that's the way life has gone, the pension is small. By comparison with how we lived before, we are poor. We don't have enough space, that's a really acute problem. We live with our children, but it's as if we're strangers in a communal flat, nobody helps anyone: they sometimes just take money from me and my husband without asking. We're waiting for the summer – it's good we've got a dacha, we've got somewhere to live properly.

The problems in this household, as was generally the case in households that were not only poor but also socially dysfunctional, included an increased risk of becoming victims of crime: almost immediately after Ol'ga Petrovna's funeral, their home was burgled and almost all their domestic appliances stolen. It was notable in that connection that the only things worth stealing from this household were a colour television and a video recorder – and these were far from new, having been bought as long ago as the mid-1990s. All the rest of the family's property consisted of things that were well over seven years old.

In 2000, according to Oksana, her husband finally found a job after a period of unemployment.

> Our material circumstances are better. Our father and my husband have started to earn more. We have some hopes of future improvement because of this work, maybe they'll get more ... In the meantime, we have had to cut back on everything, even on food. I wouldn't describe our material circumstances as 'hard', but at the same time we have to go without a lot of things.

However, these hopes turned out to be to a large extent illusory, since Oksana's husband, according to her, 'likes to have a good time': he was rarely living at home during this period and even more rarely helped out with a bit of money. In 2001, according to Oksana, despite help from her husband's father and her own mother, who lived in the country:

> there have been periods when I haven't had a kopeck.[6] I've had to accept help from a good friend of mine: she knows all about my situation and has given me both money and food.

According to her, these periods were when her husband's father was away on business and her husband was not living at home. Moreover, at these times, her husband's brother's family lived 'entirely separately' and did not help her. But even when her husband's father was there, the level of deprivation in the household was very high. As Oksana said:

> I really don't have enough money to spend even on ordinary things – eating, paying for the flat, so that Dad (she means her husband's father – N.T.) can only barely manage to cover it all now ...

It is not surprising that the indices of deprivation and social exclusion in this household were consistently high.

Household 10

This two-parent Moscow family, consisted, throughout the period of observation, of pensioner parents and their son, Igor (d.o.b. 1973); the latter joined our 1996 survey because he was officially registered with the Employment Service as unemployed. He gained this status after being dismissed for disciplinary reasons from a meat processing plant, where he worked as an unskilled general labourer, and, according to his mother, 'since then he hasn't been able to find anything suitable anywhere'. At intervals throughout the period 1996-2000 he had some occasional earnings (he sold pens in car parks, was a dispatcher and a market porter). All this employment was partial and unregistered.

He was not yet an alcoholic at the time our observation began, but he loved drinking and 'real hard boozing'. During the period when he was on the Employment Service register, he argued with the staff there, and when he was working, he was in constant conflict with the management. In later years, he took to drink. However, he blamed everyone except himself for all his misfortunes.

> My situation and my family's situation have deteriorated sharply, especially since my parents retired, as a result of the complete collapse and chaos in the country. I have to go without almost everything. The democrats have made the whole country poor – and me, too (1999).

The family's main breadwinner was the father, who, as a pensioner, supplemented his income by working, right up to early 2000, as a car park attendant. After that, the father had only occasional additional unregistered earnings from mending cars in his friend's garage.

Throughout the period of observation, this family was badly-off according to its score on the Material Deprivation Index. However, despite lack of money, each member of the household had a way of life that completely suited him or her, so it would be inappropriate to refer to any kind of social exclusion in this household, on the basis of either the Social Exclusion Index or their own feelings.

Describing the story of his own misfortunes, Igor said, in 2000:

> I had a good job at the meat processing plant, it wasn't bad. Then I fell out with my team leader, he dismissed me, everything went off the rails ... Fate has been cruel to me as far as work is concerned – one firm went bust, another was impossible to work for and I had to leave. Now I just work from time to time as a porter on the market here, the money's very low. If only someone would help me with a job, a good one, then our situation might improve. I need to take myself in hand, get myself together and everything will go smoothly. Maybe it's time I got married. In general, we live poorly, but not like some.

VORONEZH

Household 11

This household consisted of an elderly married couple. Their grown-up daughter, who worked as a lecturer in higher education, lived separately. The husband, Vladimir, joined our sample in 1996 as someone in insecure employment (he was on unpaid leave, since the factory where he worked as a gas and electric welder was in serious difficulties). As a highly skilled worker, he had always had a fairly high income before these problems arose, and he was the family's main breadwinner. By 1996, the wife had already retired, and was in receipt of both a retirement pension and a disability pension.

During the period of observation, Vladimir also retired, after which he worked only occasionally and temporarily: he was sometimes invited to his old workplace to help meet special orders. In addition, because he was highly valued at the factory as a first-class welder and, in his own words, 'an irreplaceable specialist', he had received several bonuses in kind. These included, in particular, kitchen furniture and a carpet.[7]

The family's income was made up not only of both the spouses' pensions and Vladimir's occasional earnings, but also rents from leasing out a second flat the family owned (a small bed-sit with no bathroom or toilet) and help from their adult daughter and Vladimir's two brothers, who lived in the country (as his wife said, 'we get our food mainly from the country, my husband has relatives there ... In return, we go there and help them with their land and their livestock ...'). In addition, because of their age and their comparatively low standard of education, the couple's aspirations were not high, and they were not worried whether or not they could afford leisure, holidays or modern consumer durables.

At first, the family was poised on the borderline between 'averagely well-off' and 'badly-off', but as the period of observation progressed, they settled at the badly-off level. Their material problems related not so much to insufficient income ('We have an average standard of living, we don't live any worse than others. We have no serious financial problems, but we do have various small ones', Vladimir noted in 2001), so much as with the high expenses arising from the wife's illness: she was classed as '1st category disabled' and suffered from a disease of the digestive tract. Vladimir said:

Everything started with my wife's illness. Our expenses have gone up, she has to go into hospital twice a year, there's a lot to pay for – medicine droppers, medicine ... Personally, I've had to go without a lot of things, because I've had to buy medicine and special food for my wife. There's not enough money for clothes, but I'm already at the age where I don't get too upset about that.

Despite their age and the wife's poor health, the family had maintained a very wide network of social contacts, with a permanent social circle including relatives, friends, neighbours and Vladimir's workmates. Perhaps this, as well as the feeling that he continued to be valued at the factory, meant that, in general, their material problems had no serious effect on the psychological atmosphere in the household or on their Social Exclusion Index scores. As Vladimir said, although 'our way of life is poorer than those "new Russians", on the whole we're coping'.

Household 12

This household was a lone-parent family of four people, headed by a man. The head of the family, Sergei (d.o.b. 1954), had first worked as a driver and subsequently as a fitter in a Voronezh engineering enterprise; he joined our sample in 1996 because he was under formal notice of redundancy. After being made redundant, he registered with the Employment Service, who found him a job after a few months. However, this employer (a department of a radio electronic equipment factory) was generally making cuts, so he came up against problems with wage delays and insecurity almost immediately. He worked there, at intervals, right up to 2001, but in his estimation, the job was 'bad, because they pay very little'.

Sergei lived in a one-room flat with his two school-age children and his pensioner mother. His mother had her own flat, but she had moved in with her son and rented it out in order to gain a steady additional income. The role played by any kind of regular income was especially great in this family, since in the second half of the 1990s the mother's pension payments (she received an old-age pension and a disability pension) were often delayed, the child benefit had not been paid for years and Sergei's wages from the factory were often also delayed for a long time. Given the level of inflation during this period, all these delays meant a reduction in the real purchasing power of the family's income: this was sometimes relatively small (about a third), but sometimes more.

Sergei's mother was seriously ill, which not only necessitated additional spending, but also made it impossible for her to take on the running of the household. His ex-wife, living in the same neighbourhood, had been deprived of her parental rights because of her alcoholism, so the children stayed with Sergei after the divorce. All this placed a large additional family burden on him.

Material deprivation in the family grew constantly. In 1996, the family was categorised as poor, but by the end of the decade, they were profoundly indigent. 'We are poor and we are hungry', said Sergei in 1999, and this was no exaggeration. The family could not buy any clothes, even for the children to go to school, let alone for the adults.

This situation had lasted for years, which in turn led to a continuous accumulation of problems. So, in 2000, Sergei said:

> Our material circumstances are the same, my position at the factory is insecure and there are wage delays. We are pinning our hopes on the elections: we need a complete change of leadership for both the city and the province. The hardest period was when I was unemployed. But a job hasn't changed anything especially: things have stayed the same, but now I'm being fleeced. The pay is low, prices are going up. Our spending on my mother's medicine has gone up, the children are growing, they are wanting more.

In these conditions, it is not surprising that his Social Exclusion Index score was very high.

Household 13

This was a two-parent family with a daughter, who was three years old at the start of our survey, living in their own house with an adjoining plot of land. The husband, Yevgeni (d.o.b. 1961), had worked as a physical education teacher in a school until the mid-1990s, then became a manager in a private firm. At the time our observation began, he was on unpaid leave from his last job. After quite a short period of insecure employment, Yevgeni became *de facto* unemployed and had no secure employment right up to 2000. His wife was an English lecturer in higher education and had additional earnings from tutoring. This was not a poor family: throughout the whole period of observation, they were averagely well-off on the Material Deprivation Index.

It should be said that this household was a fairly rare example – especially for Voronezh – of a case where the husband's prolonged formal unemployment had no effect on the family's standard of living. This was because of the wife's successful multiple employment, the fact that they had their own car (which Yevgeni could use to earn a bit extra if he needed to) and also the fact that they received substantial support from his wife's parents. With her father's help, they had managed to build their own house: Yevgeni did not look for a steady job for several years because he was working on this project. A lot of the building materials were obtained free from the factory where her father worked, which also supplied some free labour. As Yevgeni said in 2000:

> Our material circumstances have not changed much over all the reform years; when I haven't had work, I have been busy building the house, essentially so as to save money on labour. So I've been voluntarily unemployed.

As soon as he finished building the house, Yevgeni went back to permanent work. His training was as an Eastern martial arts instructor and in the past he had managed a martial arts club. So, having decided to go back to work, he not only started to teach physical education in a school again, but also used the facilities there to open a private club. As a result, as Yevgeni said:

> Our material circumstances have improved … If I can manage to find better work and broaden my sphere of activity (start working in another school as well), our situation will improve even more.

His wife also found 'advantageous extra work'. There was, naturally, no question of this family being affected by any kind of social exclusion.

Household 14

This household consisted of four people: a married couple, both of whom had higher education, and their two young children (born 1990 and 1994). The head of the family, Vladimir, was a builder by training and had in the past been a works superintendent, but by the mid-1990s he was a heating engineer in a large-panel construction factory. He joined our sample in

1996 as someone in insecure employment because of problems at the factory. His wife, Svetlana, was a journalist by training; in 1996, after returning from maternity leave, she was working as a senior laboratory assistant in a higher education institution, and – like all those working in the budget-funded sector in Voronezh – was suffering not only from low pay but also from constant wage delays. Nevertheless, the family was badly-off rather than poor.

In 1997, the situation at Vladimir's workplace normalised, and he had no further employment problems. His wife worked in the same institution and endured the same problems throughout the whole period of observation, except that she transferred to a post teaching laboratory methods. The household's level of welfare remained stable all this time, corresponding to 'badly-off' on the Material Deprivation Index. This was largely through help from the wife's parents, primarily her father. The latter's death in the late 1990s made the family's life considerably harder and exacerbated their financial problems, since up to then about 40 per cent of the family's income consisted of outside help. In her birth family, Svetlana had been used to a fairly high standard of living, unlike her husband (from a family that was not so well-off), who was completely satisfied with the standard of living that his income provided.

When interviewed in 2001, the family was on the verge of breakdown: Vladimir and Svetlana kept splitting up, then getting back together again. The husband tried to put into practice the model of a male-dominated, patriarchal family, which – along with his low wages and lack of willingness to get more actively involved in tackling the family's problems – led Svetlana to protest.

> The family I grew up in was very successful, and that left me with certain impressions. Everything depends on your upbringing, on your family traditions. My family has been child-centred for several generations, while in my husband's family it was usual for everyone to stick up for themselves.

By 2000, uncertainty in their personal and financial situations, prospects of a sharp deterioration in their lifestyle and lack of clear choices for the future, meant that – despite their relative external prosperity – this family had a fairly high score on the Social Exclusion Index, placing them in the risky 'grey area'.

Household 15

At the time we began our observations in 1996, this household consisted of four people: a married couple 'under forty', their 17-year-old daughter and their 13-year-old son. Over the period of observation, both the son and the daughter started work. In addition, the daughter had a child and so the household then consisted of five people.

Although Vladimir (the head of the household) entered our sample in 1996 as someone who had found work after being registered as unemployed, it turned out that he had lost his new job literally on the eve of the survey ('I lost my job yesterday!' he said as he opened the door to the interviewer). It is true that the drama of the situation was somewhat reduced by the fact that his wife's employment was secure: throughout the whole period of observation, she was a factory worker. However, Vladimir was afraid that the position of her factory was insecure, and 'the factory might let my wife go at any moment' (2000).

There were other sources of income, too. Despite being fairly young, in 1996 Vladimir was already in receipt of a pension: he had worked all his life as a ballet dancer and had to retire after 20 years service in the mid-1990s, after which he registered with the Employment Service. He was also receiving a disability pension, as he had some health problems. However, when you are not yet even 40, it is undoubtedly very hard to live on meagre pensions, with no work, two children under 18 to support and the feeling that you are no use to anyone. Neither Vladimir nor his former workmates were able to come to terms with this position. Because he had problems finding regular employment (not surprisingly, in the light of his specialised training and his poor health), he and two friends began to try and run a small business in the motor transport protection and repair line.[8] Things were not going too well for them, but Vladimir was always saying that now they were working on a new project, and he was sure this was going to be the successful one.

Throughout the whole period of observation, the household was poised on the boundary between being badly-off and actually poor, depending on the circumstances at the time: they moved from one group to the other mainly because of the ratio of number of dependents to working people at any given time. By 2001, it seemed that the household would continue to keep afloat materially for the foreseeable future, since their son had to go away on military service and then would return and start work.

However, despite their significance, material difficulties were far from being the main cause of this family's depression. As Vladimir said in 2000:

> Materially, difficult is not the right word for it – but it was even harder between 1993 and 1995: the most intolerably difficult times, just one thing after the other.

Here he was referring to the coincidence of the breakdown of all existing values and notions, the start of the reforms in Russia, the change in the family's way of life when he retired and the change in his own social status as a result of all this. In general, he perceived the last of these as more painful than the deterioration in their material circumstances. In addition, both his 'fall' into a fairly marginal type of activity, after many years of secure and respected work as an 'artist', and his prolonged failure to find a place in the new system of social relations – despite all his active efforts – led to a rapid rise in their Social Exclusion Index score.

Household 16

A two-parent Voronezh family with two children living at home, both of whom reached adulthood during the survey period (ds.o.b. 1976 and 1982). The family was 'badly-off' at both stages of observation: this is the level of welfare where social exclusion is equally likely to exist or not exist, and this household is a fairly clear example of how a family, none of whose members has had any permanent paid work for many years, successfully avoided social exclusion. For the whole period, this household's Social Exclusion Index showed low scores, they did not identify themselves as poor, and most people in the family's permanent circle were in the averagely well-off sections of the population. This might have been related to the fact that, before the reforms, the family had belonged to the prosperous section of the population.

In 1996, Valentina joined our sample as someone who had returned to work after a period of registered unemployment; she had lost her job as an engineer at a thermal power station because the enterprise was in financial difficulties, and had then been directed by the Employment Service to a job as a cashier/bookkeeper in a shop. However, she did not keep this job for long, and in 1997 she was self-employed. In later years, she worked continuously in 'casual' jobs – as an interviewer for various surveys and on the elections, of which a lot were going on in Voronezh at that time. She had moved into a new social circle, made up of people involved in election services, and her phone rang continually with offers of temporary work.

The slight fall in the family's standard of living in 1996-97 reflected not only Valentina's unemployment, but also wage delays for her husband during a period when his employer was in financial difficulties. He subsequently became self-employed; however, his small business did not bring in much money. In later years, the family noted an improvement in their circumstances, as a result of the daughter's work, greater security in the husband's situation and the son going to university.

Valentina was completely content with her family's life and had hopes that it would improve still further:

> Our material circumstances haven't changed much. But now we have work: my husband isn't earning too badly, and I've found myself some very convenient extra work, on the pre-election campaigns – Voronezh is building up to the elections for Provincial Governor. I'm sure that my children will manage to build their lives well and find good jobs: they might even be able to help us. Overall, I think that the difficult times are behind us, although who knows what life will bring – things are so complicated nowadays (2000).

Household 17

For the whole period of observation, this household consisted of four people – our respondent, Nataliya, who entered the sample in 1996 as someone who had returned to work after a period of registered unemployment, her husband and their two children under 18 (ds.o.b. 1986 and 1988).

Nataliya herself, still young and with specialised secondary education, had worked as a bookkeeper for many years, but in the mid-1990s she lost her job because her enterprise was in difficulties, and she registered with the Employment Service as unemployed. In 1997, the Employment Service found her work as a teaching assistant in a children's nursery, but she later changed her job of her own accord, and in 2000 she was working as a cutter and seamstress in a private enterprise. The job was a good one, and her pay had risen several times over the year. Throughout the whole period of observation, Nataliya generally took on a lot of work (she even took work home), and because of her heavy workload and problems with her husband, she was – despite her youth – already very tired and in poor health. Nataliya's husband was a gas welder by trade and had worked in that occupation for over ten years, right up to the mid-1990s. But subsequently, because of his alcoholism, he was not able to get work in his usual occupation, so he remained unemployed for a long time before finding work as a porter. All this time, Nataliya did not give up hope that he would 'think better of it and find some respectable work'.

In 2000, with the help of friends, he managed to get work as a welder, but it was difficult to say how much of a sustained improvement this would make in the family's life. As Nataliya herself said in that year:

> Our material circumstances have improved a little, and I hope for more improvement because my husband is working now. However, these improvements took place literally a month ago, and before that my husband hadn't been working for two years (they didn't pay his wages, he changed his job several times, he drank, he really went to pieces). Of course, it was very difficult. And it went on for a very long time.

Over the whole period of observation, the household was poor according to both the Material Deprivation Index and the self-assessment indicators. Their poverty resulted from a high dependency ratio and the husband's alcoholism. In 1999, their score on the Social Exclusion Index was close to the edge of the 'grey area', and by 2000, despite the husband's finding work, they had entered that area.

Household 18

This household was among the most underprivileged in the whole sample: it consisted of a lone mother with a large number of children, and was made up entirely of women. Our respondent, Tat'yana (d.o.b. 1963), and her three daughters (born 1981, 1988 and 1992) were later joined by Tat'yana's aunt (d.o.b. 1925), who was the official tenant of the flat where they all lived (allocated through her former employer, an aircraft factory). Throughout the whole period of observation, the head of the family worked as a cleaner in another block of flats owned by the same factory. She joined our 1996 sample as someone who had found work after a period of registered unemployment (she had first worked in the factory canteen). Although Tat'yana had secure employment throughout the period of observation, she received a low wage: she was trapped in this dead-end job partly because she wanted to ensure she got the tenancy of the flat after her aunt's death.

In a material sense, the family was going downhill, and over the period of observation, they fell from poverty into profound indigence. The household went without meat products, could not buy clothes, even for the children, or give them money to buy food at school; they had no television and could not afford to invite guests round, let alone carry out the repairs that that their small two-room flat desperately needed, or buy the simplest furniture. This household's score on the Social Exclusion Index was constantly rising.

Tat'yana associated her increasingly difficult position, firstly, with alcoholism ('If everyone who can work didn't drink, it would be easier. Both my ex-husbands went downhill that way, and I've done so too, because of them'), and secondly with her large number of dependents.

> I view my family as poor, and when you ask for help, even for child benefits, they say something crude like: 'why did you have so many kids?' So we just have to toil on … A woman on her own with children has to bring them up, shoe them, clothe them, feed them.

Tat'yana's middle daughter was disabled (by heart disease). Her older daughter was studying at a technical college and did as much as she could to help the family.

Household 19

This four-person household was yet another example of gradual degradation as a result of one family member's alcohol abuse. Our respondent, Mikhail (d.o.b. 1957), a doctor by profession, joined our sample as an insecurely employed person. Before that, he had spent all his working life as a local doctor in a district clinic. His wife, who was ten years older, worked as a cook in a student canteen. His wife's two children from her first marriage also lived with them – a 17-year-old daughter, who was already working and moved out to live separately soon after the start of our observation, and a 15-year-old son, who suffered from epilepsy and became unemployed after leaving school during the survey period.

Mikhail's wife had been widowed suddenly some years before the survey. Before that, her family was really prosperous: her husband was the head of a construction group, but he died suddenly from a heart attack. Left with no means of support, she was compelled to take on responsibility for the family, and some time later Mikhail joined her. He had also been married before and had two children from his first marriage.

In 1997, Mikhail's situation at work stabilised, but he did not return to normal permanent work, having given up the job – according to him – 'because they altered the pay'. Over the period of observation, he managed to register as unemployed, to be partly employed and even to try and start his own business, but his predominant state was unemployment. As a rule, he lost jobs because of his alcohol abuse or, as he expressed it, 'for disciplinary reasons'. The last time he had been dismissed – from the job of security guard – was not long before the survey in 2000.

Although neither Mikhail nor his wife had been poor during their previous marriages, we recorded real poverty in their household throughout the period of observation, according to the Material Deprivation Index. Moreover, their deprivation grew continuously, as did their social exclusion – the Social Exclusion Index in this household showed one of the highest scores in the sample. However, Mikhail did not get organised to go out to work. He said in 2000:

> It's impossible to live normally in this country. You can't call the situation difficult, but it isn't easy either. It would be senseless for me to work in my usual occupation now, for 600 roubles. When medicine becomes completely fee-paying, the pay will be OK again, then I'll go back into it. I'm just pinning all my hopes for improving my material circumstances on that.

His wage expectations were very high – one of the highest in the whole sample, even taking Moscow into account.

The family would most probably have been degraded and impoverished much more quickly if Mikhail had not inherited a two-room flat, following the death of his brother in 1999: he rented this out very successfully (by Voronezh standards). However, his life was not qualitatively changed – 'Our life has been bad since perestroika, and now, even though things are a bit better for us financially, money is like water', said Mikhail, who saw the rent money as his contribution to the family budget.

Notes

1. A well-known souvenir market in Moscow.
2. The fact that this respondent was receiving disability benefit throws some light on the Russian version of the tendency, well-known in welfare systems throughout the

developed world, towards fluid boundaries between unemployment, early retirement and formal disabled status as routes of exit from the labour market. During the 1990s, in common with many other countries, Russia made certain specific changes and additions to the conditions for receipt of invalidity benefit and for social security for the various categories of disability (including 2nd and 3rd category disability, covering those with general medical complaints who retained some restricted capacity to work). As a result, over the five years following the legislative changes, the number of disabled people in these two groups doubled. It is difficult to explain this phenomenon solely through a sharp deterioration in the health of Russian citizens – although that factor should not by any means be disregarded. Looking at the overall picture, and comparing the Russian experience with those of many other countries, it rapidly becomes apparent that this situation has a complex, but nevertheless direct, relationship with the issues of unemployment and poverty. As real incomes and employment opportunities have diminished, especially for older members of the population, Russians have consciously started to use disabled status and the resulting receipt of a disability pension as an economic survival strategy. Maleva asserts that the sudden growth in the number of disabled people in Russia is a distinct 'manifestation of need' among socially weak groups within the population, including those who are losing out on the labour market. (See: Maleva, T. (2000), *What Sort of Russia Has the New President Inherited?* or 'Russia's Key Social Problems', *Briefing Papers*, 2: 4, April http://pubs.carnegie.ru/russian, and – for comparison with other countries – R. Burkhauser, and M. Berkowitz (eds.) (1996), *Disability, work and cash benefits*, W. E. Upjohn Institute of Employment Research, Kalamazoo, MI; B. De Vroom and A. M. Guillemard (2002), 'From externalisation to integration of older workers: institutional changes at the end of the worklife', in J. G. Andersen and P. H. Jensen (eds.) *Changing labour markets, welfare policies and citizenship*, The Policy Press, Bristol; D. Ingles, (1998), *Older Workers, Disability and Early Retirement in Australia: Issue Paper*, Department of Family and Community Services, Canberra, Australia; OECD (1999) *A caring world. The social policy agenda*, Paris; W. Van Oorschot and K. Boos (2001), 'The battle against numbers: disability policies in the Netherlands', in W. Van Oorschot and B. Hvinden (eds.) *Disability policies in European countries*, The Hague, Kluwer Law International.)

3. Before the reforms, in the Soviet period, many economically important or socially valuable occupations entailed poor working conditions, and the enterprises concerned found themselves unable to recruit enough workers from the local population. They were therefore allocated a number of jobs – up to a defined limit – which carried the right to a temporary residence permit for the population centre where the enterprise was located.

4. Valentina lived in a house belonging to the factory where she had previously worked, which she had left in the mid-1990s because of non-payment of wages. At about the same time, her neighbour's husband died as a result of an accident sustained at work in the same factory. The factory management consequently decided that the neighbour had more right to occupy the rooms that had become free.

5. About £240: for the respondent, whose average monthly *per capita* family income was about £25, this was a huge sum of money.

6. 1/100 of a rouble - the lowest value coin in the Russian Federation.

7. The system of awarding bonuses in the form of goods rather than money relates to particular features of the Russian taxation system, as well as to the practice of product barter between enterprises, which was widespread in Russia in the 1990s.

8. This was typical 'garage self-employment' and, at the same time, social participation. In Russia today, for some people, something like an informal club has formed in each garage or parking lot, and members may find opportunities for casual – sometimes even regular – unregistered work in the garage. It is important to note that such 'garage self-employment' was frequently a man's most important channel of social contact. This was especially true of those of our sample who were in the 'grey zone' and did not have secure employment: for them, this social support was no less – perhaps even more – important than the fact that the club could be a source of extra work.

Bibliography

Abrahamson, P. (1995), 'Social Exclusion in Europe: Old Wine in New Bottles?', *Druzboslovne razprave* [*Discussions in Social Science*; a Slovenian Journal], vol. XI, nos. 19-20, pp. 119-136.

Abrahamson, P. (1998), *Postmodern Governing of Social Exclusion: Social Integration or Risk Management?*, Copenhagen: Sociologisk rapportserie nr. 13, University of Copenhagen, Department of Sociology. In part translated into Russian and published as: 'Sotsialnaya eksklusiya i bednost' ('Social Exclusion and Poverty') *Obschestvennye nauki i sovremennost (Social Sciences and Modernity)*, no. 2 [2001] Russian Academy of Sciences, Nauka, Moscow, pp. 158-166.

Akhiezer, A. (1991), *Russia: critique of a historical experiment*, Nauka, Moscow.

Alber, J. and Standing, G. (2000), 'Social dumping, catch-up or convergence? Europe in a comparative global context', *Journal of European Social Policy*, vol. 10, no. 2, pp. 99-119.

Allardt, E. (1975), *Att Ha, Att Älska, Att Vara: Om välfärd i Norden*, Argos, Lund.

Andersen, J. and Larsen, J.E. (1995), 'The underclass debate: A spreading disease?', in N. Mortensen (ed.), *Social Integration and Marginalization*, Samfundslitteratur, Frederiksberg.

Andreβ, H.-J. (ed.) (1998), *Empirical Poverty Research in Comparative Perspective*, Ashgate, Aldershot.

Antonnen, A. and Sipilä, J. (1996), 'European social care services: is it possible to identify models?', *Journal of European Social Policy*, vol. 6, no. 2, pp. 87-100.

Aronson, N. (1984), 'The Making of the US Bureau of Labor Statistics Family Budget Series: Relativism and the Rhetoric of Subsistence', paper presented to the *American Sociological Association Meetings*, San Antonio.

Atkinson, R. and Davoudi, S. (2000), 'The concept of social exclusion in the European Union: context, development and possibilities', *Journal of Common Market Studies*, vol. 38, no. 3, pp. 427-448.

Balabanova, E. (1999), 'The underclass: concept and place in society', *SOTSIS*, no. 12, pp. 65-70.

Banks, M.H., Clegg, C.W., Jackson, P.R., Kemp, N.J., Stafford, E.M. and Wall, T.D. (1980), 'The Use of the General Health Questionnaire as an Indicator of Mental Health in Occupational Studies', *Journal of Occupational Studies*, vol. 53, pp. 187-194.

Beck, U. (1992), *Risk Society: Towards a new modernity*, Sage, London.

Bell, D. (1973), *The Coming of Post-Industrial Society*, Basic Books, New York.

Berghman, J. (1996), 'Conceptualising Social Exclusion', paper for European Science Foundation Conference on *'Social Exclusion and Social Integration in Europe: Theoretical and Policy Perspectives on Poverty and Inequality'*, Blarney, Ireland, March.

Beyeler, M. (2003), 'Globalization, Europeanization and domestic welfare state reforms – new institutionalist concepts', *Global Social Policy*, vol. 3 no. 2, pp. 153-172.

Bondarenko, N. (1997), 'Interpretation of subjective assessments of personal material welfare', *Economic and Social Change*, VTSIOM Bulletin, no. 6, pp. 25-30.

Bradshaw, J. (ed.) (1993), *Budget Standards for the United Kingdom*, Avebury, Aldershot.

Byrne, D. (1999), *Social Exclusion*, Open University Press, Buckingham.

Callan, T., Nolan, B., and Whelan, C.T. (1993), 'Resources, deprivation and the measurement of poverty', *Journal of Social Policy*, vol. 22, no. 2, pp. 141-172.

Cannan, C. (1997), 'The struggle against social exclusion: urban social development in France', *IDS Bulletin*, vol. 29, no. 1, pp. 10-19.

Castel, R. (1991), 'From Dangerousness to Risk', in G. Burchell, C. Gordon and P. Miller (eds.), *The Foucault Effect: Studies in Governmentality*, Harvester Wheatsheaf, London, pp. 281-298.

Castel, R. (1995), *Les Métamorphoses de la question sociale: cronique du salariat*, Fayard, Paris.

Castel, R. (2000), 'The roads to disaffiliation: insecure work and vulnerable relationships', *International Journal of Urban and Regional Research*, vol. 24, no. 3, pp. 518-535.

Castells, M. (1998), 'The information age', *Economy, Society and Culture. Vol. 3: End of Millennium*, Blackwell, Oxford and Malden, MA.

Charles, N. and Kerr, M. (1986), 'Eating Properly, The Family and State Benefit', *Sociology*, vol. 20, no. 3, pp. 412-429.

Chernina, N. (1994), 'Poverty as a social phenomenon of Russian society', *SOTSIS*, no. 3, pp. 54-60.

Citro, C.F. and Michael, R.T. (eds.) (1995), *Measuring Poverty: A New Approach*, US National Research Council Panel on Poverty and Family Assistance Report, National Academy Press, Washington, DC.

Clark, S. and Kabalina, V. (eds.) (1999), *Employment and household behaviour: adaptation to conditions of transition to the market economy in Russia*, ROSSPEN, Moscow.

Coleman, J.S. (1988), 'Social Capital in the Creation of Human Capital', *American Journal of Sociology*, 94 (Supplement), pp. S95-S120.

Commander, S., Tolstopiatenko, A. and Yemtsov, R. (1997), 'Channels of Redistribution: Inequality and Poverty in the Russian Transition', paper prepared for the Conference on *Inequality and Poverty in Transition Economies*, EBRD, London.

Commission of the European Communities (1993), *The Future of Social Policy: options for the Union*, Green Paper, DG V, Brussels.

Coudouel, A., Manning, N. and Pascall, J. (1999), 'Women as Agents of Change', in Working Paper for *Women and Social Policy in Eastern Europe*, UNICEF Regional Monitoring Report No. 6.

Cox, D., Yezer, Z. and Himenez, E. (1998), 'Economic support of the family by private individuals in the period of transition to the market economy', in D. Klugman (ed.), *Poverty in Russia: Public Policy and Private Responses*, World Bank, Washington-Moscow.

da Costa, A. (1995), 'On the concepts of poverty and social exclusion', paper presented at the *Eighth Nordic Social Policy Seminar*, Stockholm, Sweden, February 9-11, 1995.

Davidova, N. (1998), 'Regional Specifics of Russian Mentality', *Social Sciences*, Quarterly Review of Russian Academy of Sciences, no. 1, Nauka, Moscow.

Davidova, N. (2000), 'Head of Household: Distribution of Roles and Survival Strategy', *Obschestvennye Nauki I Sovremennost (Social Sciences)*, Russian Academy of Sciences Issue, No. 3.

Deacon, B. (2000), 'Eastern European welfare states: the impact of the politics of globalisation', *Journal of European Social Policy*, vol. 10, no. 2, pp. 146-161.

Dean, H. and Taylor-Gooby, P. (1991), *Dependency Culture: The Explosion of a Myth*, Harvester Wheatsheaf, London.

de Haan, A. (1998), 'Social Exclusion: an alternative concept for the study of deprivation?', *IDS Bulletin*, vol. 29, no. 1, pp. 10-19.

Deleeck, H., Van den Bosch, K. and De Lathouwer, L. (1992), *Poverty and the Adequacy of Social Security in the EC*, Avebury, Aldershot.

Delors, J. (1996), 'Combats pour l'Europe', *Economica*.

Doyal, L. and Gough, I. (1984), 'A theory of human needs', *Critical Social Policy*, no. 10, pp. 6-38.

Doyal, L. and Gough, I. (1991), *A Theory of Human Need*, Macmillan, London.

Dubnoff, S. (1985), 'How much income is enough? Measuring public judgements', *Public Opinion Quarterly*, vol. 49, no. 3, pp. 285-299.

Durkheim, E. (1966), *The division of labor in society*, Free Press, New York.

EBRD (1999), *Transition Report 1999*, European Bank for Reconstruction and Development, London.

Economic Development Institute of the World Bank (1998), *Poverty in Russia: Public Policy and Private Responses*, World Bank, Washington-Moscow.

Eichler, M. (1988), *Nonsexist research methods: A practical guide*, Allen and Unwin, Boston.

Ellman, M. (1989), *Socialist Planning* (2nd ed), Cambridge University Press, Cambridge.

Fisher, G.M. (1993), 'From Hunter to Orshansky: An Overview of (Unofficial) Poverty Lines in the United States from 1904 to 1965', paper presented to the *15th Annual Research Conference of the Association for Public Policy Analysis and Management*, Washington DC.

Friedmann, J. (1996), 'Rethinking poverty: empowerment and citizen rights', *International Social Science Journal*, vol. 148, pp. 161-172.

George, V. and Manning, N. (1980), *Socialism, Social Welfare and the Soviet Union*, Routledge.

Giddens, A. (1998), *The Third Way: The Renewal of Social Democracy*, Polity Press, Cambridge.

Goedhart, T., Halberstadt, V., Kapteyn, A. and van Praag, B. (1977), 'The Poverty Line: concept and measurement', *Journal of Human Resources*, vol. 12, no. 4, pp. 503-520.

Goldstone, J. (1998) 'Initial conditions, general laws, path dependence, and explanation in historical sociology', *American Journal of Sociology*, vol. 104, no. 3, pp. 829-845.

Goode, J., Callender, C. and Lister, R. (1998), *Purse or Wallet? Gender Inequalities and Income Distribution within Families on Benefit*, Policy Studies Institute, London.

Goode, J., Callender, C. and Lister, R. (1999), 'Income distribution within families and the reform of social security', *Journal of Social Welfare and Family Law*, vol. 21, no.3, pp. 203-220.

Gordon, D. (2000a), 'Measuring absolute and overall poverty', Chap 4 in D. Gordon and P. Townsend (eds.), *Breadline Europe. The measurement of poverty*, The Policy Press, Bristol, pp. 49-77.

Gordon, D. (2000b), 'The Scientific Measurement of Poverty: Recent Theoretical Advances', in J. Bradshaw and R. Sainsbury (eds.), *Researching Poverty*, Ashgate, Aldershot, pp. 37-58.

Gordon, D. and Spicker, P. (eds.) (1999), *The International Glossary on Poverty*, Zed Books, London.

Gordon, D., Adelman, A., Ashworth, K., Bradshaw, J., Levitas, R., Middleton, S., Pantazis, C., Patsios, D., Payne, S., Townsend, P. and Williams, J. (2000), *Poverty and Social Exclusion in Britain*, Joseph Rowntree Foundation, York.

Gordon, D., Nandy, S., Pantazis, C., Pemberton, S. and Townsend, P. (2003), 'Child poverty in the developing world', The Policy Press, Bristol.

Gorshkov, M. (ed.) (2000), *Russia at the turn of the century*, ROSSPEN/RIISNP, Moscow.

Gorshkov, M. and Tikhonova, N. (2002), *Women in the new Russia: How do they live? What are they looking for?*, ROSSPEN, Moscow.

Goskomstat, R.F. (2000), *The Social Position and Standard of Living of the Russian Population*, Official publication, Goskomstat Russia, Moscow.

Goskomstat, R.F. (2000a), *Incomes, expenditures and consumption of households in 1999*, Goskomstat of the Russian Federation, Moscow.

Goskomstat, R.F. (2000b), 'Russian Statistical Yearbook', *Statistical collection*, Goskomstat of the Russian Federation, Moscow.

Gough, I. (1994), 'Needs Satisfaction and Welfare Outcomes: theory and explanations', *Social Policy and Administration*, vol. 28, no. 1, pp. 33-56.

Graham, H. (1992), 'Budgeting for health', in C. Glendinning and J. Millar (eds.), *Women and Poverty in Britain, the 1990s*, Harvester Wheatsheaf, Hemel Hempstead.

Granovetter, M. (1973), 'The Strength of Weak Ties', *American Journal of Sociology*, vol. 78, no. 6, pp. 1360-1380.

Halleröd, B., Bradshaw, J. and Holmes, H. (1997), 'Adapting the consensual definition of poverty', in D. Gordon and C. Pantazis (eds.), *Breadline Britain in the 1990s*, Ashgate, Aldershot, pp. 213-234.

Hanson, P. (2003), 'The Russian Economic Recovery: do four years of growth tell us that the fundamentals have changed?', *Europe-Asia Studies*, vol. 55, no. 3, pp. 365-382.

Himmelfarb, G. (1984), *The Idea of Poverty*, Faber, London.

Holman, R. (1978), *Poverty: Explanations of Social Deprivation*, Martin Robertson, London.

Jordan, B. (1996), *A Theory of Poverty and Social Exclusion*, Polity Press, Cambridge.

Katz, M.B. (1989), *The Undeserving Poor: From the War on Poverty to the War on Welfare*, Pantheon, New York.

Korpi, W. (2000), 'Contentious institutions: an augmented rational-actor analysis of the origins and path dependency of welfare state institutions in the western countries', *SOFI Working Paper 4/2000*, Stockholm: Swedish Institute for Social Research.

Kozlova, N. (1998), *Social and historical anthropology: Soviet man*, Klyuch, Moscow.

Ledeneva, A. (1998), *Russia's Economy of Favours*, Cambridge University Press, Cambridge.

Leisering, L. and Leibfried, S. (1999), *Time and Poverty in Western Welfare States*, Cambridge University Press, Cambridge.

Leonard, P. (1997), *Postmodern welfare: reconstructing an emancipatory project*, Sage, London.

Levitas, R. (1998), *The Inclusive Society? Social Exclusion and New Labour*, Macmillan, Basingstoke.

Lewis, J. (1992), 'Gender and the development of welfare regimes', *Journal of European Social Policy*, vol. 2, no. 3, pp. 159-173.

Lewis, J. (1998), *Social Care, Gender and Welfare State Restructuring*, Ashgate, Aldershot.

Littlewood, P. (ed.) (1999), *Social Exclusion in Europe: problems and paradigms*, Ashgate, Aldershot.

Lokshin, M. and Popkin, B. (1999), 'The Emerging Underclass in the RF: Income Dynamics, 1992-1996', *Economic Development and Cultural Change*, no. 4, pp. 803-829.

Lonkila, M. (1997), 'Informal exchange relations in post-soviet Russia: a comparative perspective' *Sociological Research Online*, vol. 2, no. 2, http://www.socresonline.org.uk/socresonline/2/2/9.html

Low, S. (2001), 'The edge and the center: gated communities and the discourse of urban fear', *American Anthropologist*, vol. 103, no. 1, pp. 45-58.

Macauley, A. (1996), 'Russia and the Baltics: Poverty and Poverty Research in a Changing World', in E. Øyen, S.M. Miller and S.A. Samad (eds.), *Poverty: A Global Review. Handbook on International Poverty Research*, Scandinavian University Press, Oslo, pp. 354-384.

Macauley, A., Mozhina, M.A. and Ovcharova, L. (1998), *Poverty: alternative approaches to definition and measures*, Carnegie Center, Moscow.

McCauley, M. (2003), 'From Monopoly Socialism to Bandit Capitalism: Russia since 1992', in R. Bradshaw, N. Manning, & S. Thompstone, (eds.), *After the Fall: Central and Eastern Europe since the Collapse of Communism*, Olearius Press, St. Petersburg, pp. 17-41.

Mack, J. and Lansley, S. (1985), *Poor Britain*, Allen and Unwin, London.

Manning, N. (2001), 'Copenhagen + 5: what should be done about the transition in Eastern Europe?', *Social Policy Review*, Policy Press, pp. 133-156.

Manning, N. (2003), 'Social issues and social policy in Russia', in R. Bradshaw, N. Manning, and S. Thompstone, (eds.), *After the Fall: Central and Eastern Europe since the Collapse of Communism*, Olearius Press, St. Petersburg, pp. 146-173.

Manning, N. (2004), 'OECD reports on the UK, 1979-2001', in *The OECD and European Welfare States*, Edward Elgar, Cheltenham (edited by Klaus Armingheon and Michelle Beyeler), pp. 197-210.

Manning, N. and Shaw, I. (eds.) (2000), *New risks, new welfare: signposts for social policy*, Blackwell, Oxford.

Manning, N., Shkaratan, O. and Tikhonova, N. (2000), *Work and Welfare in The New Russia*, Ashgate, Aldershot.

Mead, L. (1986), *Beyond entitlements: the social obligation of citizenship*, The Free Press, New York.

Middleton, S. (2000), 'Agreeing Poverty Lines: The Development of Consensual Budget Standards Methodology', in J. Bradshaw and R. Sainsbury (eds.), *Researching Poverty*, Ashgate, Aldershot, pp. 59-76.

Mikhalev, V. (1998), 'The expansion of poverty as a social cost of transition: A challenge for Russia', in H.-J. Andreβ (ed.), *Empirical Poverty Research in a Comparative Perspective*, Ashgate, Aldershot, pp. 359-390.

Molloy, D. and Snape, D. (2000), *Relying on the state, relying on each other*, Research Report No. 103, Social Research Branch, Department of Social Security - http://www.dss.gov.uk/asd/asd5/103summ.html

Morris, L. (1990), *The Workings of the Household*, Polity Press, Cambridge.

Moscow Carnegie Centre (1998), *Poverty: alternative approaches to definition and measurement*, Joint Monograph, Moscow.

Muffels, R., Kapteyn, A. and Berghman, J. (1990), *Poverty in the Netherlands*, VUGA, The Hague.

Murray, C. (1984), *Losing ground: American social policy 1950-1980*, Basic Books, New York.

Nathan, R.P. (1987), 'Will the Underclass Always be With Us?', *Society*, vol. 24, no. 3, pp. 57-62.

Oppenheim, C. and Harker, L. (1996), *Poverty: the facts*, CPAG Ltd, London.

Ovcharova, L. (1997), 'The definition and measurement of poverty in Russia', http://www.csv.warwick.ac.uk/fac/soc/complabstuds/russia/russint.htm

Pahl, J. (1980), 'Patterns of money management within marriage', *Journal of Social Policy*, vol. 9, pp. 313-335.

Pahl, J. (1989), *Money and Marriage*, Macmillan, Basingstoke.

Paugam, S. (1996), 'Poverty and Social Exclusion: a sociological view', in Y. Meny & M. Rhodes (eds.) *The future of European welfare: A New Social Contract?*, Macmillan, London.

Paugam, S. (1996), 'Elements of a comparative research perspective on poverty in European societies', revised version published in Y. Mény and M. Rhodes (eds.), *The future of European welfare: a new social contract?*, Macmillan, Basingstoke, 1998.

Pestoff, V. (1996), 'Reforming social services in post-communist Europe', in J.L. Campbell & O.K. Pedersen (eds.), *Legacies of Change: transformation of postcommunist European economies*, Aldine de Gruyter, New York, pp. 57-86.

Piirainen, T. (1997), *Towards a New Social Order in Russia: Transforming Structures and Everyday Life*, Aldershot, Dartmouth.

Poretskina, E. and Jyrkinen-Pakkasvirta, T. (1995), 'Social networks and the everyday life of residents of St Petersburg', *Mir Rossiya*, vol. 4, no. 2, pp. 190-201.

Procacci, G. (1993), *Gouverner la misére*, Édition du Seuil, Paris.

Puttnam, R.D. (2000), *Bowling Alone: The Collapse and Revival of American Community*, Simon and Schuster, New York.

Ravallion, M. (1992), *Poverty Comparison: A Guide to Concepts and Methods*, Living Standards Measurement Study Working Paper, No. 88, The World Bank, Washington DC.

RCTPI (Royal Commission on the Taxation of Profits and Income) (1955), *Final Report: Memorandum of Dissent*, HMSO, London.

Ringen, S. (1988), 'Direct and Indirect Measures of Poverty', *Journal of Social Policy*, vol. 7, no. 3, pp. 351-365.

Robbins, D. (1993), *Social Europe. Towards a Europe of Solidarity. Supplement 4/9*, DG V, Brussels.

Room, G. (1990), *Observatory on National Policies to Combat Social Exclusion. Synthesis Report*, University of Bath, Bath.

Room, G. (1994), 'Poverty studies in the European Union: Retrospect and prospect', paper presented at the *EU-Conference Understanding Social Exclusion: Lessons from Transnational Research Studies*, Policy Studies Institute, London, November 24-25, 1994.

Room, G. (ed.) (1995), *Beyond the threshold: the measurement and analysis of social exclusion*, Policy Press, Bristol.

Room, G. (1995), 'Poverty in Europe: Competing paradigms of analysis', *Policy and Politics*, vol. 23, no. 2.

Room, G. (1999), 'Social exclusion, solidarity, and the challenge of globalization', *International Journal of Social Welfare*, vol. 8, no. 4, pp. 166-174.

Rose, N. (1996), 'The death of the social? Re-figuring the territory of government', *Economy and Society*, vol. 25, no. 3, pp. 327-356.

Rose, R. (1993), 'How Russians are coping with transition. NEW RUSSIA BAROMETER II', *Studies in Public Policy*, nos. 215-6, University of Strathclyde, Glasgow.

Rose, R. (1996), *Evaluating Workplace Benefits: the Views of Russian Employees*, Studies in Public Policy, 277, Centre for the study of Public Policy, University of Strathclyde, Strathclyde.

Rose, R. (1998a), 'Getting things done with social capital: NEW RUSSIA BAROMETER VII', *Studies in Public Policy*, no. 303, University of Strathclyde, Glasgow.

Rose, R. (1998b), 'Getting things done in an anti-modern society: Social capital networks in Russia', *Studies in Public Policy*, no. 304, University of Strathclyde, Glasgow.

Rose, R. and McAllister, I. (1996), 'Is money the measure of welfare in Russia?', *The Review of Income and Wealth*, vol. 42, no. 1, pp. 75-90.

Rose, R. and Tikhomirov, Y. (1993), 'Who grows food in Russia and Eastern Europe?', *Post-Soviet Geography*, vol. 34, no. 2, pp. 111-126.

Rowntree, B.S. (1901), *Poverty: a study of town life*, Macmillan, London.

Runciman, W.G. (1966), *Relative Deprivation and Social Justice*, Routledge and Kegan Paul, London.

Ryan, W. (1971), *Blaming The Victim*, Pantheon Books, USA.

Sen, A. (1983), 'Poor, Relatively Speaking', *Oxford Economic Papers*, vol. 35, pp. 153-169.

Shlapentokh, V. (1989), *Public and Private Life of the Soviet People*, Oxford University Press, Oxford.

Silver, H. (1994), 'Social exclusion and solidarity: Three paradigms', *International Labour Review*, vol. 133, nos. 5-6, pp. 531-578.

Smith, A. (1776), *An Inquiry into the Nature and Causes of The Wealth of Nations*, Everyman Edition, J.M. Dent, London.

Springborg, P. (1981), *The Problem of Human Needs and the Critique of Civilisation*, Allen and Unwin, London.

Standing, G. (ed.) (1991), *In Search of Flexibility: the New Soviet Labour Market*, International Labour Organisation, Geneva.

Standing, G. (1998), 'Societal impoverishment: the challenge for Russian social policy', *Journal of European Social Policy*, vol. 8, no. 1, pp. 23-42.

Stephenson, S. (2003), 'Homeless in Russia: the mechanisms of social displacement', in R. Bradshaw, N. Manning and S. Thompstone (eds.), *After the Fall: Central and Eastern Europe since the Collapse of Communism*, Olearius Press, St. Petersburg, pp. 174-192.

Strobel, P. (1996), 'From Poverty to Exclusion: a Wage-Earning Society or a Society of Human Rights?', *International Social Science Journal*, no. 148, pp. 73-190.

Tchernina, N. (1998), 'Die Bevölkerung Russlands in der Transformationsphase', *Soziale Exklusion und Adaptionsstrategien*, Berichte des Bundesinstituts für ostwissenschaftliche und internationale Studien, no. 27, Cologne.

Tikhonova, N. (1997), 'The poor: way of life and survival strategies', in T.I. Zaslavskaya (ed.), *Where is Russia going?...* Dyelo, Moscow.

Tikhonova, N. (1999), *Factors in social stratification in conditions of transition to a market economy*, ROSSPEN, Moscow.

Tikhonova, N. (2000), 'What do Russians identify with?', in M. Gorshkov (ed.), *Russia at the turn of the century*, ROSSPEN/RIISNP, Moscow.

Tikhonova, N. and Gorshkov M. (2002), *Women in the new Russia: How do they live? What are they looking for?*, ROSSPEN, Moscow.

Touraine, A. (1991), 'Face à l'exclusion', *Esprit*, vol. 141, pp. 7-13.

Townsend, P. (ed.) (1970), *The Concept of Poverty*, Heinemann, London.

Townsend, P. (1979), *Poverty in the United Kingdom*, Penguin, Harmondsworth.

Townsend, P. (1987), 'Deprivation' *Journal of Social Policy*, vol. 16, no. 2, pp. 125-146.

Townsend, P. (1993), *The International Analysis Of Poverty*, Harvester Wheatsheaf, London.

Townsend, P., Gordon, D. and Gosschack, B. (1996), *The Poverty Line in Britain Today: What the Population Themselves Say*, Statistical Monitoring Unit Report No. 7, University of Bristol.

Townsend, P., Gordon, D., Bradshaw, J. and Gosschalk, B. (1997), *Absolute and Overall Poverty in Britain in 1997: What the Population Themselves Say: Bristol Poverty Line Survey*, Report of the Second MORI Survey, Bristol Statistical Monitoring Unit, University of Bristol, Bristol.

UN (United Nations) (1995), *Report of the World Summit for Social Development, Copenhagen 6-12 March 1995; Annex II: Program of Action of the World Summit for Social Development; Chapter II: Eradication of Poverty*, United Nations, New York.

UNDP Regional Bureau for Europe and the CIS (1999) *Central Asia 2010: prospects for human development*, UNDP, New York.

UNDP (1999a) *Human Development Report for Central and Eastern Europe and the CIS*, UNDP, New York.

UNDP (1999b), *Workshop on Poverty Statistics*, Bishkek, 27-30 September 1999.

UNICEF (2001), TransMONEE Database, UNICEF Innocenti Research Centre, Florence.

UNICEF (2003), *Social Monitor 2003*, UNICEF Innocenti Research Centre, Florence.

Van den Bosch, K. (2001), *Identifying the Poor: Using subjective and consensual measures*, Ashgate, Aldershot.

Veit-Wilson, J. (1987), 'Consensual Approaches to Poverty Lines and Social Security', *Journal of Social Policy*, vol. 16, no. 2, pp. 183-211.

Veit-Wilson, J. (1998), *Setting Adequacy Standards: how governments define minimum incomes*, The Policy Press, Bristol.

Veit-Wilson, J. (1999), 'Poverty and the adequacy of social security', in J. Ditch (ed.), *Introduction to Social Security: policies, benefits and poverty*, Routledge, London.

Veit-Wilson, J. (2000), 'Horses for discourses: poverty, purpose and closure in minimum income standards policy', in D. Gordon and P. Townsend (eds.), *Breadline Europe: The measurement of poverty*, The Policy Press, Bristol, pp. 141-164.

Vogler, C. and Pahl, J. (1994), 'Money, power and inequality within marriage', *Sociological Review*, vol. 42, no. 2, pp. 263-288.

Wacquant, L. (1996), 'The Rise of Advanced Marginality: Notes on its Nature and Implications', *Acta Sociologica*, vol. 39, no. 2, pp. 121-40.

Waldegrave, C. and Frater, F. (1996), 'New Zealand: a search for a national poverty line', in E. Øyen, S.M. Miller and S.A. Samad (eds.), *Poverty: A Global Review. Handbook on International Poverty Research*, Scandinavian University Press, Oslo, pp. 160-186.

Walker, A. and Walker, C. (eds.) (1997), *Britain Divided: The growth of social exclusion in the 1980s and 1990s*, Child Poverty Action Group, London.

Walker, R. (1995), 'The dynamics of poverty and social exclusion', in G. Room (ed.), *Beyond the Threshold: The Measurement and Analysis of Social Exclusion*, The Policy Press, Bristol, pp. 102-128.

Ware, A. and Goodin, R.E. (eds.) (1990), *Needs and Welfare*, Sage, London.

Westergaard, J. (1992), 'About and beyond the underclass: some notes on influences of social climate on British sociology today', *Sociology*, vol. 26, no. 4, pp. 575-588.

Wills, T.A. (1985), 'Supportive functions of interpersonal relations', in S. Cohen & L. Syme (eds.), *Social Support and Health*, Academic Press, New York.

Wilson, G. (1987), *Money in the Family*, Avebury, Aldershot.

Wilson, W.J. (1987), *The Truly Disadvantaged: The Inner City, the Underclass, and Public Policy*, The University of Chicago Press, Chicago, Illinois.

Wilson, W.J. and Neckerman, K. (1986), 'Poverty and Family Structure', in S.H. Danzinger & D.H. Weinberg (eds.), *Fighting Poverty: What Works and What Doesn't*, Harvard University Press, Cambridge, Massachusetts, pp. 232-259.

World Bank (1996), *From Plan to Market: World Development Report 1996*, World Bank, Washington DC.

World Bank Group (2000), *Feminization of poverty in Russia*, Research Report, http://www.worldbank.org.ru/eng/statistics/femine.htm

Yadov, V. (ed.) (1979), *Self-regulation and forecasting the social behaviour of the individual*, Nauka, Leningrad.

Yakubovich, V. (1999), 'Social opportunities and economic necessity: the inclusion of urban households in informal mutual assistance networks', in V. Kabalina & S. Clark (eds.), *Employment and household behaviour: adaptation to conditions of transition to the market economy in Russia*, ROSSPEN, Moscow.

Yeates, N. and McLaughlin, E. (eds.) (2000), *Measuring Social Exclusion and Poverty*, [Northern Ireland Government] Department for Social Development, Belfast.

Zaslavskaya, T. (1996), 'Incomes of social groups and strata: level and dynamic', *Economic and social change*, VTSIOM Bulletin, no. 2, pp. 7-13.

Zaslavskaya, T. and Kalugina, Z. (1999), 'The social trajectory of reforming Russia', *Research by the Novosibirsk School of Economics and Sociology*, Nauka, Novosibirsk.

Zubova, L. and Kovaleva, N. (1998), 'Public opinion on social issues', in D. Klugman (ed.), *Poverty in Russia: Public Policy and Private Responses*, World Bank, Washington-Moscow.

Index